POLITICAL COMMUNICATION
Issues and Strategies for Research

SAGE ANNUAL REVIEWS OF COMMUNICATION RESEARCH

SERIES EDITORS

F. Gerald Kline, *University of Michigan*
Peter Clarke, *University of Michigan*

ADVISORY BOARD

Other Books in this Series:

Volume IV

SAGE ANNUAL REVIEWS OF COMMUNICATION RESEARCH

Political Communication

Issues and Strategies for Research

STEVEN H. CHAFFEE
Editor

SAGE PUBLICATIONS / Beverly Hills / London

Annenberg Reserve
JA
86
P55

For information address:

SAGE PUBLICATIONS, INC.
275 South Beverly Drive
Beverly Hills, California 90212

SAGE PUBLICATIONS LTD
St George's House / 44 Hatton Garden
London EC1N 8ER

International Standard Book Number 0-8039-0505-x (Cloth)
0-8039-0507-6 (Paper)

Library of Congress Catalog Card No. 75-14629

FIRST PRINTING

CONTENTS

Index by Donna Wilson
Supplementary Illustrations by Albert Tims

To Sheila, who had to put up with the most

ABOUT THE CONTRIBUTORS

LEE B. BECKER is an assistant professor in the Communications Research Center of the S.I. Newhouse School of Public Communications at Syracuse University. He received his Ph.D. in mass communications from the University of Wisconsin (Madison), and has concentrated his research on the use and effects of political communications.

JAY G. BLUMLER is director of the Centre for Television Research and a reader in mass communications, at the University of Leeds. He has written widely on political communication topics, and is currently working on media and interpersonal influences on first-time voters. He is co-author (with Denis McQuail) of *Television in Politics: Its Uses and Influence* and co-editor (with Elihu Katz) of *The Uses of Mass Communications,* the preceding volume in this series.

STEVEN H. CHAFFEE is Vilas research professor in the School of Journalism and Mass Communication at the University of Wisconsin (Madison). A Stanford University Ph.D. in communication, he has published research on such diverse topics as interpersonal coorientation, the role of television in child development, and cognitive models of information processing. He is co-author (with Michael Petrick) of *Using the Mass Media: Communication Problems in American Society*, and co-author (with George Comstock and others) of *The Fifth Season: How Television Influences the Way People Behave* (forthcoming).

DENNIS DAVIS is an assistant professor in the Department of Communication at Cleveland State University. A University of Minnesota Ph.D. in mass communications, his research interests include communication theory and research methodology, and mass media and public opinion. He is co-author (with Sidney Kraus) of *The Effects of Mass Communication on Political Behavior* (forthcoming).

EVERETTE E. DENNIS is assistant professor of Journalism and Mass Communication at the University of Minnesota, where he received his Ph.D. Co-author (with William L. Rivers) of *Other Voices: The New Journalism in America* and *New Strategies for Public Affairs Reporting,* he is editor of *The Magic Writing Machine: Student Probes of The New Journalism.* A frequent contributor to

/ 9

scholarly journals and law reviews, he writes on communication law, history and media sociology.

OSCAR GANDY is a doctoral candidate in public affairs communication at Stanford University. He holds a master's degree from the Annenberg School of Communication at the University of Pennsylvania, and worked as a writer/producer for CBS in Philadelphia and lectured at the University of California's Third College before going to Stanford. His interests in political economy are currently focusing on instructional technology, and on the corporate-government partnership.

DONALD M. GILLMOR is professor of Journalism and Mass Communication at the University of Minnesota, from which he received his Ph.D. He is author of *Free Press and Fair Trial* and co-author (with Jerome A. Barron) of *Mass Communication Law: Cases and Comment.* In the mass communication and society area he is particularly interested in mass media effects, organizational theory, popular culture, and the literature of reform.

MICHAEL GUREVITCH was a senior research fellow in the Centre for Television Research at the University of Leeds during the preparation of this chapter. He received his Ph.D. in political science from the Massachusetts Institute of Technology. His research interests lie in the areas of media use and gratifications, political communication, and the study of communication networks.

SIDNEY KRAUS, professor and chairman of the Department of Communication at Cleveland State University, earned his Ph.D. at the University of Iowa. He edited *The Great Debates,* a collection of studies on the Kennedy-Nixon 1960 presidential televised debates, and has co-edited (with Steven Chaffee) a special issue of the journal *Communication Research* on Watergate and the Ervin Hearings. He is co-author (with Dennis Davis) of the forthcoming *The Effects of Mass Communication on Political Behavior.*

F. GERALD KLINE is an associate professor in the Department of Journalism, chairman of the interdepartmental doctoral program in mass communication research, and faculty associate in the Center for Political Studies at the University of Michigan. A University of Minnesota Ph.D., he is editor of *Communication Research* and co-editor of this series—the Sage Annual Reviews of Communication Research. He co-edited (with Phillip J. Tichenor) the first volume in the series, *Current Perspectives in Mass Communication Research.* During 1975 he was on leave—as a senior analyst in the Department of Communications of the Government of Canada—working on broadcasting policy.

GLADYS ENGEL LANG is professor of sociology and communication at the State University of New York at Stony Brook. A University of Chicago Ph.D. in sociology, she has specialized in studies of collective behavior, the sociology of education, and mass communication. She is co-author (with Kurt Lang) of *Collective Dynamics, Politics and Television,* and *Voting and Non-Voting.*

KURT LANG is professor of sociology at the State University of New York at Stony Brook. He holds the Ph.D. in sociology from the University of Chicago. His research interests include media and politics, collective behavior, and the sociology of the military. In addition to the works co-authored with Gladys Engel Lang (above) he is author of *The Military and the Social Order.*

MAXWELL E. McCOMBS is John Ben Snow professor and director of the Communications Research Center at the S. I. Newhouse School of Public Communications, Syracuse University. He received his Ph.D. in communication from Stanford University. His research has centered on mass communications and politics and the agenda-setting function of the media, and on applications of research findings and techniques to journalistic practice. He is co-editor of *Handbook of Reporting Methods,* a forthcoming text.

JACK M. McLEOD is professor of Journalism and Mass Communication and chairman of the Mass Communications Research Center at the University of Wisconsin (Madison). He received his Ph.D. in social psychology at the University of Michigan. His recent research focuses on political socialization and political communication. He has published a variety of studies on family communication, interpersonal coorientation, and professionalization of journalists in the U.S. and abroad.

SUSAN MILLER is a Ph.D. candidate in the Department of Communication at Stanford University. She holds the M.S. in journalism from Columbia University, and has worked as a newspaper reporter and public information officer. Her major research interests are media impacts on public officials, and media coverage of women.

GARRETT J. O'KEEFE is an associate professor in the Department of Mass Communications at the University of Denver. He holds the Ph.D. in mass communications from the University of Wisconsin (Madison). In addition to his election campaign research described here, he has worked extensively on the relationships among family communication, mass communication, child development and the life cycle.

WILLIAM L. RIVERS is Paul C. Edwards professor of communication at Stanford University. Formerly a Washington, D.C. reporter for a national magazine, he holds the Ph.D. in political science from American University. A prolific author, his books include *The Mass Media, Responsibility in Mass Communication* (with Wilbur Schramm), *The Mass Media in Modern Society* (with Theodore

Peterson and Jay Jensen), and *Other Voices: The New Journalism in America* (with Everette Dennis).

MICHAEL L. ROTHSCHILD is an assistant professor in the Graduate School of Business of the University of Wisconsin (Madison). He holds the Ph.D. in marketing from Stanford University. His research interests are in the examination of the effects of marketing communications on decision-making styles, and the application of marketing techniques in public sector and nonprofit areas.

KAREN SIUNE is an associate professor in the Institute of Political Science at the University of Aarhus. She has conducted extensive research into political communication research in Scandinavia. She was a visiting fellow at the Institute for Social Research and the Department of Journalism at the University of Michigan in 1974-75, collaborating on a national study of the 1974 mid-year elections. Her research interests are in mass communication theory and methods.

JOHN D. STEVENS is an associate professor of journalism at the University of Michigan and a past head of the History Division of the Association for Education in Journalism. He has published articles on a variety of research topics, including several aspects of popular culture. He is co-author (with Ronald Farrar) of *Mass Media and the National Experience* and (with William Porter) of *The Rest of the Elephant: Perspectives on the Mass Media.*

ASKING NEW QUESTIONS ABOUT

COMMUNICATION AND POLITICS

Steven H. Chaffee

THE WORLD OF POLITICS and the techniques of mass communication have intersected in fundamental and fascinating ways, at least since the days when Julius Caesar posted his version of the day's news, the *Acta Diurna*, to neutralize the speeches of his opponents in the Roman Senate. The difficulty most thinkers have had in coming to a unified interpretation of communication and politics is exemplified by Thomas Jefferson. Practically everyone is aware that this Founding Father once wrote, "were it left to me to decide whether we should have a government without newspapers, or newspapers without a government, I should not hesitate a moment to prefer the latter." Not so widely publicized is his complaint, during the latter stages of his presidency, that "the man who never looks into a newspaper is better informed than he who reads them; inasmuch as he who knows nothing is nearer to truth than he whose mind is filled with falsehoods and errors."

Ambivalence has also characterized the posture toward communication and politics of scholars who have subjected this complex field to their special forms of scrutiny in this century. Walter Lippmann, surely one of our greatest journalists, became sensitized early on to the fact that reporters perceive and pass on information that is organized in terms of stereotypes they hold. For them as for their readers, he noted that "we have to appraise not only the information which has been at their disposal, but the minds through which they have filtered it" (Lippmann, 1922). Much later, commenting on the inadequacy of public opinion as a guide to foreign policy, he stated, "Strategic and diplomatic decisions call for a kind of knowledge—not to speak of an experience and a seasoned judgment—which cannot be had by glancing at newspapers, listening to snatches of radio comment, watching politicians perform on television, hearing occasional lectures, and reading a few books" (Lippmann, 1955).

And yet the principle of a freely operating press in a participant democracy is a deeply ingrained assumption throughout the social sciences that have taken on the study of political communication. Carey (1974) points out that this has been the single-minded concern of historians of journalism in the United States. The authors of the first major surveys of voters during an election campaign spent their final chapter coming to grips with the somewhat embarrassing fact that they had found that "certain requirements commonly assumed for the successful operation of democracy are not met by the behavior of the 'average citizen' " (Berelson, Lazarsfeld and McPhee, 1954). Just as medieval churchmen labored mightily to make posthumous Christians of the great minds of ancient Greece, there has been considerable latent anguish in the social sciences in attempting to reconcile normative beliefs in democracy and press freedom with persistent evidence of less-than-ideal levels of competence and performance on the part of either the electorate or the mass media.

But this conflict between cherished values and scientific inquiry is no more inevitable in research on political communication than it is in molecular biology or solid-state physics. It is a product of an intellectual perspective, and such things should be seen as replaceable. In the physical and biological sciences, normative value questions like the perfectibility of the universe have long since been replaced by intellectual traditions based on clearly explicated theories and concrete attempts to test them. The continuing vacillation of the social and behavioral sciences between value judgments and empirical inquiry can be attributed largely to the lagging pace of theory construction and methodological invention. It is quite likely that we will never "know" the laws governing human processes of political communication with the same degree of precision that characterize our understanding of the movement of particles in space or of the mathematics of genetic inheritance. But those sciences have advanced through the postulating of theories about idealized conditions that do not exist in empirical reality—no ball has yet rolled down an inclined plane under conditions of zero friction, but Newtonian physics replaced earlier pre-scientific conceptions because of an idea that such a ball was worth theorizing about anyway. The existence of imperfect citizens and media need not impede scientific study of them, unless we allow it to.

This book has been produced by social scientists who are willing to assume, in some degree or another, that the study of political communication needs to be approached from fresh intellectual perspectives, and with new tools. Their goal is not the achievement of positive certitude about human behavior; it is the more pragmatic aim of developing vigorous and challenging fields of inquiry. By devising new kinds of questions to ask about communication and politics, and by sharpening the methodological procedures for this work, the contributors to this volume are striving toward lines of investigation that can free social scientists from the eternal normative conundrums of the past.

Far from relieving us of issues of democratic values, these new research directions are quite likely to lead to the crystallization of ever more problems in the realm of human and societal judgment. Modern science, after all, has posed new ethical concerns—nuclear weapons, eugenics, and environmental pollution are obvious examples—and has failed to solve more than a handful of traditional ones. Similarly new dilemmas have been created by such fruits of political communication research as modern techniques of "selling" candidates, and the projection of election winners from survey and early-precinct data before polls have closed in some areas. Empirical investigation is not a magical procedure for finding all the answers, it is a constant process of setting more penetrating questions. What is sought in this book is a set of research paradigms through which we can extend the depth and breadth of our understanding of the role of communication in political processes. To the extent that these efforts eventually succeed, we will have clarified what is going on and gained some ideas of what can be done to cope with this massive problem of modern society. And even were the entire enterprise to fail in all its purposes, there remains something to be said on behalf of tilting at new intellectual windmills.

The material presented in this volume is a collection of invited papers on aspects of political communication research that have either been very productive in recent years and thus stand in need of summing up, or that have been neglected to date and thus could stand some stimulation and direction. While the ancestral bloodlines of this effort may be dubious, its immediate genesis can be attributed to several sources. Most directly, it was conceived by the editors of this Annual Review series, Peter Clarke and F. Gerald Kline, as a research topic whose time had come—or, more exactly, would be coming soon after publication, with the onset of the 1976 election season. Our editorial apprehension that politics and communication might be too narrow a focus to sustain a full collection of papers was resolved by developing a broader conception of that field than has been traditionally held—in terms of both the substantive scope of research and appropriate methodologies. Professor Kline was particularly instrumental in conceptualizing the total package and in securing the participation of other contributors.

Beyond the immediate editorial responsibilities, several institutions helped stimulate this project. Perhaps the most important is the John and Mary R. Markle Foundation, which funded several of the projects from which chapters of this book were produced. Through the sustained efforts of Forrest Chisman of the Markle staff, the past few years have seen not only a rejuvenation of research on political communication, but the establishment of a standing committee of the Social Science Research Council devoted to Mass Communication and Political Behavior. In addition to reviewing and generating proposals for research on the 1976 election (Patterson and Abeles, 1975), this committee has served as a point of contact between those planning this book and other branches of political behavior research.[1] Essential, too, have been several academic organizations,—notably the Association for Education in Journalism—whose conventions have provided a locus for reporting findings, exchanging viewpoints, and discussing new directions for the study of political communication. Meetings of the American Association for Public Opinion Research and the International Communication Association have been similarly helpful as gathering places for many of the ideas and persons represented in the pages that follow.

The support of the University of Wisconsin and its Mass Communications Research Center has been essential to the preparation of this volume. In addition to financial sustenance from the Wisconsin Alumni Research Foundation through the Research Committee of the Graduate School, and from the William F. Vilas Trust Estate, there have been numerous contributors to the editorial task. Among those helping with thinking have been Jack M. McLeod, Harold L. Nelson, Mary Ann Yodelis, Albert R. Tims, Richard Martin, Jean Lewin and Donna Wilson. And nothing would have been possible without the expert secretarial skills of Mary Ann Coffman.

The authors who have contributed chapters here took on extraordinary tasks. Rather than simply summarize their own research, or that of a field in which they had been working recently, they were asked to address specific topic areas from a new perspective. Since the purpose of the volume is to look ahead to new types of research, each author was asked to (a) organize the assigned field from a theoretical perspective that would lead to the asking of new empirical questions and (b) discuss the pragmatics of research procedures and methodology appropriate to that perspective. These two foci are not equally applicable to every topic area, of course. The resulting chapters lay greater emphasis on theory in some cases, and practical methodology in others.

The first three chapters are heavily substantive and theoretical in their focus, and follow a progression from individual to system as levels of discourse. Becker, McCombs and McLeod provide a compendium of recent research on the development of political cognitions in individuals. Two dominant themes in this area have been the role of communication in political socialization, and the effects of the mass media in setting the agenda of political topics that people consider. Kline and Siune consider a different level of analysis, the concept of "mass" political communication that has suffused so much normative and critical writing regarding this domain of social behavior. Chaffee attempts to combine several bodies of theory and research on social and political systems into an agenda for research on macro-political processes as they involve individuals within the system as a whole.

The following four chapters attack in depth specific types of research that seem to hold considerable promise for the future. The first of these, the study of election campaigns, is of course a well established tradition in the field. But as O'Keefe's chapter makes clear, new ways of organizing both conceptualization and data-gathering in election studies are being developed that are likely to alter substantially the conclusions that future investigators will reach. Blumler and Gurevitch present a careful rationale and agenda for a type of research that to date has scarcely been discussed, much less actually performed. This is cross-national comparative study of political communication processes; as they point out, some of the most important questions cannot be addressed by data from less ambitious research undertakings. Kraus, Davis, Lang and Lang explore the possibilities of organizing research around major discrete events that test the relationship between mass media and politics, rather than around generic concepts. They set out a proposal for establishing "fire house" teams that can be rushed into the field during critical periods. Rivers, Miller and Gandy review what we know—and consider how we might learn more—about relationships between the media and government officials and bodies. As they observe, this area has been characterized by highly descriptive research that has suffered from the lack of organizing themes and programatic work.

The final three chapters discuss methodologies whose applications to political communication have been overly limited in the past. Rothschild brings the perspective of marketing and consumer behavior to the political arena, and demonstrates how experimentation and multiple operationalism can enrich the field—both by providing convergent evidence for the replication of existing findings, and by opening up new kinds of questions that could not be studied with traditional methods. Stevens looks at political communication research from the perspective of a historian, and shows how the methods of social science can be applied to archived material. This can be seen as a form of comparative research, on a par with the cross-national comparative approach of Blumler and Gurevitch; while the latter advocate comparative examination of different systems in the future, Stevens notes that there is much to be learned from comparison of the same (U.S.) system at different points of its development in time past. Finally, the reader will sense a distinct change of environment in the last chapter, in which Gillmor and Dennis combine an introduction to methods of legal scholarship with a prospectus for the study of judicial institutions. Since they must use the footnoting format of the legal discipline, this paper may superficially strike the reader as different in kind from the earlier chapters. But substantively the Gillmor and Dennis chapter can be seen as a part of the whole; legal questions grow out of political ones, and research on the law and judicial institutions is a necessary extension of political communication research. While most legal scholars could be faulted for their lack of expertise in social research methods, it is at least as unfortunate that so few who work in the behavioral tradition are competent to analyze the legal principles that place so many constraints on political communication processes. Gillmor and Dennis are more at home in the law library than in the computing center, to be sure, but their appreciation of the practices and potentialities of many branches of social science for their area of study is a welcome attempt at bridging one of the widest gaps in the field.

Despite the diversity of viewpoints, disciplines, and levels of analysis represented in these chapters, there is at least one major theme that is common to most, if not all of them. At least since the publication in 1960 of Klapper's major synthesis of the Columbia University findings of only limited political effects of the mass media, it has been typical in academic circles to assume that communication campaigns can make only minor dents in the political edifice. Citizens' processing of media information has been thought to be highly selective, conditioned by partisan predispositions, and subordinate to interpersonal influences (the "two-step flow"). Almost any message received, so it has seemed, would stand a good chance of having at most the net effect of reinforcing the person's existing cognitive state.

This limited effects model is simply not believed by the authors of the chapters that follow. The possibility that media effects on politics are only minor remains, but it is not *assumed* in this book. Instead many of these chapters are devoted to an analysis of the narrow range of studies from which limited effects have been inferred—and to proposing alternate directions for research that might demonstrate how limited the limited-effects model is. This has to be an exciting prospect for any student of political communication.

Public policy regarding the mass media has traditionally been established by politicians, lawyers, bureaucrats, and media management personnel, with only tangential (and often tendentious) reference to research findings. The limited effects model has historically been exploited to justify limited public constraints on the media, a position that happily jibes with normative beliefs in the rightness of First Amendment protections of freedom of press and of speech. In recent years a number of constraints have been imposed—again without much in the way of empirical evidence to support the assumption of their wisdom. The authors of this book are technical specialists in research disciplines, but they also manifest the generalist's concern for policy questions. In opening up new lines of study, and in proposing better ways of studying time-honored questions, their highest hope might well be to specify those elements of the communication-politics nexus that stand in need of public control—and those that ought to be left free of it.

NOTE

1. This committee has been chaired by SSRC President Eleanor Bernert Sheldon, and staffed by David Statt and Ronald Abeles of SSRC. Members, in addition to Kline, Chaffee and Chisman, have been Ben H. Bagdikian, Leo Bogart, Richard A. Brody, Philip E. Converse, Herbert Hyman, Thomas E. Patterson and Ithiel de Sola Pool.

REFERENCES

BERELSON, B. R., P. F. LAZARSFELD and W. N. McPHEE (1954) Voting: A Study of Opinion Formation in a Presidential Campaign. Chicago: Univ. of Chicago Press,

CAREY, J. W. (1974) "The problem of journalism history." Journalism History 1 (spring) 3-5.

KLAPPER, J. T. 1960) The Effects of Mass Communication. New York: Free Press.

LIPPMANN, W. (1922) Public Opinion. New York: Macmillan.

---, (1955) The Public Philosophy. Boston: Little, Brown.

PATTERSON, T. E. and R. P. ABELES (1975) "Mass communications and the 1976 presidential election." Items 29 (20) 13-18. New York: Social Science Research Council.

Chapter 1

THE DEVELOPMENT OF POLITICAL COGNITIONS

Lee B. Becker, Maxwell E. McCombs and
Jack M. McLeod

ON THE AVERAGE WEEKDAY, the typical U.S. newspaper devotes about 4 per cent of its non-advertising items to editorial
comments, according to a study by the Newspaper Advertising
Bureau (1972). Another 12 per cent of the content is set aside for
various kinds of columns, some dealing with politics and public
affairs. On the same day, the television networks are likely to set
aside about 16 per cent of their evening news broadcasts for commentary, a study by the American Institute for Political Communication (1974) has shown. Local stations, however, rarely include
editorial comment in their programming.

Many of these editorials and commentaries are intended to tell
readers and viewers how to evaluate personalities in the news or what
opinions to have on current events. Many others, however, are not.
Only about 24 per cent of the dailies in the U.S. even endorse a
candidate for president.[1] Editorials often take no stand on important issues; readers are presented with interpretive information and
left to derive their own opinions.

Readers and viewers do report relatively high levels of exposure to
the editorials carried. The Advertising Bureau study, for example,
finds that 25 per cent of newspaper readers report reading the
average editorial; readership of selected, typical public affairs news

AUTHORS' NOTE: The first two authors acknowledge the support of the John Ben
Snow Foundation in preparation of this chapter. The John and Mary R. Markle
Foundation also assisted in preparation of the chapter through a grant to the third
author.

items is also 25 per cent. And a recent national study showed that 41 per cent of newspaper readers reported reading editorials and opinion columns "frequently," compared with 38 per cent for stories about local politics and 37 per cent for national politics.[2]

But these relatively high exposure levels may be misleading. Blume and Lyons (1968), in a study of potential voters in Toledo, Ohio, found that only about one-third of the respondents could correctly say which gubernatorial candidate the local newspaper favored, and less than two of every ten respondents knew the paper's endorsement for a state senate race. Three-fourths of the voters said the paper's endorsements were immaterial to them in deciding how to vote. Similarly McCombs (1967) has shown that relatively few people even meet the minimum requirements necessary for demonstrating newspaper endorsement effects. In his study of six California races, McCombs found that as few as 4 per cent of the voters for a state senate race reported that their votes matched those of their newspapers editorial endorsements and that they had made up their minds after seeing the editorials. The largest percentage of voters "eligible" for the effect was 19 per cent for a technical taxation proposition on the ballot. While such factors do not render the effects of newspaper endorsement totally immaterial, they do suggest they may be relatively unimportant when other media content and effects are considered. Robinson (1974), using national survey data from the last five presidential elections, concluded that there is about a 3 per cent differential effect that could be attributed to newspaper endorsements when the voter's party identification and twelve other predictors of voting behavior were controlled statistically.

INFORMATION TRANSMITTAL VS. PERSUASION

Most of the resources of newspapers and news staffs of television and radio stations are devoted to information transmittal, not persuasion. The reporter covering the city council meeting may hope his or her readers form certain opinions as the result of the information placed in the news story, but the purpose of the story is to provide the information. The sports desk editor who sets aside space for baseball standings cares little what evaluations the readers makes of the teams, or the sport itself, based on the statistics. The editor simply is concerned with presenting the materials. Providing the audience members with information, as any introductory reporting text will say, is the primary function of the modern journalistic profession. Commenting on the information and trying to shape public opinion through editorial persuasion is of secondary importance.

It is ironic, then, that the literature of political communications has focused extensively on the persuasive function of the media and attitude change and relegated to minor study the information transmittal function and information holding. The kinds of messages that occupy most of the time of practicing journalists have gone largely unstudied *in their own right*. While much of the research literature has considered information transmittal an important intermediary effect, the ultimate criterion has been assumed to be persuasion, and the information transmittal findings have been obscured by those pertaining to attitude change. As a result, we know less about the effectiveness of the media in doing what they do most often than we know about what occupies a relatively small amount of their energies and attention.

Historical Basis for Persuasion Emphasis

This imbalance in favor of the study of persuasive effects is more understandable when viewed from its historical perspective. The use of the mass media by such political leaders as Father Coughlin in this country and Mussolini and Hitler in Europe to stir public sentiments and form fascistic political attitudes caused many social scientists to worry about the impact of "manipulative media" on a "susceptible citizenry" in the 1930s and 1940s. Sears and Whitney (1973) have noted that the social scientists responding to these fears shared four distinct orientations. First, they were socially motivated, particularly by a fear for democracy's future. Second, their primary goal was to reduce the impact of the demagogues by providing citizens with insight into the mechanisms by which propaganda had its impact. Third, they assumed a totally gullible audience. And fourth, they focused almost exclusively on the propagandist's tricks of rhetoric in explaining the effects of the message. For them, the audience was monolithic and effects could be assumed; the message was the important variable for study.

In this atmosphere of assumed "hypodermic-type" effects of the media, two of the most important programs of research in the field of communications were begun. The Information and Education Branch of the Army began recruiting sociologists and psychologists to study communications effects, particularly those related to the use of orientation films such as *The Battle of Britain*. The Army wanted to know how best to teach needed skills to World War II inductees, and how to change their attitudes in the direction of "good morale." Under learning psychologist Carl Hovland, experiments were designed to determine the impact that message and communicator variables had on persuasion and learning—a focus continued when the research program was moved to Yale University after the war. The series of publications resulting from Hovland's Yale Communication and Attitude Change Program have been some of the most influential in the short history of communication research (Hovland, 1957; Hovland and Janis, 1959; Rosenberg, Hovland, McGuire, Abelson and Brehm, 1960).

While the Yale laboratory findings can be seen in retrospect as challenging some of the assumptions of the "hypodermic" model of media effects, a more serious threat to that perspective came from field studies conducted in the same era by Columbia University's Bureau of Applied Social Research. Their first survey was conducted during the 1940 presidential campaign in Erie County, Ohio, with the expectation that the mass media would be influential in affecting the vote outcome (Lazarsfeld, Berelson and Gaudet, 1948). Little evidence of strong media effects on voting was found, however, and the emphasis of the analysis in this and succeeding studies was on the role of interpersonal influence in voter decision making. The Erie County study, despite its limitations due to site selection (the county went Republican in a Democratic landslide) and historical timing (it was long before the age of television), has had lasting impact on the field of political communications. Klapper (1960) summarized much of this research and concluded the media effects are limited, and when they do occur are mediated by other variables such as interpersonal communications and *the orientations of the audience members themselves* to the communicated message. Beginning in 1952 the major election studies have been conducted by the Survey Research Center at the University of Michigan rather than at Columbia, but the limited effects model has remained very much in vogue. The impact of this model, as well as the "hypodermic" model, on communication research has been recounted by Blumler and McLeod (1974), McLeod and Becker (1974), McLeod, Becker and Byrnes (1974) and McCombs and Bowers (1975), among others. We will make reference to the impact of these models again when we discuss in greater detail the Columbia and Michigan studies.

Cognitions vs. Attitudes

It would be misleading to conclude that the Yale and Columbia projects were unconcerned with communication effects other than persuasion. Some of the more dramatic findings reported by Hovland and his associates are for information gain, not attitude formation or change. Hovland, Lumsdaine and Sheffield (1949), in fact, found information gain and attitude change to be unrelated to one another in their study of the effects of the indoctrination film, *The Battle of Britain*. The Columbia studies also assessed political information levels. But both programs of research maintained a primary focus on the factors leading to attitude change; information was studied only as an intermediary process of relatively little interest for its own sake.

McGuire (1969), in his review of the theoretical definitions of attitudes, does note that many theorists have attempted to differentiate between the effects of educational and persuasive appeals. These attempts have led to a cognition/attitude distinction that is of particular interest here. McGuire (1968, 1969) has posited a model of persuasive effects that attempts to differentiate between variance explained in persuasion due to the attention of the message recipient to (and his or her comprehension of) the message, on the one hand, and yielding to the message's persuasive appeal on the other. Comprehension would be labeled a cognition, as separate from the attitude which is either changed or left as before the persuasive message.

The position we take in this chapter is that attitudes are summary evaluations of objects by individuals while cognitions are stored information about those objects held by individuals. The evaluations may be based on cognitions the individual has about the objects, but the dynamics of the relationship between the cognitions and the attitudes are complex, allowing for seemingly idiosyncratic assemblages of cognitions. For example, the evaluation of the object "the Republican Party" that underlies the summary statement, "The Republican Party is bad for the country," would be termed an attitude. The information the individual holds which is used to form the evaluation we would call cognitions. Not all cognitions, of course, are used to form attitudes.

Implicit in our cognition/attitude distinction is the assumption that cognitions can be measured independently of attitudes and have the potential of being evaluated against some external, objective criterion of communicated information. While no one can assert that an individual holds the "correct" attitude of a given object, it is usually possible to determine if the information being held by the individual is correct. This theoretical assumption has implications for the research we discuss here, and it will be dealt with in greater detail later. It only need be said now that not all researchers working in the area seem to agree on the best method of measuring and evaluating cognitions—or even whether it is profitable to evaluate them.

While other types of distinctions are made in the literature of attitude change, we are not attempting further differentiation here. We are treating as equal the terms attitude, value and opinions. Our key distinction is between cognition, which does not imply an evaluation by an individual, and attitude, which does. The distinction between cognition and attitude becomes hazy at times, particularly as we deal with such global objects as political systems and institutions. But it is one we feel is worth making to help refocus attention of media effects studies away from persuasion.

The Range of Possible Effects

The historical focus on persuasion has particularly drawn attention away from those cognitions thought to be most independent of atttitudes. Only recently have researchers begun to study the media's impact on the views of reality held by audience members and the consequences of these cognitions for the audience. A number of studies, beginning with the seminal work by McCombs and Shaw (1972), have dealt with media effects on the saliences of public issues. This research, which has developed from consideration of the media's role as determiner of the community's agenda, will be discussed in detail in this chapter. Socialization research also has begun to focus on the media's role in creating the cognitive images we hold of our political and social system as well as the impact of these cognitions on subsequent behavior.

The attitudinal focus of the field in previous decades also resulted in the slighting of a host of other possible media effects. Relatively unstudied are media effects on voter turnout and political activity or interest in general. Also given little attention are media effects on information seeking, particularly that directed at one medium such as newspapers resulting from exposure to the content of another, such as television or radio. Media effects on interpersonal communications have largely been ignored, although it is likely that the content and extent of people's interpersonal discussion are determined at least in part by what they see and read in the media. The style of such discussions and the nature of the interpersonal contacts formed are also likely to be productive areas of research. Similarly, we know relatively little about the effects of the media on types of child-rearing and general living habits. While child and adolescent research has focused extensively on such anti-social effects of the media as violent responses to social situations, relatively little is known about learning from the media of pro-social behaviors. Considerable research also has been done on consumer behavior, but here too the focus has been largely on the formation of favorable evaluations of products and not information holding about them. The effects of the media on the emotions of the audience members beyond specific object-centered attitudes have also received surprisingly little attention. The arousal of fear, passion or affection, as well as changes in mood state or levels of sexual arousal, are important areas that remain in need of investigation from a communication research perspective.

The Concept of Development

Most of what each of us knows about the political environment is provided by the media since our own personal experiences are limited by temporal and spatial restrictions. Most of the political world comes to us as a second-hand reality. The media have helped us form our first political cognitions and have led to changes in them across time. The media have played a key role in the development of what we know about the world around us.

Much of our detailed knowledge about the power of the media to form and develop political cognitions comes from those classical studies of media effects conducted by the Columbia researchers, plus the literature on information campaigns, and some socialization research. But new programs of research are developing, contributing to our understanding of the link between "the world outside" and "the pictures in our heads" (Lippmann, 1922).

THE COLUMBIA AND
MICHIGAN VOTING STUDIES

No other series of studies has had as much impact on the study of political communication as that conducted in the 1940s and 1950s by Columbia University's Bureau of Applied Social Research. And the most important study in the series, because of its impact on both the subsequent Columbia work and that conducted elsewhere, was the 1940 Erie County project. The intent of the study, Lazarsfeld, Berelson and Gaudet (1948) report, was "to discover how and why people decided to vote as they did" (p. 1). To achieve that end, personal interviews were conducted each month from May through November of the election year with a panel of 600 residents of the Ohio county.

The Columbia research team found that only limited change was taking place during the 1940 campaign. Almost half of the voters who went to the polls in November had already known in May (the time of the first interview) how they would vote; they maintained their choices throughout the campaign, and voted accordingly in November. Another block of voters (more than a quarter of the sample) decided on a candidate during the convention period, and maintained that choice in November. For this group, the decision had been finally determined by the end of August. Only about 25 per cent of the voters made their final vote decision during the major phases of "the campaign."

Even for these undecided voters, however, the issues of the campaign were judged to be relatively unimportant. Only 8 per cent of the total sample was found to actually change vote intentions substantially during the campaign. Most of this change was in the direction of consistency with pre-campaign "predispositions", as indexed by the person's religion, social class, and place of residence. Little change appeared to be the result of campaign developments.

While such factors limit the possible impact of the media during a campaign, Lazarsfeld, Berelson and Gaudet did not conclude that mass communication was unimportant. Rather, they found evidence the media play a decisive role in increasing interest in the campaign, which had the important subsequent effect of stimulating more information seeking about the election. But the researchers found what they interpreted as *selective exposure* to the "propaganda" in the media; they concluded that voters used the content of the media to support the vote conclusion they would have reached because of their social predispositions. Similarly, the Columbia researchers concluded that the block of voters who exposed themselves to the media during the campaign despite firm earlier decisions on vote choice were seeking *reinforcement* of their decision, not new information.

The key finding on selective exposure to the media is based on analysis of 122 persons who had not made a vote decision by August.

The researchers reported that 54 per cent of the 79 persons in this group with a Republican predisposition exposed themselves mainly to Republican campaign materials. Similarly, 61 per cent of the 43 persons categorized as predisposed toward the Democratic candidate exposed themselves mainly to Democratic materials. Among the Republicans, 11 per cent exposed themselves to an equal balance of materials, while the comparable figure for Democrats is 17 per cent. But 35 per cent of the Republicans did expose themselves predominantly to Democratic materials, while 22 per cent of the Democrats saw mostly Republican materials.

The selectivity interpretation becomes somewhat suspect, when considered in light of the media content of the election period. The researchers judged 55 per cent of the campaign materials to be Republican, 25 per cent Democratic, and the rest neutral. This makes the Republican exposure to Democratic materials more difficult to explain in terms of selectivity; and both Democratic and Republican exposure to Republican materials are easier to explain without inferring selectivity. Only Democrats exposed primarily to Democratic materials, and those individuals with a decidedly neutral level of exposure were clearly behaving selectively.

Furthermore, the Columbia researchers found some rather striking evidence of political effects that could be attributed directly to the media. Among persons with Republican predispositions *and* predominantly Republican media exposure, only 15 per cent voted for the Democratic candidate; but the Democratic vote among Republicans with predominantly Democratic exposure is 47 per cent. For the Democrats with predominantly Republican exposure, 49 per cent voted Republican, compared to 25 per cent of the Democrats who received predominantly Democratic exposure. The Columbia researchers nevertheless concluded that interpersonal influence was the more important force in explaining this effect, although no direct evidence for this conclusion was presented.

The interpersonal-versus-mass communication influence interpretations are based, in part, on the findings that on the average day, 10 per cent more people reported participating in a discussion of the election than listened to a major speech or read about campaign items in the newspaper. In addition, people who made up their minds later in the campaign were more likely to mention personal influences in explaining their decision.

The Erie County study focused on only one media effect: persuasion leading to a vote choice. The only intermediary effect, information seeking, was not pursued because of the dominant selective exposure interpretation. No attempt was made to measure information received from the media, or other relevant cognitions. Despite the fact that a key conclusion of the Erie County study regarding the relative impact of interpersonal forces and media content was based on "impresssions . . . (and) summarized without much formal statistical data" (p. 150), its conclusions form the basis for much of what we "know" about media effects in campaigns today.

While the Erie County study focused on the aspects of the campaign expected to influence voter decision making, the next study in the series, conducted in Elmira, N.Y., in 1948, examined the social forces leading to voting *consistency across campaigns* (Berelson, Lazarsfeld and McPhee, 1954). The majority of the approximately 1,000 persons interviewed in the southern New York community were found to have personal associations, group contacts, and family traditions largely supportive of their political positions. And while the homogeneity of the voters' social contacts was found to be negatively related to discussion of politics, those persons reporting discussion with homogeneous groups were less likely to change their positions during the campaign than were persons reporting political discussions with heterogeneous social contacts.

Again, there was considerable evidence of vote stability in Elmira during the campaign. Almost two-thirds of the voters had made up their minds by the time of the first interview in June and did not change during the campaign. Another 15 per cent reached final decisions during August, and 11 per cent more during October. The remaining 10 per cent made their final decisions at election time. Of the total voting sample, only 16 per cent wavered between parties during the campaign, with another 13 per cent moving from "undecided" to an eventual party choice. The researchers remained more impressed with the stability of the vote than with change.

In examining the relationship between exposure to the media during the campaign and the evidence of voter decision making, Berelson et al. found that those persons reporting extensive use of the media during the campaign were less likely to change their votes than were the sample members who reported lower media exposure. This finding held up even after controlling statistically for the effects of the person's interest in politics.

The Columbia researchers did find dramatic evidence of other media effects during the campaign. Again, media exposure was positively related to increase in interest during the campaign. Similarly, media use led to a strengthening of the voters' support for their candidates, and to higher turnout at the polls on election day. In addition, those voters high in media exposure demonstrated a better understanding of the candidates' support among the diverse groups making up the electorate than among those using the media less, and they were more likely to be able to identify accurately both candidates' stands on the issues. Both of these information findings held up after controls for the political interest and level of education of the voter.

A more dramatic finding regarding the media's role in the campaign comes from an analysis of those 1948 voters who, by social background and 1944 vote, were not likely to vote Republican in 1948. For these voters, movement toward the Democratic candidate as the campaign progressed was associated with an increase in the salience of issues such as the Taft-Hartley labor bill and the cost of living. Such issues in that time were clearly associated with the Democratic party. The salience of these "Democratic issues" overrode the voters' unfavorable image of President Truman, with the shift being strongest among those groups holding the least favorable opinion of Truman. To the extent that the voter saw these traditionally Democratic issues as important ones in the campaign, he or she was more likely to support the candidate of that party, even if the candidate was personally evaluated unfavorably.

The Elmira data also provide some evidence as to the origin of the late-campaign increases in the salience of those consumer-labor issues. An analysis of the content of the major campaign speeches of the candidates, which were covered extensively by the media, shows that Truman stressed his stand on the Taft-Hartley Law, inflation, housing, social security and taxation, devoting 39 per cent of his speech content to them. Dewey, on the other hand, devoted only 18 per cent of his speech content to these issues. The Republican candidate, instead, attempted to stress general themes, such as unity and governmental style. But largely because the Democratic candidate decided to stress them, the issues of labor and the consumer were the dominant theme of the media campaign. And among those non-Republican voters exposing themselves to this media content there was an increase in the salience of the Democratic issues during the late campaign. The media played an important role in determining which issues were before the voters, and, via this indirect route, in the outcome of the election. The role of the media in placing these issues before the voters is a theme we will return to.

Many of these findings regarding non-persuasive media effects were replicated in the final major election study undertaken by the Columbia Bureau of Applied Social Research. During the 1950

Congressional elections, panels of voters were interviewed in Colorado, Iowa, Minnesota and Washington, to ascertain the generalizability of the findings from the presidential studies. Glaser and Kadushin (1962) concluded that there was general support for the earlier findings. Media exposure during the campaign was negatively related to indecision; it was positively related to increases in interest and strength of voting decision, to accuracy of information about the candidates' stands on the issues, and to turnout. For the most part, exposure was again found to be negatively related to change in vote intention during the campaign, though the Iowa panel did not show this effect.

With the 1952 presidential election, the University of Michigan's Survey Research Center became the dominant research force in large-scale voter studies. After a small pilot study in the 1948 election, (Campbell and Kahn, 1952) the SRC launched in 1952 (Campbell, Gurin and Miller, 1954) the first in a series of major studies relying on panels of potential voters drawn to represent the entire U.S. electorate rather than a single community. The shift to SRC represented a conceptual as well as a methodological change. The SRC studies clearly moved away from data-gathering aimed at the sociological explanations of voting which characterized the Columbia work, and toward data that would lead to cognitive and attitudinal explanations of voting decisions. For the first time, voters were asked to *indicate* their party affiliation; the Columbia researchers had studied party via the *predispositions* that led people to vote for one party rather than another. Attitudes and evaluations of candidates played a prominent role in the SRC studies, in the tradition of V. O. Key Jr., a prominent critic of the Columbia studies.

But the choice of a methodology also had impact on the kinds of problems that the SRC researchers *could* study. The Columbia researchers had focused on single communities for their major studies, investigating the traditions of the communities, their sociological structure and composition, and the nature of major institutions in those communities. The national studies conducted by SRC made this kind of contextual consideration impossible. To a large extent, each voter was considered to have an identical social environment; voting was considered to be an individual phenomenon that produced aggregate national effects, not a local one with a community base.

This shift from the community to the nation as a center for study had tremendous impact on the study of the role of the media in the election. Despite the long tradition in this country of local media institutions, the SRC studies, particularly as represented in the summaries of the 1948 through 1960 elections (Campbell, Converse, Miller and Stokes, 1960, 1966), forced a conception of the media as national. The rise in prominence of the broadcast networks and the news magazines, as well as broadly regional newspapers such as the New York Times and the Los Angeles Times, seemed to justify this shift. But such a decision ignores peculiarities of media roles within a community that may serve to counter the influence of the national media or limit their influence to select audiences. The SRC research made content analysis of the local media institutions extremely difficult and forced researchers to guess what users of the media were receiving. The result was that the potential effects of the media on the voter's "cognitive and affective map of politics"—on which the SRC studies focused—was left largely unexplored. Media use was considered an individual political activity, in the same category as attending political rallies and contributing financial support to one of the parties.

Interpersonal communication, identified by the Columbia team as one of the most important sources of influence in decision making, similarly was relegated to a relatively unimportant position in the SRC model. The "two-step flow" notion of information diffusion pursued by Columbia researchers Katz and Lazarsfeld (1954) in non-campaign settings, has not been made the major subject of inquiry in political settings. In fact, Sheingold (1973) has argued that the national focus of the Michigan studies has made impossible the pursuit of the role of social networks in the study of voting, despite the strong suggestion in the Columbia data of the merit of this line of inquiry. The national concern of SRC also has drawn attention away from the study of the mass media and interpersonal relationship as it relates to political campaigns. Social network research could help us understand both *what* campaign information is transmitted by the media to the individual voter and *how* it is transmitted—or through which networks. In short, pursuit of this avenue of study might help us isolate contingent conditions that govern media influence.

INFORMATION CAMPAIGNS

A second area of research with lasting impact on our understanding of the communication of political and public affairs materials has dealt with the effects of information campaigns. Despite their descriptive title, however, these studies have tended to center more on the media's role in persuasion than on simple information transmittal; the latter has, however, been examined as an intermediary process.

Hyman and Sheatsley (1947), using data gathered by the National Opinion Research Center of the University of Chicago, reported evidence that despite the prominence of the issues in the media, the general population remained relatively ignorant of developments in Palestine, aspects of atomic energy, a proposed loan to England under debate in Congress, and other international matters. But the more important finding, the researchers argued, was the relationship between lack of knowledge in one of these areas and low levels of knowledge in others. The researchers concluded that they had identified a group of "chronic know-nothings" who successfully isolated themselves from the effects of information campaigns. The "know-nothings" were uninterested in public affairs, an attitude found to be highly related to lack of knowledge about such matters.

Hyman and Sheatsley did not have direct measures of exposure to the content of the media; to the extent that interest in public affairs can be considered a surrogate for media use, their findings can be interpreted as potentially supportive of inferred media effects on information levels. Those individuals most interested in public affairs were most knowledgeable about them. Further analysis, however, seemed to indicate that information level was unrelated to a change in attitude on the American loan to England for those people with a negative *predisposition* toward that nation—a finding which the authors emphasized over any possible effect of media exposure.

The Cincinnati information campaign on the United Nations, also evaluated by NORC (Star and Hughes, 1950), seemed to offer further support for the Hyman and Sheatsley findings. Information levels regarding the U.N. were found to remain relatively constant in the Ohio city despite an extensive media and interpersonal campaign aimed at increasing awareness of and knowledge about the international governmental body. Star and Hughes found that those people who reported exposing themselves to media messages about the U.N. were the well-educated, younger members of the community—precisely the group most likely to know a great deal about the organization before the campaign began. Similarly, those highest in exposure were persons who were most favorably inclined toward the international organization before the campaign. Media effects seemed to be blocked by the predispositions of the audience members; from the point of view of the researchers, the media were not successful mechanisms for transmitting information nor for changing community attitudes.

Despite the limitations of these early studies, the interpretations have become part of the accepted findings of the field, reinforcing the conclusions of the Columbia program. These interpretations, however, have been undermined in a small way by Douglas, Westley and Chaffee (1970), who not only found evidence that an information campaign did change community attitudes, but also showed that variation within the community of level of information about the test subject (mental retardation) was related to level of media exposure. Similarly, Mendelsohn (1973) has argued that the null effects interpretation of the early information campaign studies has placed the blame on the audience, rather than on the transmitter of the message. To make a campaign succeed, the message must be designed to meet the needs and interests of the audience. Only then can media effects be judged.

POLITICAL SOCIALIZATION

These early studies of voting and information campaigns dealt with changes in cognitions over relatively short periods, usually less than a year. The development of political cognitions over longer periods has been the focus of a rapidly growing body of research on political socialization (see Sigel, 1965; Dawson and Prewitt, 1969; Sears, 1969; Dennis, 1973; Kraus, 1973).

Socialization research is of particular interest here since it deals with the early stages in the life cycle when critical political cognitions are being formed. By the time children reach second grade, recognition of important government leaders is about at adult levels. But young children tend to see government in terms of the people involved in them, not the roles these people play or the institutions they represent. As a result, children over-estimate the importance of the president in government, thinking he "runs the government" or makes law. Research of the 1960s showed that children also expressed extremely positive affect for the president, seeing him as protective and benevolent. More recent research, however, shows that this "universal" finding may have been time-bound; children raised in the shadow of Vietnam and Watergate show drastically lower levels of affect for the office of the president and even for government in general (Dennis and Webster, 1975; Rogers and Lewis, 1975). There has been a cognitive shift toward perceiving the president as a less powerful figure, less knowledgeable, and less helpful.

The years of adolescence were once thought of as quiescent in terms of political development. It is true that little gain is shown in levels of party affiliation, political efficacy, or trust in the political system (McLeod, Chaffee, and Wackman, 1975). On the other hand, significant increases between the seventh and eleventh grade in level of political knowledge and in the abstract conception of community are found. While time spent with television declines about 10 per cent during this period (from a peak level at about age 12), the level of attention to news and public affairs content on television and in newspapers moves from very low to at least moderate levels. While it is possible that growth in both public affairs media use and political sophistication during this period are merely coincidental, a functional argument would seem to have some merit. Unfortunately, the political socialization literature fails us on this point. For the most part, youthful exposure to public affairs content is usually treated as an indicator of political development—a dependent variable related to age.

Direct investigation of the media as socializing agents has been infrequently attempted; instead most attention has been directed to the role of the family and of schools. The media are assumed to exert influence on political cognitions "somehow," though evidence for this is largely intuitive. Since exposure to television begins early in life and occupies as much of the young school child's time as does school (Schramm, Lyle and Parker, 1961; Lyle and Hoffman, 1971), it is "obvious" that it must be a source of influence. A more exact specification of the role of media is needed. Exposure to news content could be simply the process by which social class distinctions are manifested, or it could be a mechanism evening out gaps in information. Its effect could be direct or it could interact with a host of other variables to have such a socializing effect. Or the correlation between media use and political cognitions could be spurious, and hence media would have little role in development.

Fortunately, there is relevant empirical evidence for some of these questions (see Chaffee, Jackson-Beeck, Lewin and Wilson, 1975). We do know that the media constitute the primary source of political information for children and adolescents (Johnson, 1967; Hollander, 1971; Dominick, 1972). And Chaffee, Ward and Tipton (1970) used cross-lag correlation techniques to test the hypothesis that public affairs media exposure leads to knowledge gain. Shortly after the presidential primaries in 1968, the media use and political knowledge of Wisconsin junior and senior high school students were measured. Comparable measures were obtained after the November election that year. The data suggest that media use leads to knowledge gain during the campaign more strongly than the reverse causal sequence. Since controls for education and other potentially contaminating influences did not disturb the media-to-knowledge relationship, the impact of media cannot be said to be a simple extension of educational or social class differences. The news media also seem to convey information to younger children. Atkin and Gantz (1975) used longitudinal data to show that attention to television news predicted to gains in knowledge of public figures and current events. Other types of cognitions also may be affected by the media. Using cross-lag analysis of young voters in 1972 and 1974, McLeod, Brown and Becker (1975) found that those who were relatively frequent users of newspaper and television public affairs content tended to increase their sense of political efficacy in the face of the Watergate scandal while others came to feel less efficacious.

The question remains, however, as to how these media use patterns developed in the first place. Many studies have shown that higher levels of parental education and social class are related to the child's media use, but the dynamics of that influence are not clear. The Wisconsin data discussed above showed that parent-child communication patterns were related to public affairs media use of adolescents even after educational and other factors were controlled (McLeod, Chaffee and Wackman, 1975). Homes where the child is taught to express ideas and is exposed to public controversy, and where there is little emphasis on deference to parents and on harmony, are apt to produce adolescents who use media public affairs content and are less interested than others in the entertainment aspects of television. Atkin and Gantz (1975) found that the extent to which parents discussed current events with their young children was antecedent to both television news watching and knowledge increase among grade school youngsters.

While these and other findings testify to the importance of the media in the political socialization of adolescents, a great number of questions remain unanswered. One of these is the permanence of patterns established during adulthood. Chaffee, Jackson-Beeck, Lewin and Wilson (1975) present data showing that the influences of *adolescent* media use on political knowledge decrease substantially compared with these effects some eight years later. McLeod and O'Keefe (1972) suggest that the continuance of adolescent influence is contingent upon the continuity of experiences in occupational and sex roles encountered in young adulthood. The longitudinal data of Himmelweit and Swift (1975) appear to support this formulation.

Another remaining question is the appropriate model for the media's socializing effects. Some of the studies support direct effects inferences while others suggest various types of contingent and contributory conditions. Recent work on the gratifications sought from political content suggests that the motivational bases of use may be as important as exposure per se in determining political effects (McLeod and Becker, 1974). This work has examined only young and older adults; it might be usefully extended into the study of the political socialization of younger age groups.

THE AGENDA-SETTING HYPOTHESIS

Recent socialization research is illustrative of the trend in political communications to specify areas of likely media effects other than direct persuasion. One of the most fruitful branches of research to result from this reconsideration has been studied under the functionalist rubric of media "agenda-setting." Clearly here the focus has moved away from the question of opinion formation, to specification of the media's role in development of specific cognitions about issues in the public domain.

This notion of an agenda-setting function of the mass media specifies a strong, positive relationship between the emphases of mass media coverage and the salience of these topics in the minds of individuals in the audience. The relationship is explicitly stated in causal terms: increased emphasis of a topic or issue in the mass media influences *causes* increased salience of that topic or issue for the public. Here may lie one of the most important effects of modern mass communication—the ability of the media to structure our world for us. As Cohen (1963) has summarized it, the mass media may not be successful much of the time in telling people what to think, but the media are stunningly successful in telling their audience what to think *about*.

Research on the agenda-setting function of mass communication has its base in the writings of many of the early communication researchers. Lippmann (1922) sketched the role the media necessarily play in shaping our perceptions of public affairs and our considerations of that vast world beyond our immediate sensory experience. Park (1925) was concerned with the effects of the press's

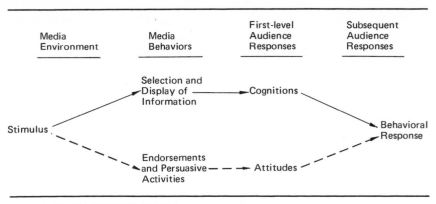

Figure 1: MEDIA EFFECTS MODEL

NOTE: The solid arrows represent the relationships of concern in agenda-setting research. The broken arrows are of concern in attitude change studies.

presentation of news on the topics of conversation within a community. Lasswell (1948) wrote of the media's "surveillance" function. And Schramm (1957) spoke of the media's role in helping readers anticipate events in the world around them. But these notions became obscured by the narrow focus on persuasion effects, and only recently have these ideas about the media's cognitive effects been reformulated and empirical evidence gathered to test them.

What has developed from this reformulation is a concern with the role the media play in putting issues in the fore—or forcing them onto the agenda of a community for discussion and action. Rather than a single relationship, this reformulation has led to specification and examination of a set of relationships between the environment of the media institutions, the resulting media activities, the effects of these behaviors on the audience members, and the consequences of these immediate media effects in terms of subsequent behavior. These relationships are represented in Figure 1 by solid arrows. (Note that agenda-setting is not concerned with the broken arrows in this figure; they are the relationships of concern in attitude change research and they are important in agenda-setting only as they impinge on the other specified relationships.)

Antecedents of Media Behaviors

To a large degree, agenda-setting research to date has dealt with the relationship between the selection and display of issues in the media, and audience cognitions. Less attention has been given to forces in the environment of the media that produce the relevant media behaviors. The available literature on the gatekeeping behavior of reporters and editors, however, can be reconsidered in the agenda-setting framework. This behavior, as Donohue, Tichenor and Olien (1972) note, can be viewed as including all forms of information control that may result from decisions about message encoding, including selecting, shaping, display, timing, withholding, or repetition. Only attitudinal shaping, in this list, would *not* be relevant to agenda-setting.

White (1950), in his classic study of gatekeeping, focused on the selection or rejection of messages. One of the key findings of the gatekeeping literature is that media gatekeepers making these selection decisions seem not to have the audience in mind. Their perceptions of the audience have been found to be somewhat inaccurate (Tannenbaum, 1963; Martin, O'Keefe and Nayman, 1972), and their decisions are more a function of what they think the publisher wants used than what the audience is interested in (Donohew, 1967). In addition, Gieber (1956) and Gold and Simmons (1965), in studies of editors on small daily newspapers in Wisconsin and Iowa, found evidence that the news wire services were making many of the decisions for the editors, i.e. effectively setting the agenda for them. While the editors couldn't use all the copy sent by the Associated Press wire (the percentage used ranged from 5 to 58 per cent in the Iowa study), they used stories on a given topic in the same proportion as provided by the wire. When the AP moved a large number of stories on crime, the editors selected from this set—but they did print a large number of crime stories. When the wire sent only a couple of stories on a topic, the editors again sampled, using roughly the same proportion of these stories as of the other categories. McCombs and Shaw (1974), in a reanalysis of data from earlier gatekeeping studies, replicated this finding of wire service effects on editors.

Additional evidence about antecedents of media behaviors comes from a study of foreign affairs reporters by Cohen (1963). These reporters, interviews indicated, began their day by reading the work of other reporters in an effort to learn what the important news of the day was. In this way, the reporters not only were learning about the *general* types of stories likely to be used by the competition, but they also were obtaining *specific* ideas on what breaking events they needed to cover. News, Cohen's data showed, was clearly defined by the reporters in terms of what the other reporters were reporting as news. Similarly, Crouse (1972), in his participant observation study of reporters covering the 1972 presidential campaign, found that, particularly for difficult stories, reporters checked their versions of what happened with each other (especially with recognized authority figures in the group) to determine if they had decided to report the right thing. If they all agreed, the reporters apparently assumed they had handled the matter correctly.

Additional information about how news decisions are made comes from a study by Sigal (1973) of the front-page content of the New York Times and the Washington Post. Almost 60 per cent of the content was found to have its origin at official proceedings, with press releases or at press conferences, or as the result of some non-spontaneous event such as a speech or ceremony. Another 15 per cent resulted from less formal sources, leaks, nongovernmental proceedings such as organizational meetings, or news reports from other news organizations. Only slightly more than 25 per cent of front-page content in these "prestige papers" could be attributed to reporter enterprise, such as interviews conducted at the reporter's own initiative, spontaneous events witnessed by the reporter, independent research, or the reporter's own conclusions.

This lack of evidence that reporters spend much of their time working on their own initiative does not necessarily indicate the media merely reflect the world around them. Funkhouser (1973b) has shown that media coverage of such crucial stories of the 1960s as the Vietnam War, crime, and urban disorders did not relate well to objective criteria indexing development of these stories. News coverage of the war peaked two years before the number of American troops in Southeast Asia. Similarly, coverage of urban disorder peaked in 1967, while the actual number of disturbances was highest a year later. And crime coverage failed to increase while the number of crimes committed per capita did. The media seem not to mirror perfectly the events of the day, but the image they create through news coverage isn't entirely of their own making. A study of the 1971 Danish general elections by Siune and Borre (1975) suggests that in that country reporters get some cues on what to cover from the politicians; the audience, again, seems to have little real impact.

Settings for Agenda-Setting Research

The basic hypothesized relationship forming the core of agenda-setting is a positive one between the attention given various issues in the media and the saliences assigned these issues by the audience members. A cataloguing of the studies undertaken to date gives some indication of the breadth of problems studied as well as the general flexibility of the model.

By far the most popular setting for agenda-setting research has been election campaigns. And the most studied campaign has been presidential. McCombs and Shaw (1972), in the first empirical test of the agenda-setting relationship, interviewed a sample of "undecided" Chapel Hill, N.C. voters during the 1968 campaign. (That particular subsample of the general population was chosen because it was considered to be the most likely to show media influence.) Analysis indicated that the issues given prominent play in the media during the election were the same ones considered to be important by the voters studied. In 1972, four studies with agenda-setting components were undertaken: Chapel Hill (Mullins, 1973); Charlotte, N.C. (Shaw and McCombs, 1975); Madison, Wisconsin (McLeod, Becker and Byrnes, 1974); and Syracuse, N.Y. (McClure and Patterson, 1973). Though the findings vary by study, some support for the agenda-setting hypothesis surfaces in each case. During the 1971 election in Kentucky, Tipton, Haney and Baseheart (1975) extended the study of agenda-setting to a local election setting, and the media's effects on determining the issues in gubernatorial and mayorality campaigns were considered.

Funkhouser (1973a), Kline (1973), and Martin (1975) have examined the agenda-setting phenomenon using national polling data as an indication of public opinion in non-campaign settings. Again, the issues emphasized by the media during the period of study show high positive correlations with the issues mentioned by the people as important concerns. McCombs (1974) similarly has looked at non-election effects of agenda-setting using data from a local setting.

Other variations on the agenda-setting hypotheses have been tested by Gormley (1975), who found impact of the media on North Carolina state legislators, and by Bowers (1973) and Shaw and Bowers (1973), who examined the relationship between political advertising content and issue saliences. The latter two studies are unique in that they alone have examined the effect of media content other than news. In a largely speculative paper, McCombs and Schulte (1975) have extended agenda-setting to the area of modernization. This process of nation-building, the authors argue, can be thought of as a shifting of agendas. Long-standing social practices—the traditional agenda—must be replaced by a more flexible agenda of new topics. Chaffee and Izcaray (1975), however, were unable to demonstrate more than minor agenda-setting effects in a regional capital of Venezuela—an oil-rich but still developing nation.

Issues Surfacing in the Research

The research undertaken on agenda-setting has generated a series of questions, or dimensions, along which future research is likely to run. These dimensions can be considered in terms of the nature of the effect itself, the process through which it is registered, and the type of content producing the effect.

Nature of the Effect. McLeod, Becker and Byrnes (1974) have argued for conceptual distinctions between three types of saliences likely to be affected by the content emphasized in the media. The first variable, labeled "individual issue salience," is defined as the importance assigned to an issue by an individual in terms of his/her own set of priorities. The second variable, labeled "perceived issue salience," is defined as the importance the individual thinks others are assigning to the issue. As such, it is a reality concept, or an estimate of what relevant others hold to be important. The third criterion variable is the actual amount of importance assigned to an issue by the community; it should be partially indexed through the amount of interpersonal communication. McLeod, Becker and Byrnes called this third kind of salience "community issue salience."

The distinctions made here are crucial to an understanding of the general model of effects being discussed. The first two types of saliences, "individual" and "perceived", are cognitive in nature and individual in focus. The "community" salience variable, however, is behavioral and focuses on social units. Though no data have been gathered that allow for a precise test of this expectation, the two *intrapersonal* concepts would be expected to fall into the class of variables labeled "first-level responses" in Figure 1. The *interpersonal* concept would be expected to be in the "subsequent responses" group and be, in part, a consequence of the intrapersonal variable.

Evidence of the distinctiveness of these concepts is provided by two unpublished studies conducted in Syracuse, N.Y. within the last two years. In the fall of 1973, personal interviews were conducted with a sample of sophomores at Syracuse University. Each student was asked which issue was most important to him personally, and which issue he discussed most often. The order of the open-ended questions was alternated in the questionnaires to control for system-

TABLE 1
RESPONSES TO TWO SALIENCE MEASURES: FALL 1973

	Issue important personally	Issue talked about most
Watergate	63%	70%
Middle East	13	19
Inflation	10	3
Other	14	8
TOTAL (n = 275)	100	100

NOTE: Respondents could select only one issue for each measure.

atic effects of one question on the other. The results, reported in terms of simple marginals in Table 1, indicate the answers to the two questions are not identical. More students reported Watergate was their most talked about issue than thought it most important to them; the Middle East situation showed a similar difference. Inflation, on the other hand, showed the reverse pattern.

The second study, which asked not only that respondents indicate the issue most important to them personally and the issue most discussed, but also the issue they thought was given the most attention in the media, was conducted the following fall (1974) with Syracuse voters. The results of these three open-ended questions, reported in Table 2, show high similarity between the responses to the two measures used in the study of college sophomores, but an interesting discrepancy between these responses and those recorded for the media coverage measure. A larger percentage of the voters thought Watergate was the most important issue in the news than felt it was important to them personally or in their interpersonal discussions. Economic issues, however, were clearly dominant for all three categories.

Subsequent analysis of the data from the Syracuse sophomore study by McCombs (1974) and Agnir (1975) suggests that the effects of the media's agenda may be even stronger on discussion salience than on personal salience. Almost half of the students who selected Watergate as the issue most often discussed said they did so because it was in the news at the time; none of them used this reason to justify selecting Watergate or any other issue as the most important personally. Correlatively, the match between the current media agenda and the interpersonal discussion measures was generally stronger than it was for the intrapersonal salience measures. These stronger effects on discussion, however, may result from different time lags for the effects on the two variables, and for the effects of

Becker, McCombs, McLeod / Political Cognitions [45]

TABLE 2
RESPONSES TO THREE SALIENCE MEASURES: FALL 1974

	Issue important personally	Issue talked about most	Issue in the news
Inflation	68%	67	63
Watergate	8	8	21
Other	24	24	17
TOTAL (n = 339)	100%	99%	101%

NOTE: Respondents could select only one issue for each measure.

the media on the other discussion partners. The topic of discussion in a conversation is not usually controlled by only one of the participants.

The Process of Effects. The effects of media content on the saliences of various issues, regardless of the salience concept studied, are expected to be cumulative, resulting from the cycle of buildup and decline of issue coverage in the media. For this reason, the saliences measured by the researcher at a given point in time should reflect the media's content emphasis back to some identifiable point; the saliences, however, would be expected to change as the cumulative balance changes.

Evidence that the issue saliences do in fact reflect this cumulative buildup has been provided by Stone (1975), who content analyzed national news magazines for periods before the study, and matched these content emphasis findings with individual issue saliences. His analyses show that as the pre-study content analysis period is increased in size, the match between the media's emphasis and students' responses increases—up to about four months. After that, the match seems to show slippage, indicating that the student saliences reflect a cumulative agenda that has built up over a four-month period. Analysis of the period following the study offers additional evidence of the cumulative nature of the effect. Within two months after the study, the media's emphasis is unrelated to the study-period audience saliences. Shaw and McCombs (1975) show similar evidence supporting the cumulative nature of the media's effect in their analysis of the Charlotte, N.C., data. The best match between content and the responses of individual audience members comes from a cumulative indication of media content. Again, the period is about four months.

The audience members seem to be somewhat aware of the cumulative effect of the media, at least in retrospect. Respondents from the 1972 study by McLeod, Becker and Byrnes (1974) in Madison, Wisc., when reinterviewed two years later, indicated considerable shift in what they thought *should have been* the key issues of the 1972 race—given what they eventually learned about Watergate. While only 8 per cent of the young voters had indicated they thought Honesty in Government was the most important issue when first interviewed, 47 per cent later said it should have been the most important. The change for older voters is equally dramatic: from 14 per cent to 58 per cent. Watergate, of course, did not seem to catch on with the press until several months after the 1972 election, and we can only speculate on its potential impact had that not been the case.

Content and Effects. The effects of nuances of emphasis used by editors—a central element in agenda-setting research—has been investigated by Shaw (1973) who compared the match between the content displayed on the front page of a Durham, N.C., newspaper and the content on the inside pages, with the individual saliences of a small sample of Durham residents in 1972. The relationship between the content emphasis on the front page and the saliences was greater than the relationship between the content of the inside pages and the saliences. The front page, of course, is the major display page for the editor; the data suggest the reader also recognizes the difference between a front page and an inside page story, probably paying less attention to the latter.

There is also some evidence in the literature (Agnir, 1975; Chaffee and Izcaray, 1975; McClure and Patterson, 1974b; McCombs, Shaw and Shaw, 1972; Tipton, Haney and Baseheart, 1975), that television news is less effective in transmitting its agenda to its audience than are newspapers. The relationship is tenuous and based on indirect comparisons of the two media. To the extent that the relationship holds, however, it may reflect the limitations in techniques of emphasis available to the producers of television news programs. There is nothing quite equivalent to the inside page, and little difference between a story used as lead item and one used midway through the broadcast, or after a pause for a commercial. The number of stories

TABLE 3
SALIENCE OF HONESTY IN GOVERNMENT: FALL 1972 TO FALL 1974 SHIFTS

	Actual 1972 salience	Reconsidered 1972 salience, in 1974
Honesty in Government		
Young voters (n = 85)	8%	47%
Older voters (n = 100)	14%	58%

NOTE: Young voters are those who in 1972 were eligible to participate in their first presidential election (18-25 years old); older voters were all others.

which can be used for television news also is limited, suggesting that the cumulation of effects discussed above may not be operating.

Little research has been done on the differences between issues, and inherent limitations on the agenda-setting relationship resulting from such differences. One typology that might be used would distinguish between issues with a definite origin (e.g. the Watergate corruption story, which began early on June 17, 1972 with the bungled burglary of the National Democratic Headquarters) and economic issues, which seem not to have such a starting point. We would expect the media to have more impact when the issues provide "breaking news", as with Watergate, than with the long-established issues with their intricate, established webs of relationships. In addition, the media's influence may be limited to those issues for which some "solution" seems possible and is being widely discussed.

It also would be possible, though no one has attempted to do so yet, to study the salience of these various solutions, and the media's impact on them. In addition, the media's role in establishing the salience of various attributes of candidates has not been researched. Many campaigns, however, seem to turn on such attributes as "honesty" and "poise"–aspects of a candidate's image–and their contribution to our understanding of the electoral process seems potentially fruitful. The media also determine, to a large degree, which candidates get seriously considered, but this effect remains unresearched.

Methodological Decisions

In addition to the conceptual distinctions in the research on agenda-setting discussed above, certain methodological differences exist. Many of the conceptual points have methodological implications, leading to the differences discussed here. These differences deal with the unit of analysis, the model of effects tested, specification of comparison groups, and the use of static vs. time-series designs.

Unit of Analysis. Most of the early research in agenda-setting relied on comparisons of media content with aggregated indices of audience saliences. The Funkhouser (1973a) study, for example, compared the rank of 14 issues based on a cumulative index of their coverage in the media during the 1960s, with the rank of these same issues determined by the number of people who had listed them as the most important to them in Gallup polls. The resulting .78 rank-order correlation indicates that the issues given the most coverage were, with minor discrepancies, the ones considered important by the largest number of people, and the issue given the least attention was considered important by the fewest individuals.

More recent research, however, has shifted away from such aggregate comparisons, toward comparisons that indicate the degree of fit between the content emphasized in the media and the issues considered important by each individual. McClure and Patterson (1973, 1974b) and Weaver, McCombs and Spellman (1975) have examined the changes in the saliences of selected issues across time—arguing that an individual's rating of the importance of an issue should change as coverage of the issue progresses in the media. McLeod, Becker, and Byrnes (1974) employed a more complicated indicant of the fit of an individual's salience of four issues with their play in the local media.

Model of Effects. Differences in the unit of analysis indicate differences in the methodological model of effects studied. McCombs (1975) has noted that at least three different models exist in the literature. The first, labeled the "awareness" model, is concerned only with the presence or absence of an issue on the agenda of the audience, and seems to underlie the aggregate comparisons discussed above. The second or "salience" model, is concerned with only two or three issues, and allows for some rough indication of their relative importance. But it does not look for exact replication of the media's full agenda by the audience. Operationally, this would require that audience members indicate which issues were important, rather than only seeking a single issue. The final model, labeled the "priorities" model, is concerned with the full ranking of issues by the individual— and the match between this ranking and the attention given the issues in the media.

The three models require not only different operationalizations in terms of numbers of issues, but also distinct differences in inputs from and restrictions placed on the respondents. The awareness and salience models implicitly call for open-ended questions, while the priorities model clearly requires some way of getting comparable data from each individual. This latter requirement seems to necessitate more structured questions—most likely with the interviewer determining which list of issues is to be evaluated in terms of comparative salience. To the extent that subsequent analysis will require comparisons based on rank order, the same requirement must be made for the individual respondent data. A rank-order technique, or paired-comparison approach, is indicated.

Comparison Groups. The ideal design (seldom realized in the real world) would allow for comparison of persons exposed to one agenda from a specified medium outlet and similar other persons exposed to a different agenda from another similar medium outlet. McCombs and Shaw (1972), however, have shown strong similarities between the content of various national and local media, indicating how difficult it is to find the ideal situation. McLeod, Becker and Byrnes (1974) did find differences in the issues given attention by the two Madison, Wisconsin, newspapers, and were able to make such comparisons. Chaffee and Izcaray (1975) exploited major differences between local newspapers and network television in Venezuela, where there is no local origination of TV news.

A second strategy, employed in the other studies on agenda-setting, has been to form comparison groups on the basis of variables expected to change the agenda-setting relationship. Individuals exposing themselves to large amounts of media fare, for example, ought to show a stronger agenda-setting effect than those exposing themselves to lesser amounts, and comparisons have generally supported this expectation. Such comparisons, however, run the risk of producing spurious results because of other differences in the control groups.

Static Versus Time-Based Designs. Most of the early research has relied on static comparisons of media content with the audience saliences, providing only correlational data. Stronger designs employing evidence on time-order have appeared recently. Tipton, Haney and Baseheart (1975), for example, employed cross-lagged panel correlation techniques to their analysis of the 1971 Kentucky elections; Weaver, McCombs and Spellman (1975) have used this technique to measure order of effects for the Watergate developments. Both studies suggested that while there is some evidence that the media merely mirror the community rather than determine which issues are salient, the effect of the media emphasis on the audience is more prominent. The Stone (1975) study, discussed above, similarly offers evidence that the media are not merely reflecting the agenda of local voters. McClure and Patterson (1973, 1974b) have used change scores for their analysis of salient issues during the 1972 campaign, again providing evidence for agenda-setting that is more powerful than that provided by correlational designs.

Contingent Conditions

Even in its early formulation, the effect of the media's play of issues on the audience was not expected to be universal. The persuasion research had warned against such an expectation, and McCombs and Shaw (1972) designed their study to maximize the possibility of media effects. Only undecided voters were interviewed in that survey, indicating which group those researchers thought most likely to be influenced by the media's agenda.

Much evidence of the factors affecting the media-emphasis to individual-salience relationship is developing in the literature, supporting the early expectation of restrictions on the scope of the agenda-setting influence. McCombs, Shaw and Shaw (1972) found that the agenda-setting relationship is strengthened among persons who display high perceived need for information and frequent media use, and *low* levels of interpersonal discussion. Mullins (1973) found some evidence indicating that *high* interpersonal discussion facilitates agenda-setting, along with low group membership, high newspaper exposure, high news interest, and registration to vote. McCombs and Weaver (1973), in an attempt to synthesize these findings, suggested that a variable called "need for orientation" might serve in a contributory or contingent capacity. They found that agenda-setting occurred only for respondents who were highly interested in the election and yet uncertain in their voting choice. These findings, based on aggregate comparisons, were replicated using individual-level data by Weaver, McCombs and Spellman (1975).

McLeod, Becker and Byrnes (1974), using perceived issue salience as their criterion variable, found that age played an important role in restricting the agenda-setting effect. Young voters, eligible to vote in a presidential election for the first time in 1972, showed no evidence the media had any influence on the issues they thought were important in the campaign; but the older voters did show a significant effect. This simple analysis obscured the picture that developed when additional variables were examined; several controls were found to be more important for the young than older voters. When the samples were divided according to the strength of their partisan commitment, the data showed that the young who were weak partisans evidenced the agenda-setting effect while the young, strong partisans did not. For the older voters, this control made little difference, with both partisan groups showing agenda-setting. In contrast with the need for orientation findings, McLeod, Becker and Byrnes found that those *less* interested in the campaign, for both age groups, were more likely to reflect the newspaper's agenda than were the more interested. In addition, those persons who reported they did *not* use the newspaper for aid in decision making, nor for information for future interpersonal communications, showed the *greatest* agenda-setting effect. The authors concluded that the "skimmers" of the newspaper and those relatively uninterested in the campaign were most affected by the media's content emphasis.

The contradictory evidence on contingent conditions may reflect differences in the media's effects on the types of saliences studied, or differences in the media stituations. McLeod, Becker and Byrnes were only using newspaper readers for their analysis of the two distinct agendas presented by the competing Madison newspapers. Many of the other studies cited have used global indices of media content, in one-newspaper communities. Clearly these findings on limiting conditions are more suggestive of the restrictions and of the value of that type of analysis, than indicative of strong relationships likely to allow for easy replication.

Subsequent Effects

The importance of agenda-setting as a research endeavor is increased to the extent we can show that the saliences resulting from media exposure have subsequent effects, such as candidate choice, turnout at the polls, or other relevant behaviors or attitudes.

Some of the strongest evidence of the importance of issue saliences in determining actual election results was provided by the Elmira study. As has been indicated, Berelson, Lazarsfeld and McPhee (1954) found strong evidence that those voters predisposed to vote Democratic were more likely to shift to Truman during the campaign to the extent they thought labor and consumer issues were the ones salient in the campaign. The shift to Truman occurred despite negative evaluations of the candidate.

Since agenda-setting is concerned only with the effects of the media on the saliences of issues, the control for evaluative components in assessing subsequent effects is crucial. Kovenock, Beardsley and Prothro (1970) found no evidence that saliences predicted vote choice after controlling for the match between the individual voters' and candidates' positions on the issues. Beardsley (1973), however, has argued that this may be a methodological artifact resulting from the measures of saliences used. Shapiro (1969) and RePass (1971) seem to have supported the individual predictive power of saliences. Becker and McLeod (1974) similarly found evidence that saliences had an impact on candidate choice even after controlling for partisan direction and agreement with the candidates on the issues. Also, those Democrats who saw the issues of the campaign that were favorable to McGovern as the most important were more likely to vote than were their Democratic counterparts not having these perceptions about the campaign. For the Republicans, those thinking the McGovern issues the most important were less likely to turn out than were other Republicans thinking Nixon issues were more important.

Becker and McLeod also found evidence that the salience of the Honesty in Government issue from the 1972 campaign had long-lasting impact as the Watergate scandals developed. Those young voters who thought the Watergate-related Honesty issue important during the campaign were more likely to report high levels of media use and interpersonal discussion about Watergate during the time of the Ervin Committee Senate hearings of 1973 than were other young voters with a lower salience rating for the Honesty issue. The interpersonal discussion findings are particularly important since they are generally supportive of Kline's (1973) findings and seem to indicate that interpersonal discussion is a consequence of individual saliences.

One of the most innovative studies of subsequent effects of issue saliences has been provided by Bloj (1975), who examined the relationship between the sales of airline tickets and flight insurance, and news of air disasters. During heavy coverage of air crashes, ticket sales decreased and flight insurance sales increased. Bloj did not have measures of individual issue saliences, but the findings are rather convincing evidence that subsequent behavioral effects of some importance result from media content.

The relationship between saliences and attitudes is difficult to differentiate causally, yet important to understand from the point of view of subsequent effects. The relationship between these two groups of variables has been left unspecified in Figure 1, in part because of the lack of direct evidence bearing on it. Data from the 1972 study in Charlotte, N.C., however, do offer some insight into this relationship. Respondents were asked to indicate both their relative individual saliences on six issues then in the public domain and also to indicate their attitudes on prominent facets of those same issues. As Table 4 indicates, the correlation between these two sets is relatively weak across the issues. Only three of the relationships—for Drugs, Environment, and Detente—are significant at traditional levels.

While the relationships shown in Table 4 are small and generally would have limited impact in terms of control in examining effects

TABLE 4
RELATIONSHIPS BETWEEN ISSUE SALIENCES AND ATTITUDES: FALL 1972

Issue/Attitudinal Statement	*Pearsonian correlation between salience of issue and attitude*
Vietnam/U.S. should keep some troops there	−.11
Busing/Busing is good for our children	−.07
Inflation/U.S. is in good economic condition	−.11
Drugs/Drugs are no longer a problem	−.13
Environment/Pollution is not a problem	−.15
Detente/U.S. should improve relations with Russia and China	+.19
	(N = 268)

NOTE: A high score for the attitudinal statements indicates agreement; a high score for salience indicates high salience.

following from the saliences, caution should be exercised in generalizing from these data to other samples. Researchers should examine these relationships in subsequent effects analysis. Becker and McLeod (1974), after controlling indirectly for the evaluative component, found that the salience of the Honesty issue during the 1972 campaign was related significantly to the attitudes the respondents had the following spring on the resignation of Nixon. Given the knowledge of time-order, the findings indicate that attitudes and saliences may be functionally related under some circumstances.

MEDIA EFFECTS ON INFORMATION HOLDING

In addition to the evidence of media effects from agenda-setting research, evidence is now being accumulated that the media are relatively effective transmitters of political information. In part, this evidence has resulted from a reexamination of the findings of the Columbia political studies as well as reconsideration of the findings from the information campaign research. New research is being undertaken, however, reflecting differences in perspective and methodological orientation, but focusing on the media's power to determine the information stored by individuals.

General Findings

The media are relatively successful in providing information to their audiences on breaking news. In a classic study of the diffusion of such an event, the stroke suffered by President Eisenhower in 1957, Deutschmann and Danielson (1960) found that roughly two-thirds of their sample had heard of the illness within 10 hours of its development, and 82 per cent of those interviewed indicated they first learned of the event via the media. Greenberg (1964) similarly found that the preponderance of persons who learned of the assassination of President Kennedy early learned about it first from the media.

Robinson (1972), drawing primarily on national data from SRC studies, also has shown that those individuals highest in media exposure are generally the most knowledgeable about matters of more duration and more depth. The relationship holds up even after controlling for education; in fact, the relationship tends to be stronger for those low in education, though they are the people least likely to expose themselves to media news. The relatively low level of exposure of the low education groups to the media suggests that the transmittal of information through media should lead to a knowledge gap between educational levels—an expectation supported by a series of studies of small Minnesota communities (Tichenor, Donohue and Olien, 1970; Tichenor, Rodenkirchen, Olien and Donohue, 1973; Donohue, Tichenor and Olien, 1975). The Minnesota program, however, has focused only indirectly on the media exposure to information-holding relationship, and the authors have noted several exceptions to the knowledge-gap expectation.

Some of the most convincing evidence of the media's impact on the knowledge levels of individuals about election issues and developments has been provided by two studies of British general elections. Trenaman and McQuail (1961) found that increasing television exposure by the electorate during the 1959 elections was related to the acquisition of increasingly accurate information about party policies. These findings occurred despite the lack of a relationship between exposure and attitude change toward the parties. Blumler and McQuail (1969) replicated these findings in the general election five years later. Increased exposure to the media led to an increase in knowledge about issues during the campaign. McClure and Patterson (1974a) found comparable results in change of understanding of the issues of the 1972 presidential campaign in the United States.

Measuring Information Holding

Clarke and Kline (1974) have argued that one of the reasons media effects studies have failed to produce clear results is that they approach the problem from the point of view of the researcher. The researcher, of course, is a relatively atypical member of the media audience, generally better educated than most media users and of a somewhat higher social position. Research concepts and operationalizations should be more audience oriented, Clarke and Kline argue. Debate over appropriate measures is particularly important in studies of information holding; it is impossible to index the entire array of material stored, yet necessary to gather data reflective of the variations within the population being studied. Two general strategies for solving this problem can be identified: those relying on "textbook" definitions of knowledge, and those relying on more idiosyncratic determinations of people's information holdings.

"Textbook" Definitions. The standardized type of knowledge question can best be illustrated by those used extensively by SRC to ascertain political knowledge in various areas. A typical item asks the respondent: "Do you happen to know what kind of government most of China has right now—whether it's Democratic, Communist or what?" (Robinson, Rusk and Head, 1968). Other questions designed to measure knowledge about U.S. governmental affairs would ask the terms of office holders, or number or names of Congressmen from a given state. Such information is easily verifiable, and a knowledge score simply computed.

A slight variation on this operational approach can be used for specific issues, particularly those developing over a relatively short period of time. Many election studies, for example, have attempted to index the accuracy of information voters hold about the candidates' stands on the issues. The Columbia voting studies illustrate this approach well. In the 1948 Elmira study, for example, the researchers asked voters to indicate the stands the two candidates had taken on such issues as the Taft-Hartley bill and Price Control. The media were found to have impact on the accuracy of these answers. Becker (1975) employed this approach in the study of Watergate effects, again showing media effects on knowledge level about the scandal.

Idiosyncratic Definitions. The "textbook" definitions are restrictive in that they not only determine which topics are to be asked about but also which types of answers are to be accepted. It is possible, of course, to predetermine the areas of questions, and still not limit the kinds of information accepted. Tichenor, Rodenkirchen, Olien and Donohue (1974), for example, specified the topic in their Minnesota studies, but then asked the respondents to tell about the "important" aspects of the topic. These open-ended responses, then, were evaluated by the researchers to derive an index of the accuracy of the statements. Essentially, these questions allow the respondent to determine which attributes of the topic he or she wishes to discuss. The researcher only evaluates the responses on the attributes, not the choice of attributes.

Clarke and Kline (1974) and Palmgreen, Kline and Clarke (1974), however, reject the researcher evaluation of the information provided by the respondent—a procedure common to all the measures discussed to this point. Instead, their respondents are first asked to nominate a topic, and then to tell the researcher what he or she knows about the topic. This subsequent information is structured via various probes. For example, *actor information* holding is indexed as the number of answers provided to the question: "Are there any groups, persons or organizations that are trying to influence or affect what is done about the problem?" *Proposal information* is indexed through the question: "Are there any proposals for how to deal with the problem?" The researcher does not evaluate the answers, but instead treats as equivalent those responses clearly "incorrect" (from the researcher's point of view) and those "correct".

The standard measures of media exposure also are not respondent-oriented, Clarke and Kline argue. In their research, the respondent is asked to describe "each thing you've read, seen or heard" about the topic, and then the source of this information. The total number of "things" described are labeled "content unit discriminations." The number of such items attributed to each medium also is scored. The latter index replaces the more standard level-of-exposure measures used in most communication research.

Using these innovative measures of information holding and media exposure in a study of Toledo, Ohio, residents, Palmgreen, Kline and Clarke (1974) showed significant effects for newspaper message discriminations in five of six information-holding tests. Television message discriminations were related in only two of the six comparisons. Standard newspaper exposure indices, by contrast, showed relatively strong effects in three of the six comparisons; the standard television news exposure index showed no significant relationships. These findings seem to suggest some superiority of the discrimination approach, though the results are not totally persuasive. The departure from normal measures of information holding and media use represents more than a mere shift in operationalizations. The nature of the "information" has changed radically, from something that accurately meets external criteria, to something with no *required* link with any criterion. Both are cognitions, but they are quite different in nature.

CONCLUSIONS

These recent studies dealing with media effects on information holding, together with the increasing body of research on agenda-setting, manifest a major shift in the field away from studies of attitude effects. The growing assumption is that if attitudes are important for study, they should be examined as part of a model specifying intermediate effects such as those on cognitions. Media effects are not only expected to be more pronounced when examining such intermediate effects, but a fuller understanding of the process should result. By examining such intermediate level consequences, which in turn have effects on areas other than attitudes, the whole domain of communication effects is broadened.

It is important, however, to reconsider in terms of its long-range impact much of what we have learned of media effects from the literature examined here. Most of the studies have been short-term, examining the media's effects over periods not in excess of six months. But cognitions, particularly those dealing with such broad concepts as the "political system" and the "office of the President," should develop over rather long periods of time, changing only slightly during a few months. These kinds of global cognitions are not being studied adequately, although they are tremendously important.

The agenda-setting framework is both a valuable guide for future research in the area of political cognitions and an important area of study in its own right. It specifies a set of relationships, beginning with the impact of the social system on media institutions, and, then, on their members, particularly reporters and editors. These media operatives make decisions which, the evidence shows, have impact on the cognitions of the media audience members. These cognitions, for example, have been shown to affect voter turnout and election choice. Both behaviors can be seen as central to the political and social system. So the model takes us full circle. It is illustrative of the types of approaches to media studies that can and should be taken in the future.

The findings from this avenue of inquiry, however, also have importance in terms of our general understanding of media effects.

The audience is not so malleable as merely to follow in the ways advocated on the editorial pages of the newspapers or in the commentaries of the networks. But its members do take their cues about the nature of the world about them from the media. And these cues influence what they do. To be sure, not every one fits this model; the agenda-setting research has indicated serious limitations on the media's effects. But the effects that have been found seem to be real.

To date, much of the agenda-setting research has been limited to political campaigns, and all of it has dealt with adults. But the effects of the media's content emphases on younger audience members are probably at least as strong—and perhaps stronger. It remains for someone to examine these effects on younger children. It may well be that children tend to see government in terms of key figures, such as the president, not because of their inability to handle the abstractions of structure and power, but because the reportage in the media—reinforced by the simplicity of their textbooks—make *only* these figures salient. In other words, they may be mistakenly attributing power to the figures that are salient.

At the same time that we should think about extending the domains of agenda-setting research, we should also be cautious of overextension. If the conceptual model is to retain its value, it should be kept within its existing framework. In other words, it should be applied to the study of saliences, since these are the core of the model. Other kinds of media effects can of course be studied—but from other perspectives. Agenda-setting's richness results, to a large degree, from its functionalist underpinnings, which point out likely avenues of fruitful research.

Saliences, of course, are only one kind of cognition. Information holding is another, a more general concept about which we know too little. The tendency seems to be to apply subconcepts such as selectivity and distortion—with their attitudinal origins—to this area as well. These may be inapplicable to the study of cognitions. At least their relevance should be demonstrated empirically, rather than assumed on the bases of past attitudinal research.

The available evidence on media effects is quite consistent. The Yale studies, those conducted at Columbia, many of the information campaign studies, and the new programs of research in agenda-setting, socialization, and information holding, demonstrate the media's impact on cognitions. Further specification of the relationships and subsequent effects need to be explored. That dominant activity of the media—information transmittal—seems to be quite important from this new perspective.

NOTES

1. Endorsement data are compiled every four years by Editor and Publisher and are presented in the last October or first November issue of the magazine. Those papers which do not endorse candidates tend to be the smallest in terms of circulation.
2. The authors thank F. Gerald Kline, University of Michigan, for making these data from the 1974 national study of the Center for Political Studies available.

REFERENCES

AGNIR, F. (1975) "Testing new approaches to agenda-setting: a replication and extension," in M. McCombs and G. Stone (eds.) Studies in Agenda-Setting. Newhouse Communications Research Center, Syracuse University, Syracuse.
American Institute for Political Communication (1974) The 1972 Presidential Campaign: The Nixon Administration—Mass Media Relationship. Washington, D.C.
ATKIN, C. K. and W. GANTZ (1975) "The role of television news in the political socialization of children," presented to the International Communications Association, Chicago, Ill.
BEARDSLEY, L. (1973) "The Methodology of the electoral analysis: models and measurement," pp. 30-92 in D. Kovenock and J. Prothro (eds.) Explaining the Vote: Presidential Choices in the Nation and States, 1968. Chapel Hill, N.C.: Institute for Research in Social Science.
BECKER, L. B. (1975) "A uses and gratifications approach to Watergate effects analysis." Presented to the SUNY Conversations in Disciplines Conference, Utica, N.Y.
———and J. M. McLEOD (1974) "Political consequences of agenda-setting." Presented to conference on the agenda-setting function of mass communications, Syracuse University, Syracuse, N.Y.
BERELSON, B., P. LAZARSFELD and W. McPHEE (1954) Voting. Chicago: University of Chicago Press.
BLOJ, A. G. (1975) "Into the wild blue yonder: Behavioral implications of agenda-setting for air travel," in M. McCombs and G. Stone (eds.) Studies in Agenda-Setting. Newhouse Communications Research Center, Syracuse University, Syracuse.
BLUME, N. and S. LYONS (1968) "The monopoly newspaper in a local election: the Toledo Blade." Journalism Q. 45 (summer) 286-292.
BLUMLER, J. G. and J. M. McLEOD (1974) "Communication and voter turnout in Britain," pp. 265-312 in T. Legatt (ed.) Sociological Theory and Survey Research. Beverly Hills: Sage Pubns.
———and D. McQUAIL (1969) Television in Politics. Chicago: University of Chicago Press.
BOWERS, T. A. (1973) "Newspaper political advertising and the agenda-setting function." Journalism Q. 50 (autumn) 552-556.
CAMPBELL, A. and R. L. KAHN (1952) The People Elect a President. Ann Arbor: Survey Research Center, University of Michigan.
———, G. GURIN and W. E. MILLER (1954) The Voter Decides. Evanston, Ill.: Row, Peterson and Company.
———, P. E. CONVERSE, W. E. MILLER and D. E. STOKES (1966) Elections and the Political Order. New York: Wiley.
———, P. E. CONVERSE, W. E. MILLER and D. E. STOKES (1960) The American Voter. New York: Wiley.
CHAFFEE, S. H. and F. IZCARAY (1975) "Mass communication functions in a media-rich developing society." Communication Research 2 (October).
———, L. S. WARD and L. P. TIPTON (1970) "Mass communication and political socialization." Journalism Q. 47 (winter) 647-659.
———, M. JACKSON-BEECK, J. LEWIN and D. WILSON (1975) "Mass communication in

political socialization," in S. Renshon (ed.) Handbook of Political Socialization (in press).

CLARKE, P. and F. G. KLINE (1974) "Media effects reconsidered." Communication Research 1 (April) 224-240.

COHEN, B. C. (1963) The Press, the Public and Foreign Policy. Princeton: Princeton University Press.

CROUSE, T. (1972) The Boys on the Bus. New York: Random House.

DAWSON, R. E. and K. PREWITT (1969) Political Socialization. Boston: Little, Brown.

DENNIS, J. (1973) (ed.) Socialization to Politics: A Reader. New York: Wiley.

––– and C. WEBSTER (1975) "Changes in children's images of the president and of government between 1962 and 1974." American Politics Q. (October).

DEUTSCHMANN, P. J. and W. A. DANIELSON (1960) "Diffusion of knowledge of the major news story." Journalism Q. 37 (summer) 345-355.

DOMINICK, J. R. (1972) "Television and political socialization." Educational Broadcasting Rev. 6 (February) 48-57.

DONOHEW, L. (1967) "Newspaper gatekeepers and forces in the news channel." Public Opinion Q. 31 (spring) 61-68.

DONOHUE, G. A., P. J. TICHENOR and C. N. OLIEN (1972) "Gatekeeping: mass media systems and information control," pp. 41-69 in F. G. Kline and P. J. Tichenor (eds.) Current Perspectives in Mass Communication Research. Beverly Hills: Sage Pubns.

–––, P. J. TICHENOR and C. N. OLIEN (1975) "Mass media and the knowledge gap: a hypothesis reconsidered." Communication Research 2 (January) 2-23.

DOUGLAS, D. F., B. H. WESTLEY and S. H. CHAFFEE (1970) "An information campaign that changed community attitudes." Journalism Q. 47 (autumn) 487; 492.

FUNKHOUSER, G. R. (1973a) "The issues of the sixties: an exploratory study in the dynamics of public opinion." Public Opinion Q. 37 (spring) 62-75.

––– (1973b) "Trends in media coverage of the issues of the sixties." Journalism Q. 50 (autumn) 533-538.

GIEBER, W. (1956) "Across the desk: a study of 16 telegraph editors." Journalism Q. 33 (fall) 423-32.

GLASER, W. A. and C. KADUSHIN (1962) "Political behavior in midterm election," pp. 251-272 in W. N. McPhee and W. A. Glaser (eds.) Public Opinion and Congressional Elections. New York: The Free Press.

GOLD, D. and J. L. SIMMONS (1965) "News selection patterns among Iowa dailies." Public Opinion Q. 29 (fall) 425-30.

GORMLEY, W. T. (1975) "Newspaper agendas and political elites." Journalism Q. (in press).

GREENBERG, B. S. (1964) "Diffusion of news of the Kennedy assassination." Public Opinion Q. 28 (summer) 225-232.

HIMMELWEIT, H. and B. SWIFT (1975) "Principles of continuities and discontinuities in media use and taste: a longitudinal study of adolescents reexamined at ages 25 and 33." J. Social Issues, (in press).

HOLLANDER, N. (1971) "Adolescents and the war: the sources of socialization." Journalism Q. 48 (autumn) 472-479.

HOVLAND, C. I. (ed.) (1957) Order of Presentation in Persuasion. New Haven: Yale University Press.

––– and I. L. JANIS (eds.) (1959) Personality and Persuasibility. New Haven: Yale University Press.

–––, A. A. LUMSDAINE and F. D. SHEFFIELD (1949) Experiments on Mass Communication. Princeton: Princeton University Press.

HYMAN, H. H. and P. B. SHEATSLEY (1947) "Some reasons why information campaigns fail." Public Opinion Q. 11 (winter) 413-423.

JOHNSON, N. (1973) "Television and politicization; a test of competing models." Journalism Q. 50 (autumn) 447-455, 474.

KATZ, E. and P. F. LAZARSFELD (1955) Personal Influence. New York: The Free Press.

KLAPPER, J. T. (1960) The Effects of Mass Communication. New York: The Free Press.

KLINE, F. G. (1973) "Sources and impact of political information in the 1972 elections," presented to the American Association for Public Opinion Research, Ashville, N.C.

KOVENOCK, D. M., R. L. BEARDSLEY, and J. W. PROTHRO (1970) "Status, party, ideology, issues and candidate choice," presented to the International Political Science Association, Munich, Germany.

KRAUS, S. (1973) "Mass communication and political socialization: a reassessment of two decades of research." Quarterly J. of Speech 59 (December) 390-400.

LASSWELL, H. S. (1948) "The structure and function of communication in society," in L. Bryson (ed.) The Communication of Ideas. New York: Institute for Religious and Social Studies.

LAZARSFELD, P., B. BERELSON and H. GAUDET (1948) The People's Choice. New York: Columbia University Press.

LIPPMAN, W. (1922) Public Opinion. New York: Macmillan.

LYLE, J. and H. R. HOFFMAN (1971) "Children's use of television and other media," pp. 129-256 in E. A. Rubinstein, G. A. Comstock and J. P. Murray (eds.) Television and Social Behavior, Washington, D.C.: National Institute of Mental Health 4.

MARTIN, R. R., G. J. O'KEEFE and O. B. NAYMAN (1972) "Opinion agreement and accuracy between editors and their readers." Journalism Q. 49 (autumn) 460-468.

MARTIN, S. A. (1975) "Youth unrest on the national agenda: studying a decade of public opinion," in M. McCombs and G. Stone (eds.) Studies in Agenda-Setting. Newhouse Communications Research Center, Syracuse University, Syracuse.

McCLURE, R. D. and T. E. PATTERSON (1974a) "Television news and political advertising." Communication Research 1 (January) 3-31.

――― and ――― (1974b) "Agenda-setting: comparison of newspaper and television network news," presented to the conference on the agenda-setting function of mass communications, Syracuse University, Syracuse, N.Y.

――― and ――― (1973) "Television news and voter behavior in the 1972 presidential election," presented to the American Political Science Association, New Orleans, La.

McCOMBS, M. E. (1975) "Agenda-setting: a new perspective on mass communication." Presented to the SUNY Conversations in the Disciplines Conference, Utica, N.Y.

――― (1974) "A comparison of intra-personal and inter-personal agendas of public issues," presented to the International Communications Association, New Orleans, La.

――― (1967) "Editorial endorsement: a study of influence." Journalism Q. 44 (autumn) 545-548.

――― and T. A. BOWERS (1975) "Television's effects on political behavior," in G. A. Comstock, D. Armor, S. H. Chaffee, N. Katzman, M. E. McCombs and D. Roberts (eds.) The Fifth Season: How TV Influences the Way People Behave. Santa Monica, Cal.: Rand Corporation (in press).

――― and H. F. SCHULTE (1975) "Expanding the domain of the agenda-setting function of mass communication," presented to the World Association for Public Opinion Research, Montreux, Switzerland.

――― and D. L. SHAW (1974) "Our unseen environment: media influence on political agendas," presented to the conference on the agenda-setting function of mass communications, Syracuse University, Syracuse, N.Y.

――― and D. L. SHAW (1972) "The agenda-setting function of the media." Public Opinion Q. 36 (summer) 176-187.

――― and D. WEAVER (1973) "Voters' need for orientation and use of mass media," presented to the International Communication Association, Montreal, Canada.

―――, D. L. SHAW and E. F. SHAW (1972) "The news and public response," presented to the Association for Education in Journalism, Carbondale, Ill.

McLEOD, J. M. and L. B. BECKER (1974) "Testing the validity of gratification measures through political effects analysis," pp. 137-166 in J. G. Blumler and E. Katz (eds.) The

Uses of Mass Communication: Current Perspectives on Gratification Research. Beverly Hills: Sage Pubns.

——— and G. J. O'KEEFE (1972) "The socialization perspective and communication behavior," pp. 121-168 in F. G. Kline and P. J. Tichenor (eds.) Current Perspectives in Mass Communication Research. Beverly Hills: Sage Pubns.

———, L. B. BECKER and J. E. BYRNES (1974) "Another look at the agenda-setting function of the press." Communication Research 1 (April) 131-166.

———, J. D. BROWN and L. B. BECKER (1975) "Decline and fall at the White House: A longitudinal analysis of communication effects," presented to the Association for Education in Journalism, Ottawa, Canada.

———, S. H. CHAFFEE and D. B. WACKMAN (1975) Communication and Political Socialization. Beverly Hills: Sage Pubns. (in preparation).

McGUIRE, W. J. (1969) "The nature of attitudes and attitude change," pp. 136-314 in G. Lindzey and E. Aronson (eds.) The Handbook of Social Psychology Vol. 3. Reading, Mass.: Addison-Wesley.

——— (1968) "Personality and susceptibility to social influence," pp. 1130-1187 in E. F. Borgatta and W. W. Lambert (eds.) Handbook of Personality Theory and Research. Chicago: Rand-McNally.

MENDELSOHN, H. (1973) "Some reasons why information campaign can succeed." Public Opinion Q. 37 (spring) 50-61.

MULLINS, L. E. (1973) "Agenda-setting on the campus: the mass media and learning of issue importance in the '72 election," presented to the Association for Education in Journalism, Fort Collins, Colo.

Newspaper Advertising Bureau (1972) A National Survey of the Content and Readership of the American Newspaper. New York.

PALMGREEN, P., F. G. KLINE and P. CLARKE (1974) "Message discrimination and information holding about political affairs: a comparison of local and national issues," presented to the International Communication Association, New Orleans, La.

PARK, R. E. (1925) The City. Chicago: University of Chicago Press.

RePASS, D. E. (1971) "Issues salience and party choice." Amer. Political Science Rev. 65 (June) 389-400.

ROBINSON, J. P. (1972) "Mass communication and information diffusion," pp. 71-93 in F. G. Kline and P. J. Tichenor (eds.) Current Perspectives in Mass Communication Research. Beverly Hills: Sage Pubns.

——— (1974) "The press as King-maker: what surveys from last five campaigns show." Journalism Q. 51 (winter) 587-594.

———, J. G. RUSK and K. B. HEAD (1968) Measures of Political Attitudes. Institute for Social Research, University of Michigan, Ann Arbor.

ROGERS, H. R. and E. B. LEWIS (1975) "Consequences of negative attitudes toward a president for political system support." Amer. Politics Q. (October).

ROSENBERG, M. J., C. I. HOVLAND, W. J. McGUIRE, R. P. ABELSON and J. W. BREHM (1960) Attitude Organization and Change. New Haven: Yale University Press.

SCHRAMM, W. (1957) Responsibility in Mass Communication. New York: Harper.

———, J. LYLE and E. B. PARKER (1961) Television in the Lives of Our Children. Stanford: Stanford University Press.

SEARS, D.O. (1969) "Political behavior," pp. 315-458 in G. Lindzey and E. Aronson (eds.) The Handbook of Social Psychology Vol. 5. Reading, Mass: Addison-Wesley.

——— and R. E. WHITNEY (1973) "Political persuasion," pp. 253-289 in I. Pool and W. Schramm (eds.) Handbook of Communication. Chicago: Rand-McNally.

SHAPIRO, M. J. (1969) "Rational political man: a synthesis of economic and social-psychological perspectives." Amer. Political Science Rev. 63 (December) 1106-1119.

SHAW, D. L. and T. A. BOWERS (1973) "The influence of TV advertising on the voter's political agenda," presented to the Association for Education in Journalism, Fort Collins, Colo.

――― and M. E. McCOMBS [eds.] (1975) The Emergence of Public Issues: Political News and Voter Learning. University of North Carolina School of Journalism and Newhouse Communications Research Center, Syracuse University.

SHAW, E. (1973) "Front page versus total coverage." University of North Carolina, Chapel Hill: Working papers on agenda-setting, series #1.

SHEINGOLD, C. A. (1973) "Social networks and voting: the resurrection of a research agenda." Amer. Sociological Rev. 38 (December) 712-720.

SIGAL, L. V. (1973) Reporters and Officials. Lexington, Mass.: D. C. Heath.

SIGEL, R. [ed.] (1965) "Political socialization: its role in the political process." Annals of the American Academy of Political and Social Science 361 (September).

SIUNE, K. and O. BORRE (1975) "Setting the agenda for a Danish Election." J. of Communication 25 (winter) 65-73.

STAR, S. A. and H. M. HUGHES (1950) "Report on an educational campaign: the Cincinnati plan for the United Nations." Amer. J. of Sociology 55 (January) 389-400.

STONE, G. (1975) "Cumulative effects of the media," in M. McCombs and G. Stone (eds.) Studies in Agenda-Setting. Newhouse Communications Research Center, Syracuse University, Syracuse.

TANNENBAUM, P. H. (1963) "Public communication of science information." Science 140 (May) 579-583.

TICHENOR, P. J., G. A. DONOHUE and C. N. OLIEN (1970) "Mass media and differential growth in knowledge." Public Opinion Q. 34 (summer) 158-170.

―――, J. M. RODENKIRCHEN, C. N. OLIEN, and G. A. DONOHUE (1973) "Community issues, conflict, and public affairs knowledge," pp. 45-79 in P. Clarke (ed.) New Models for Mass Cummunication Research. Beverly Hills: Sage Pubns.

TIPTON, L. P., R. D. HANEY and J. R. BASEHEART (1975) "Media agenda-setting in city and state campaigns." Journalism Q. (spring) 15-22.

TRENAMAN, J. and D. McQUAIL (1961) Television and the Political Image. London: Methuen.

WEAVER, D., M. E. McCOMBS and C. SPELLMAN (1975) "Watergate and the media: a case study of agenda-setting." American Politics Q. (October).

WHITE, D. M. (1950) "The gatekeeper: a case study in the selection of news." Journalism Q. 27 (fall) 38-390.

Chapter 2

COMMUNICATION, MASS POLITICAL BEHAVIOR,

AND MASS SOCIETY

Karen Siune and F. Gerald Kline

THE PREVIOUS CHAPTER by Becker et al. points to historical reasons for concern with mass persuasion. Implicit in their commentary was the notion that the persuasive effects of carefully constructed messages would reach *large* numbers of people. The size of the audience was crucial to early studies. The previous chapter also concentrated on the development of political cognitions in the individual. We will look at the implications of aggregating individuals to see how these relate to political communication. We will also look at the role of media structures.

At the outset we should define our terms. One often sees or hears references to mass media, mass communication, mass persuasion, mass behavior and mass society.[1] The term "mass," as it modifies media and communication, usually (but not accurately) describes particular structures or delivery systems for the formulation and communication of messages to large numbers of people. Janowitz (1968) for example says they "comprise the institutions and techniques by which specialized groups employ technological devices (press, radio file, etc.) to disseminate symbolic content to large, heterogeneous, and widely dispersed audiences." The word mass, however, as it refers to persuasion and behavior, usually describes the activities of people who are related to each other in a particular kind of way; the *number* of people involved is a secondary consideration. Blumer (1946, p. 186) says

...the mass consists of individuals belonging to a wide variety of local groups and cultures ... the object of interest which gains the attention of those who form the mass is something which lies on the outside of the local cultures and groups; and therefore, that this object of interest is not defined or explained in terms of the understandings or rules of these local groups. The object of mass interest can be thought of as attracting the attention of people away from their local cultures and spheres of life and turning it toward a wider universe, toward areas which are not defined or covered by rules, regulations, or expectations. In this sense the mass can be viewed as constituted by detached and alienated individuals who face objects or areas of life which are interesting, but which are also puzzling and not easy to understand and order ... Further, in not being able to communicate with each other, except in limited and imperfect ways, the members of the mass are forced to act separately, as individuals.

We will focus our attention on the way the audience members relate to each other, the implications this has for the reception and impact of messages, and the structure of media institutions in linking elites and non-elites.

In this chapter we will use the term "large-scale" media when we refer to newspapers and television, reserving the term "mass" for the audience relationships that have implications for the ways the messages are received. We intend to examine mass behavior as a more extreme example of communication effect. Our concern is less with showing how such outcomes can be linked to other more common outcomes and the various psychological theories that are offered in explanation, and more with pointing to societal structural variables that are antecedent to all kinds of outcomes.

MASS SOCIETY

Following Kornhauser's (1959) terminology we will delineate the major elements in his conception of society and apply them directly to the role of the large-scale media in the political process. Kornhauser begins by stating:

The Theory of mass society has two major intellectual sources, one in the nineteenth century reaction to the revolutionary changes in European (especially French) society, and the other in the twentieth century reaction to the rise of totalitarianism, especially in Russia and Germany. The first and major source may be termed the *aristocratic* criticism of mass society; the second, the *democratic* criticism of mass society. The first centers in the intellectual defense of elite values against the rise of mass participation. The second centers in the intellectual defense of democratic values against the rise of elites bent on total domination. (p. 21)

Two key dimensions run through Kornhauser's presentation. The first has to do with the *loss of exclusiveness of elites* and the concomitant rise of mass participation in cultural life. He cites Burckhardt (1955), Le Bon (1947), Ortega y Gasset (1932) and Mannheim (1940) as leading aristocratic critics of this trend. The second dimension has to do with the *loss of insulation of non-elites* and the rise of elites bent on total mobilization of the population. Two democratic critics who have analyzed this theme are Lederer (1940) and Arendt (1951). Kornhauser distilled these two major concepts into a more general view of "mass society as a system in which elites are readily accessible to influence by non-elites and non-elites are readily available for mobilization by elites." Dichotomizing the two dimensions, he generated four societal types: mass, totalitarian, communal and pluralist.[2]

The key elements for our purposes are the lack of independent group ties (Blumer, 1946) or *atomization of the individual* (Arendt, 1951; Mills, 1956); the means for mobilization, *the use of large-scale media* to reach enough non-elites to count in the world of politics; the *communication and feedback* pressures on the elites, referenda, petitions, letter writing, and public opinion polls; and the possible *dependent outcomes* such as knowledge, attitude change and behavioral activation of which mass behavior is the most extreme example.

Mass behavior is rare in a totalitarian society because of the coercive power of the elites; when it does occur, though, it has to do with vital questions. In communal societies, mass behavior seldom occurs, and then only in peripheral spheres. It is also peripheral in a pluralist society due to offsetting intermediate relations; it occurs, however, at a rate second only to that in mass society because so many remote symbols have an opportunity to vie for attention through so many communication channels. Mass behavior is most common, as the terms imply, in a mass society.

Contemporary societies are not purely one type or the other, but there are times when the elements of one type are most predominant. Mass society is the least likely to be found of the four, while communal societies are less likely in this age of modernization. Pluralist and totalitarian, in varying degrees, are in our time much easier to identify. It is in the mass society, or at least the mass society of the moment, that we should expect to find the volatile mass behavior and its associated political and social instability.

ATOMIZED MAN

Many early students of media effects were influenced by what they saw as man's loss of ties. They worried that industrialization and urbanization had robbed individuals of their sense of community, first by eroding small towns and then neighborhoods of cities, and perhaps even by eradication of the family as an effective social unit. In such a situation, according to Kornhauser,

> people are divorced from their community and work, and they are free to unite in new ways. Furthermore, those who do not possess a variety of relations with their fellows are disposed to seek new and often remote sources of attachment and allegiance. Where proximate concerns are meaningful, people do not spend much time or energy seeking direct gratification from remote symbols . . . On the other hand, people may respond to their lack of proximate relations with apathy; as a result their availability for mobilization may be hidden. Apathy born of alienation from community may persist under more or less stable conditions. However, the underlying disaffection of which apathy may be an expression readily leads to activism in times of crisis, as when people who have previously rejected politics turn out in large numbers to support demagogic attacks on the existing political system. (pp. 60-61)

A fairly large and apathetic segment of the population in any society does not take the opportunity to be exposed to political information; but Converse (1962) has pointed out that these same persons respond most strongly to it when the correct message strategy and delivery are employed. If they vote, the limited political information they have received tends to be decisive.

Although the concept of man as an atom isolated from social groupings has been abandoned as a generalized perspective (Friedson, 1954; Katz and Lazarsfeld, 1955; Kline, 1972) it was particularly important in conceptualizing early research on persuasion and propaganda. With the recent growth of topic-based analysis of media effects (Morrison, Kline and Miller, 1975; Palmgreen, Kline and Clarke, 1974) one can conceive of the atomization concept in a restricted way as it relates to specific topics. For example, a tie to a social group that has no information or stated position on a particular topic will be of little help in assessing any new information or persuasive appeal attached to that topic. One should expect to find a greater susceptibility on that topic than on those where knowledge exists or predispositions are held.

A salient contemporary example of such a phenomenon is the movie "Jaws." The amount of information held or available concerning sharks was quite probably minuscule for the bulk of the population—even in coastal communities where sharks are found in their natural habitat. Within weeks after the film was seen in 460 theatres in the U.S. by millions of people, the incidence of reported shark sighting along coastal beaches soared. Fear of swimming more than a few yards offshore was a widespread reaction. Despite criticisms in the press by marine biologists and well known naturalists about the misleading information conveyed in Jaws, the lack of information guaranteed general susceptibility to the presentation. Much of the agenda-setting research in the communication research literature (see Becker et al. chapter) points to this way of viewing media message consequences in the cognitive realm. The ability of the media to put new issues on the agenda, or to determine what people should think about, is a potent kind of persuasive power even though it may not directly change attitudes. Siune and Borre (1975) observe that, although agenda-setting studies are usually not labeled mass persuasion, they could be.

We might push this notion of topic atomization slightly further by considering those areas where newness is not so much in question as is the social acceptability of discussing something openly. Sexual topics certainly fall in this category, as does the widespread response to large-scale media coverage of breast cancer in the wives of both the President and Vice-president of the U.S. (Medical clinics and doctor's offices were overwhelmed within days after the first news reports.) By extending the original notion of atomization of persons along sociometric lines to atomization by topic and by social acceptability, we can extend our understanding of knowledge acquisition, changes in attitude, and changes in behavior.

LARGE-SCALE MEDIA IN THE SOCIETY

Most people assume that democracies need large-scale media for intercommunication between those who govern and their constituents. Part of this ideal is that democratic societies must have an informed public and, according to McQuail (1969), these societies have a need for consensus. There is also a need for continuity (Park, 1923) and for the creation of an informed public through the diffusion of political information (Key, 1961; see also Chaffee chapter).

Studies of diffusion have shown that large scale media, especially radio, are efficient instruments for spreading new information in developing countries, and can lead to changing attitudes towards innovations (Rogers, 1962). But in western societies this function of the media has been evaluated negatively because of a failure to emphasize alternatives to existing ways of doing things; the media are criticized for reinforcing the status quo. Mills (1956) and Marcuse (1964) especially stress this negative evaluation, arguing from a leftist perspective that is gaining increasing credence. How efficient are large-scale media in performing these tasks? In the next few pages we will outline a perspective on the media's role.

In Figure 1 we present a simplified view of the communication linkages between the major societal elements. The top level, the elite, contains relations inclusive of the whole population, notably the state. We should, however, go beyond the formal governmental aspects of the state, and include the major corporate and financial

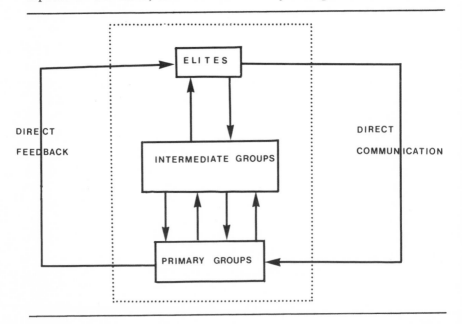

Figure 1

components that are interrelated at the top in most complex societies.

At the bottom level are the primary groups, the highly personal relations that include neighbors, friends and especially the family. In the middle, acting as a buffering, filtering and contextualizing mechanism can be found the intermediate relations. These include local community agencies, voluntary associations, and occupational group ties. These intermediate relations function as links between the individual and the centers of power. Of particular importance to us is the inclusion of the local media as a part of these linkages. Kornhauser concentrates on the area within the broken lines of Figure 1 and does not consider the direct links upward and downward that are a result of more recent technological developments. We explicitly wish to consider these.

Kornhauser argues that when the intermediate relations are weakened, we have a situation where there is very little or no insulation between elites and non-elites. Under this condition we would find high accessibility to the elites with tremendous mass pressures and inclinations toward majority rule, and high availability of non-elites for mobilization and total domination by the elites. Such a situation, the archetypal mass society, would provide great opportunity for instability and mass behavior. In a pluralistic society, although the rate of mass behavior is lower, it is still possible because of the many accessible channels of communication that can carry remote symbols and messages for behavioral activation. Note that a major requirement for this to come about is the use of large-scale media to carry messages directly from the power centers of the society to the citizenry with a minimum of filtering or contextualizing by the local media, local groups or other intermediate relations. It also requires, for effective mass behavioral outcomes, that there be the equivalent of atomization of the individual where he or she is not equipped with a primary group contextualization that would offset the impact. This might be most likely to take place where the messages contain new or unique information. Additionally there would be a higher probability for direct activation where the message was more symbolic than real, and more indefinite than definite.[3] Let us now consider what large-scale media look like.

It has only been a short time since the demise of the large circulation weekly general magazines that reached millions of readers across the U.S. By virtue of their audience size they had to cater to tastes that were common to most. With the changing demand for more specialized topics, changes in advertiser choices, and increased distribution costs, the likes of *Life, Look* and *The Saturday Evening Post* eventually disappeared. In their death throes they attempted to cut their subscriptions to match carefully selected demographic groups that were desired by advertisers, and to tailor their content to those same readers. The changes came too late and were not drastic enough in their narrowing. Not suffering the same fate, however, were the many specialized magazines that have since come to flourish with small audiences; they have met specific content needs of specialized groups, and advertisers willing to pay to reach them. There is a similar story to tell for radio. When television arrived the economics of national network radio were shattered. To survive, the stations sought specialized formats and audiences that were economically viable. The history of radio since that time has been one of specialization in a few quite diverse areas—and financial success. Both magazines and radio, although referred to by many as "mass media", are not large-scale media as we are using the term here. They are much more accurately thought of in connection with the intermediate relations portrayed in Figure 1. They offer a great deal of diversity in presenting viewpoints across the many channels of communication they occupy, but are distinctly homogeneous within each channel.

The truly large scale medium of the present day is television. As organized in most western countries (in large part due to the economics of program production) a single broadcast reaches many people simultaneously through network structures. Depending on the political system, these television networks can be commercially competitive, publicly supported, or a combination of both. Often networks that compete for the same viewers are quite similar in their programing at a particular point in the daily schedule, but offer some degree of diversity within each channel over time. Except for minimal local programing the content is usually nationally oriented and caters to tastes that are common to the largest audience.

The newspaper is a hybrid with its local, national and international content. Although many U.S. cities still have competing newspapers, the trend in general has been toward one major newspaper organization per city. The papers usually rely on cooperative newsgathering agencies to collect, write and disseminate national and international news, while covering their local areas with their own staffs. This arrangement, and traditional journalism practice, dictates that the local staff provide a "local angle" on national and international stories whenever possible. This is one kind of contextualization that can be provided by a community-based medium.

There are forces at work, again economic in nature, that can offset this. The first is the increasing loss of intra-city competition between newspapers (above). The second is a trend toward chain ownership of many newspapers, with concomitant economies of scale on crucial costs such as paper, common content, and administration. A third, and also growing, factor is the development of technology that can reduce manpower costs. The most obvious is the use computer-based news transportation techniques. Where an editor used to take the wire copy, scan it, edit it and send it to be processed for delivery, a machine now provides versions of the story of varying lengths which are set automatically with a minimum of editorial intervention. Additionally, the wire service sends model headlines along with its stories, to reduce local labor. The net result is a homogenization of non-local content and the integration of traditionally local media into a large-scale medium at least for national and international content.

In various parts of the world, either through historical accident, conscious ideological choice, or financial capability, differing media structures and patterns of control have developed (Siebert, Peterson and Schramm, 1956). In many ways the media structure is seen as a necessary component for carrying forward national goals. It is sometimes also seen as an adjunct to the structure of the intermediate relations that exist, either to undermine their strength where centralized control is a goal, or to support weak intermediate relations where diversity and pluralism are sought. The combinations of media structures, intermediate relations and societal feedback mechanisms operate in conjunction with one another. Let us now turn to those feedback mechanisms that have traditionally been available to the non-elites, and to the new ones that have arisen with technological development.

COMMUNICATION AND FEEDBACK

It has been said that one of the major scientific breakthroughs of the 20th century has been the explication of statistical sampling theory. With it came the development of public opinion polling and survey research as we know it today. Despite fiascos such as the mispredictions of the 1936 and 1948 U.S. presidential elections, or more recently the poll errors in recent British elections, the accuracy of modern sample surveys is such that all modern societies rely on them to a large degree for surveillance. Opinion polling, both public and private, is not the only means of determining citizen claims, but it is one of the most ubiquitous approaches used today.

There are other, intensity-weighted, ways in which the non-elites can communicate or bring pressure to bear on the elites. Letter-writing campaigns have a long and honorable tradition, as does circulation of petitions and their presentation to the political leadership. On a more activist front, demonstrations and rallies have served a similar purpose. Within the last decades the use of such techniques, in conjunction with media coverage, has become a common tool of minority groups with grievances. All of these, although we are sensitive to the depth of feeling of those writing, signing or rallying, are only rarely representative of the population as a whole. Occasionally one outcome of such specialized campaigns is the extension of the issue to the majority of the population via a referendum. Although a voting act, this can be applied at times other than those specified for traditional electoral activity and it can be very issue specific.

The complexities of modern life, and the ways methods of feedback are used for minority views, push the burden of rapid and *representative* citizen pressure onto opinion polling in a modern society. Returning to Figure 1 we can see that polling is a direct link between non-elites and elites. Other methods (aside from referenda) fall into the group - mediated communication categories to the elite, each having a group-related weight and consequent bias. Competing information channels of this kind help provide the buffering that Kornhauser evaluates so positively in a pluralistic society.

One thing that must be kept in mind is that the organizers of opinion polls are rarely if ever representative of the whole population, nor are the concerns that they organize questions around necessarily everyone's concerns. Where the poll questions and issues become centralized and allied with elite strata we do not really have feedback. Schiller (1971b) claims that the use of polls to foster the illusion of popular participation is conscious manipulation and mind management. And Singer (1973) points out that polls are often not a sufficient answer to the need for feedback. They are expressive in nature, mostly confined to responding to stimuli that are chosen by authorities, and not representative of the universe of concerns that is imbedded in the population. He contrasts this *expressive* feedback, which does not have a specific instrumental objective, with *determinative* feedback, which does—and which would be analogous to "civic participation" in the sense of Almond and Verba (1965). Whether communication and feedback as pursued through group related ties necessarily fits the expressive or determinative mode is a major question in politics. Ziegler (1970) has criticized the conception of group membership having anything to do with representation and substantial political activity as misleading at best.

We have to understand intermediate relations and ties to groups in two ways. The first is active participation, where individuals make an effort to communicate upward. The second is psychic or social belonging and identification, which provides a context for receiving messages. From our point of view the lack of groups would prevent both, while the bypassing of groups with downward communication would still have to contend with the latter.

A recent event on the American scene exemplifies Kornhauser's concern for the buffering of elites and non-elites from one another. In 1969 President Nixon was faced with an imminent executive decision concerning Lieutenant William Calley, a confessed killer of Vietnamese civilians at My Lai in Vietnam. The death penalty was the likely punishment to be meted out by the court martial. Prior to the judicial decision a national poll was released that overwhelmingly supported clemency for Calley. Within days President Nixon asked for national radio and television time so that he might speak directly to the nation. He agreed with the poll results, he said, and promised executive clemency should the military court ask for the maximum sentence. The rapidity and directness of both the upward and downward communication is a prime example of what Kornhauser saw as a lack of insulation of elites and non-elites from each other. It is crucial to note here that the lack of buffering was not due to a paucity of intermediate relations but due to the technological capacity of large-scale media and national public opinion polling. The strategy of using direct patriotic appeals to the whole populace, where there can be no contextualizing and filtering by groups linked to the same population, has been a hallmark of the U.S. presidency since the inception of large-scale electronic media. Its use in conjunction with public opinion polling poses the same problem Kornhauser confronted—except here the decimation of the intermediate groups is not the only way in which mass behavior and instability might occur.

From a different national perspective, one that operates in the shadow of the American media, current debate in Canada centers on preservation of a centralized (versus weakened but diverse) regional electronic media structure. The fear is that Canada cannot cope with the dominant and culturally centralized U.S. media; it may lose its national identity. Similar arguments, usually more economic than geographic, have been made by Schiller (1971a) and Varis (1974). Although much of our discussion has been (and will continue to be) couched in national or societal terms, we should not lose sight of international implications.

DEPENDENT OUTCOMES OF COMMUNICATION

The concept of persuasion has been widely used but not always defined. The term is commonly meant to indicate a change in attitudes, opinions or behavior that is caused by communication. Because of our interest in the political system we find it useful to separate the dimension "behavior" from the dimension "attitude", and to include opinions as expressions of attitudes (Katz, 1960) and not as behavior. Hovland and Janis (1959, p. 2) use the term *attitude change* "as a clear cut indication that the recipient has internalized a valuational message, as evidenced by the fact that a person's perceptions, affects, and overt actions, as well as his verbalized judgment, are discernibly changed." The use of changes in overt actions as part of the definition of changes in attitude is an example of a belief in tight linkages between attitudes and behavior. But does attitude always take place *before* a change in behavior? And will change in behavior always take place after and as result of a change in attitude? Katz and Stotland (1959) demonstrate that attitudes are not the sole determinants of behavior, and changes in behavior are not necessarily a result of changes in attitudes. McQuail (1969) has argued that the steps in the linkage seem as logical and rational: a change in knowledge should take place before a change in attitude takes place, and a change in attitude is necessary before a change in behavior takes place.

It is our intention to keep the three dimensions (knowledge, attitudes and opinions, and behavior) separate as an indication that they are not always linked in a particular logical order. Himmelstrand (1960) has also specified the conditions under which attitudes will predict behavior, working from the assumption that attitudes will not always be predictive of behavior. Wiecker (1969) has shown that relevant attitudes do not always change before behavior, and that it is not always safe to infer behavioral outcomes from information about attitudes.

In specifying what we mean by mass behavior we have to return to Kornhauser's notions of the term "mass" in this context. We mean to describe direct activity of people where (a) the focus of attention is remote from personal experience and daily life, and (b) the mode of response to remote objects is direct. Symbolic appeals that lack a sense of reality or definition are prime candidates for activating mass behavior. Ties of family, friends, work, class, church, unions, or other social groups tend to bring proximity to objects—specifying a reality and definiteness that undermines the capability of these remote symbols to activate behavior. Should the activation take place, however, and not be mediated by other persons, the response is usually direct and immediate.

It should be clear that there is a difference between mass behavior and other behavior that is related to knowledge acquisition or attitude change. This is not to say that knowledge acquisition or attitude change are not related to mass behavior. It is simply that studies of mass behavior events to date have not focused on the knowledge or attitude conditions that are antecedent to or a consequence of mass behavior; so we know little of the sequential arrangements. It is reasonable to assume that the conditions that are paramount for mass behavior will provide real opportunities for other knowledge, attitude change or behavioral outcomes. In fact, it is our contention that by including mass behavior as extreme examples of media effects we will be able to make more general statements about related changes.

STUDIES IN MASS BEHAVIOR

A classic example of mass persuasion and mass behavior was that of the marathon war bond sales drive undertaken in the U.S. in 1943. The eighteen-hour plea by singer Kate Smith for purchase of the bonds was carried on the CBS national radio network (Merton, 1946). A repeat of the same format later during World War II met with even greater success. The basic pleas for money and the presentation of Kate Smith as the hostess for the program represented support for abstract patriotic symbols along with a topic that had little, if any, experiential definition for the populace. The radio network reached large numbers of people across the U.S. during the program, with an outcome not unlike the massing of large groups of anonymous persons. Thousands phoned their purchase pledges to appropriate locations, and could do so as often as they wished. The measurement of impact was also a factor that helps make this event, and its study by Merton, stand out. Purchases of war bonds represents a nonambiguous outcome, something often missing in media effects research.

Marten Brouwer[4] has studied a similar event in The Netherlands, where the opportunity to donate money was the dependent outcome. When the facilities at the broadcasting outlet could not handle the crowds, additional opportunities had to be made available to handle the behavior. Here we have an even more extreme example of not only giving, but of traveling to give, as the activity triggered by the communicated appeal.

Another classic study in the communication research literature was The Invasion from Mars (Cantril, Gaudet and Herzog, 1940). This study attempted to capture the mass behavior that came about when Orson Welles' radio program was broadcast, in 1938. The show, a simulation of a news program that reported the landing of invaders from the planet Mars, provided messages in a context that emphasized abstract symbols remote from personal experience where the response could have been direct. The media reported that a large number of people fled their homes, but there was no accurate estimate as to how many. The large number was relative rather than absolute. Rosow (1973) using the word "mass" as synonymous with large, refers to the program as frightening half of the nation. Rosengren, Arvidson and Sturesson (1974), however, estimate that only about two per cent of the audience reacted in a clear behavioral fashion. In many ways the program's effect has a place in the literature because of the assumed size of the outcome or because it was caused by the mass media. Although (as we have pointed out) it does have a mass character to it because of the direct communication of a message that was abstract and unreal, it was not necessarily as important as many events that may have gone unheralded because they have not been formally studied.

The Rosengren team's evaluation of The Invasion from Mars was reported in a study of an event in Sweden that had many of the same characteristics. In 1973 a program was broadcast on radio, telling of an accident in a nuclear plant in Bärseback. The fictitious event was set in 1982 with the objective of dramatizing the risks associated with nuclear energy. The plant referred to was under construction at the time of the broadcast. The media coverage of the audience's reaction to the program, if left unchallenged, would have provided another example of mass behavior similar to that reported in the media following the Welles program. But Rosengren and his colleagues found that few fled or could be considered as acting in a mass behavioral way. Still, the intention of the program to create awareness of the topic was achieved in large part; this other, less dramatic, outcome fits the schema at hand.

THE DANISH REFERENDUM

We observed earlier that direct communication about topics that were removed from personal experience or had abstract symbolic qualities generated some mass behavior. For large proportions of the population there were probably other outcomes. Let us turn now to the 1972 referendum in Denmark on the European Economic Community, to examine vote choice as one of these other outcomes.

The question posed was whether Denmark should join the EEC; 68 per cent said "yes." The turnout was very high (90 per cent) and the coverage by all of the large-scale media was extensive. The central argument by the proponents of entry, and the one supported by the majority of newspapers, was the economic. The selection of economics for successful emphasis squares with Allardt's (1975) estimate of what is salient politically in Denmark. Little, if any, counterarguing on this issue occurred; instead, opponents emphasized the long-term political implications—not the short-term economics.

It is clear from surveys of the population five months before the referendum that the turnout could not be interpreted as mass behavior. At that time 87 per cent had said they would cast their ballots in October. In May nearly 75 per cent had some interest in the issue (although only 42 per cent knew something about the European Community). In August, just one month before balloting, the first wave of a panel study was launched.

The turnover of voting choice that took place during the intense campaign that was waged by the various factions is highly significant. Nearly one-fourth of those who had intended to cast a negative ballot switched in favor of the Danish entry; and of the some 30 per cent who did not have a clear position in August, three-quarters

TABLE 1
VOTING ON DANISH EEC REFERENDUM, BY AUGUST VOTE INTENTION

In October, voted . . .	In August, intended to vote . . .			
	Yes	No	In doubt	Total
Yes	99%	21%	74%	67%
No	1	79	26	33
(N)	(119)	(102)	(93)	(314)

Source: Siune and Borre (1975)

voted for entry. The parties with the largest membership solidly supported entry and the major businesses and corporations advertised extensively in favor of a "yes" vote. Taken across all media, the preponderance of information and persuasion was for entry and centered on one major issue—the economic one. We might also speculate that many who were in doubt in August were largely those who (more than 50 per cent) had known nothing about the EEC in May. This would support our point (above) about the uninformed and apathetic. Although not a typical example of direct communication by one centralized agency, the relatively concentrated campaign apparently caused a large shift that carried the day.

It should be clear from the above examples that we need to take media structure and media concentration as necessary components of a general media effects model when we are concerned with relatively large-scale outcomes. It is also clear that the character of the message, the way in which behavior can be undertaken, and the way in which intermediate relations are organized in a society, are all major elements one should consider.

FUTURE TECHNOLOGY, MEDIA AND SOCIETY

We have tried to argue so far that many of the media effect outcomes that one finds in the communication research literature need to be considered in a larger social context. We have used the societal model offered by Kornhauser to elucidate some key elements for consideration. One was the role of intermediate groups in providing social anchors for evaluating and contextualizing messages that one sees or hears. A second and a third centered on the direct communications that are now technologically available between elites and non-elites by virtue of media structure and feedback mechanisms.

Donohue, Tichenor and Olien (1972) have pointed to the continuing relationships that various subsystem structures have with each other as the overall system maintains an equilibrium. This balancing takes place with upward and downward communications predominately between the elites and non-elites through the intermediate relations. When information channels are opened to bypass these various contending groups we have to consider seriously what the outcomes might be for overall system stability.

Kenneth Boulding has also been concerned with the issue of technology and information. He says, "The rise of modern technology and the growth in the complexity of the knowledge structure of the society is perhaps the dominant factor in the political process of modern society" (1971, p. 107). With the technological potential of many channels of information and entertainment via cable, direct broadcasting of television programs to the home only years away, and the assembly and delivery of newspapers by electronic means no longer a futurist's pipe dream, we should consider what the implications are for some of the dependent outcomes mentioned above.

Owen, Beebe and Manning (1974) have addressed, at least in the realm of television, the implications of moving away from monopolistic competition and outright monopoly of communication channels to competition—where the scarcity of channels is not a major constraint. The demands on the radio spectrum from users not involved in public communication have risen rapidly in the last decade, putting pressure on regulators for more spectrum allocation. These constraints, though real enough in certain areas, seem less so when one considers the potential of cable where penetration is very high (as in Canada, The Netherlands and Belgium); the use of restricted-power drop-in television channels; newer technologies of spectrum compression techniques; and the direct broadcast satellite developments. The key issue of course is the use of technology for many channels of information and drawing economic and viewer sustenance from the many intermediate groups who will use these as channels, rather than for the centralization of information sources that would undercut (or otherwise not involve) the many pluralities that exist in most countries. As we have tried to show, the implications are important where the goals of individual choice of competing voices are important to political stability. We can also see that where the national goal is stability without individual choice of information, the technology can be implemented to assist that end.

SUMMARY

Our concern has been with the way in which political outcomes can be seen as a product of communication and feedback structures in the society, as well as of the group structures that provide contextual linkages to one's family, friends, co-workers and other affiliations. We have relied on the mass society perspective that Kornhauser advanced in the 1950s. We have added to that the technologically centralized communication and feedback channels that play such an important role in modern polities. Using examples of mass behavior as extreme examples of communication effects, as well as the voting outcome in a recent Danish referendum, we have argued that the aggregate outcomes were partially a product of the systemic properties being discussed. Finally we discussed some of the future possibilities that new media technologies might provide for offsetting information centralization.

NOTES

1. We could have included mass culture in our list of terms often found in the communication research literature. Although beyond the scope of this chapter, it can be linked to this mass society approach. In fact, the preservation of critical values that require the social insulation of those segments of society that embody them, so central to the debate over mass culture, is a key tenet paradoxically taken over from the aristocratic critics by the democratic critics. Although disagreeing on the values to be preserved, both camps agree on the pressure relationship that exists between elites and non-elites, and on the need to provide protection against direct access to each other.

2. *Mass society* will occur when (a) the elites are accessible and (b) the non-elites are available, and it will exhibit a high rate of mass behavior. This situation comes about when the few independent groups between the state and the family become greatly weakened. In the absence of these independent forces large numbers of people are pushed and pulled toward activist modes as elites mobilize and in turn are susceptible to upward pressure.

The Communal Society requires the sustenance of traditional structures. Elite element standards are selected and fixed by traditional ascription. Non-elites are firmly bound by kinship and community, and are difficult to mobilize. The erosion of communal ties in the Late Middle Ages brought about by the very early beginnings of urbanization and industrialization is the kind of force required to free populations for mobilization such as that found in the millennial movements that flourished then.

A Pluralist Society can sustain its freedom and diversity by minimizing the potential for mobilizing the non-elites and maximizing accessibility to elites. These elites will be accessible where there is competition among independent groups with the concomitant many channels of communication and power. The non-elites, on the other hand, possess multiple commitments to diverse and autonomous groups. To mobilize such a population would require the destruction of such groups or group ties so that messages directed to them would not be encumbered by competing interpretations and viewpoints.

A Totalitarian Society requires elite monopoly of accession either by coercion or persuasion, and a non-elite population that can be mobilized because there are so few independent social formations that might lessen resistance to messages emanating from a centralized agency or agencies.

3. In a communal situation as defined by Kornhauser there would be very few messages traveling from top to bottom, and those that did would always pass through the intermediate level. In a totalitarian society most of the messages would travel from top to bottom either directly or through intermediate groups that were not autonomous from the state in a way that would provide any different message even if they put a group contextualization on it. In a pluralistic society we would expect little in the way of direct communication up or down, but a good deal more up through the intermediate groups so that the elites would know the will of the people and act accordingly.

4. Personal communication to the author (Siune).

REFERENCES

ALLARDT, T. E. (1975) "A comparative study of need-satisfaction, alienation and discontent in the Scandinavian countries," presented to conference on "Recent Political Trends in the Scandinavian Countries," Washington, D.C.

ALMOND G. and S. VERBA (1965) The Civic Culture. New York: Little Brown.

ARENDT, H. (1951) The Origins of Totalitarianism. New York: Harcourt-Brace.

BLUMER, H. (1946) "The mass the public, and public opinion," in A. M. Lee, New Outline of the Principles of Sociology. New York: Barnes and Noble.

BOULDING, K. E. (1971) The Image. Ann Arbor: University of Michigan Press.

BURCKHARDT, J. (1955) Force and Freedom. New York: Meridian Books.

CANTRIL, H., H. GAUDET and H. HERZOG (1940) The Invasion From Mars. Princeton: Princeton University Press.

CONVERSE, P. E. (1962) "Information flow and the stability of partisan attitudes." Public Opinion Q. 26: 578-599.

DONOHUE, G. A., P. J. TICHENOR and C. N. OLIEN (1972) "Gatekeeping: mass media systems and information control," in F. G. Kline and P. J. Tichenor (eds.) Current Perspectives in Mass Communication Research. Beverly Hills: Sage Pubns.

FREIDSON, E. (1954) "Mass communication research and the concept of mass." Amer. Soc. Rev. 18: 313-317.

HIMMELSTRAND, U. (1960) "Verbal attitudes and behavior: a paradigm for the study of message transmission and transformation." Public Opinion Q. 24: 224-250.

HOVLAND, C. I. and I. L. JANIS (1959) Personality and Persuasibility. New Haven: Yale University Press.

JANOWITZ, M. (1968) "The study of mass communication," International Encyclopedia of the Social Sciences. New York: Macmillan-Free Press.

KATZ, D. (1960) "The functional approach to the study of attitudes." Public Opinion Q. 24 (summer):163-204.

––– and E. STOTLAND (1959) "A preliminary statement to a theory of attitude structure and change," in S. Koch (ed.) Psychology, A Study of a Science. New York: McGraw-Hill.

KATZ, E. and P. LAZARSFELD (1955) Personal Influence. New York: Free Press.

KEY, V. O. (1964) Public Opinion and American Democracy. New York: Alfred A. Knopf.

KLINE, F. G. (1972) "Theory in mass communication research," in F. G. Kline and P. J. Tichenor (eds.) Current Perspectives in Mass Communication Research. Beverly Hills: Sage Pubns.

KORNHAUSER, W. (1959) The Politics of Mass Society. New York: The Free Press.

LeBON, G. (1947) The Crowd. London: Ernest Bonn Ltd.

LEDERER, E. (1940) State of the Masses. New York: W. W. Norton.

MANNHEIM, K. (1940) Ideology and Utopia. London: Routledge and Kegan Paul.

MARCUSE, H. (1964) One Dimensional Man. London: Routledge and Kegan Paul.

McQUAIL, D. (1969) Towards a Sociology of Mass Communications. London: Collier-Macmillan Ltd.

MERTON, R. K. (1946) Mass Persuasion: The Social Psychology of a War Bond Drive. New York: Harper Bros.

MILLS, C. W. (1956) The Power Elite. New York: Oxford University Press.

MORRISON, A., F. G. KLINE and P. V. MILLER (1975) "Aspects of adolescent information acquisition about drugs and alcohol," in R. E. Ostman and H. Mowlana (eds.), Communication Research and Drug Education. Beverly Hills: Sage Pubns.

ORTEGA y GASSET, J. (1932) The Revolt of the Masses. New York: W. W. Norton.

PALMGREEN, P., F. G. KLINE and P. CLARKE (1974) "Message discrimination and information holding about political affairs: a comparison of local and national issues," presented to International Communication Assn.

OWEN, B. M., J. H. BEEBE and W. G. MANNING, Jr. (1974) Television Economics. Mass.: D. C. Heath and Co.

PARK, R. E. (1923) "The natural history of the newspaper." Amer. J. of Soc. 29: 273-289.

ROGERS, E. (1962) Diffusion of Innovations. New York: Free Press.

ROSENGREN, K. E., P. ARVIDSON and D. STURESSON (1974) The Bärseback Panic. Lund University mimeo.

ROSOW, I. (1973) "The social context of the aging self." The Gerontologist 13: 82-87.

SCHILLER, H. I. (1971a) Mass Communications and American Empire. Boston: Beacon Press.

——— (1971b) "The polling industry: The measurement and manufacture of opinion," presented to the Society for the History of Technology.

SIEBERT, F. S., T. PETERSON and W. SCHRAMM (1956) Four Theories of the Press. Urbana: University of Illinois Press.

SINGER, B. D. (1973) Feedback and Society. Lexington, Mass.: D. C. Heath.

SIUNE, K. and O. BORRE (1975) "Setting the agenda for a Danish election." J. Communication 25: 65-73.

VARIS, T. (1974) "Global traffic in television." J. Communication 24: 102.

WIECKER, A. W. (1969) "Attitudes versus actions: The relationship of verbal and overt behavioral responses to attitude objects." J. Social Issues 25: 41-78.

ZIEGLER, H. (1970) "The communication revolution and the future of interest groups," in H. Sackman and N. Nie, The Information Utility and Social Choice. Montvale, N.J.: AFIPS Press.

Chapter 3

THE DIFFUSION OF POLITICAL INFORMATION

Steven H. Chaffee

THE MOST PERVASIVE IMAGE of political activity that one can extract from common parlance is that of a *system*. Shrewd operators are said to have "learned the system", quixotic rebels try to "buck the system", and youthful drop-outs "reject the system." Speech-makers glorify the "genius of our system", while others bemoan the "failure of our system" to cope with new challenges. The Cold War is characterized as the inevitable clash between two great rival systems. And so on.

There has been, however, precious little systematic discourse or evidence to substantiate this easy use of the term. In particular, research on political communication has rarely been organized in terms of system-level concepts. Instead we have had studies of communication at the level of the individual, as typified by the survey of public opinion, and studies of political systems that con- centrate on identifying enduring structural properties—a standpoint from which communication processes are either assumed as a given, or treated as a source of error.

While a great deal has been learned, and can be learned, from studies at the individual and structural levels of investigation, there is good reason to believe that some unique kinds of understanding of political communication processes might be gained by research that

AUTHOR'S NOTE: The thoughtful suggestions of Albert Tims throughout the preparation of this paper are gratefully acknowledged. Rebecca Quarles, Kim Smith and Jean Lewin also made helpful comments on a draft of the theoretical portion. Support for this work came from the Graduate School of the University of Wisconsin.

is specifically conceived in system-level terms. It is the actions of individuals that give life to the structural properties of political systems, just as the latter in turn constrain the behaviors of individuals. Communication, being by definition a process, should presumably be studied in connection with changes *over time* in the state of a system, or of individuals within a system. This chapter is devoted to outlining an agenda for research on parameters of communication processes that are relevant to a general model of political systems (Easton, 1965a, 1965b).

COMMUNICATION IN TERMS OF CONSTRAINTS

When we are dealing with empirical questions that are amenable to statistical inference, it is necessary to have a baseline, or zero point, against which to compare observed results (cf. McLeod and Chaffee, 1971). In studies of the effects of communication on attitudes, for example, this "null model" purpose is served by the measurement of *change,* specifically the difference between the person's expressed opinions prior to receiving the message and comparable opinion statements afterwards. In the study of political systems, it has been usual to assume that an analogous change-of-level measurement would serve as an appropriate indicator of significant effects. For example, a change in foreign policy, a revised tax structure, or an amendment to the constitution, are all palpable signs of change in the system's behavior that are likely to send historians, political scientists and other types of social researchers into action to determine the causes of the change.

Communication, despite the high importance it is accorded in discussions of political change, rarely gets identified as an important causal mechanism in analyses of major systemic shifts. Instead, when the communicatory activities of individual actors within the system are examined across time, they turn out to have been fairly constant before, during, and after the period in which the policy change occurred. For instance, one's time spent reading the daily newspaper, or one's frequency of interpersonal contact with work peers, would be unlikely to vary much from one month to the next; even if momentous events were going on, an individual deeply involved in that change is likely to substitute one class of communicatory activity for his habitual ones, rather than to "communicate more" in any empirically discernible way. This kind of evidence is usually interpreted as forcing us to the conclusion that, while communication in general is manifestly essential to the political process, communication *variables* did not govern the course of the particular change.

This paradox suggests that our conception of the research question may have been in error. Instead of assuming that the generic problem is that of *facilitating change* in political outcomes via communication, we could examine *constraints* on communication that affect the *intervening process* through which the political system operates—and which might just as easily result in political stability as in change. That is, the important questions about communication—the ones that are likely to yield theoretically generalizable answers—may not be those that inquire into specific agents of change in individual behavior, but instead those that identify structural barriers that are properties of the socio-political system. If, as it appears, communicatory behavior exhibits great *stability within individuals* over time but considerable *variation between individuals* at any given time, we might reasonably suspect that there are constraining factors in the system that account for these habitual individual differences. Within the boundaries of those constraints, which research could presumably help to identify, communication might indeed be assumed to be a given—an inter-individual transmission process that operates simply, steadily, and efficiently enough to justify our not attempting to engineer facilitation factors that might render it "more complete" or "more effective." These constraining factors would then be looked upon as independent variables that control the process through which the political system functions, rather than as potential mechanisms through which one interest-sector within the system might facilitate political change in a particular direction. This would shift emphasis to the quality of political decision-making for the system as a whole. To develop this approach, it will be necessary to say much more precisely what is meant by the functioning of a political system, by complete or perfect communication, and by factors that constrain these things.

DIFFUSION AS A GENERIC PROBLEM

The specification of an appropriate null model is the point of departure for this task. A well-established tradition in communication research is the study of diffusion of new ideas and practices, and of news information (Rogers and Shoemaker, 1971; Deutschmann and Danielson, 1960; Greenberg, 1964a). The findings from diffusion studies can be thought of generally in terms of a simple two-dimensional graph in which time is represented on the horizontal axis, and the cumulative number of persons who have adopted the new idea or practice, or learned of the news item, is plotted on the vertical axis. When presented in this way, which is usually the case in reports of diffusion analyses, the graph characteristically takes on the form of an S-curve. That is, in the earliest phase only a few people are "adopters" or "knowers", and the cumulative curve representing this group builds very slowly over time. Gradually, the diffusion curve accelerates; the greatest number of new adopters or knowers per unit time occurs when about half of the population has reached that status. After this, the curve decelerates, until finally only a few additional adopters or knowers are being added per unit time.

Although some writers have considered this S-curve a substantive finding, and have even remarked on the frequency with which it has been "replicated" as evidence of its theoretical import, it should be obvious to the student of introductory statistics that it is a null or random model—at least from the perspective of constraints on communication. The S-curve is a *normal ogive,* which is statistical terminology for a cumulative plot of the familiar normal or bell-shaped curve. Let us assume for purposes of illustration that we are examining the itinerary through the population in a system composed of 100 individuals, of an item of knowledge, and that there are no constraints on communication; the item will "diffuse" any time a knower interacts with a non-knower. We can also assume that interactions are totally random, which means that the probability of any one person interacting with some other particular person at a given time is 1/99; there are 4,950 different possible two-person interactions. Now to start the diffusion process at Time 1, only one person should have the information. At Time 2 he will interact with one other person, so that both will thereafter be knowers. We can calculate the probability of a "diffusion interaction", i.e. one between a knower and a non-knower, for any number of knowers. When there are only two knowers and 98 non-knowers, for instance, there are 196 different possible diffusion interactions, plus 4,753 possible interactions between pairs of non-knowers and one between the two knowers; the probability of diffusion is only 196 ÷ 4,950 or about 4%. The same low probability of diffusion would hold at the other end of the S-curve, when there remain only two non-knowers along with 98 knowers; in this situation, 4,573 of the possible 4,950 interactions would involve two knowers, neither of whom could transmit the information to the other since both already have it. These low probabilities of diffusion at the extremes of the S-curve contrast dramatically with the situation when diffusion has reached the halfway point. If 50 of the 100 persons know the information, the probability of a diffusion interaction is 2,500 ÷ 4,950, or slightly greater than 50%–about 13 times as great as the probability when there are only two knowers or only two non-knowers. This 50% mark is the highest probability of a diffusion interaction that is reached in the course of diffusion, which explains why the "speed" represented by acceleration of the S-curve tends to be greatest at this point.

The only remarkable conclusion to be drawn from the frequent

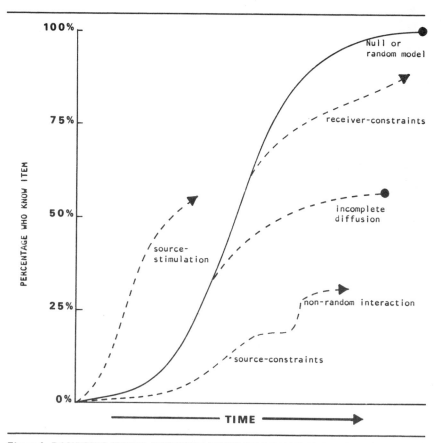

Figure 1: RANDOM S-CURVE AND SOME TYPES OF DEVIATIONS FROM IT

discovery of cumulative curves that approximate the S-form in diffusion research is not that this represents some behavioral imperative
that facilitates or "causes" diffusion to proceed at an S-curve pace;
instead we should conclude that an empirical S-curve is simply
evidence of an *absence of constraints* and a *randomness of interaction* within the system population under study. The interesting
instances accordingly become those where diffusion does *not* follow
the S-curve; here we should suspect structural factors that constrain
communication or that render interactions non-random. There are
several general patterns of deviation from the normal ogive, which
should point us in different research directions. One is the fairly
frequent case where diffusion falls far short of 100% of the population; if the S-curve eventually flattens out at, say, 60% diffusion, we
should direct our inquiry to constraining factors in the remaining
40% of the population that might render them impervious to the
item that is being diffused.

On the other hand, if the S-curve accelerates more (or less) rapidly
than might be expected under the null conditions discussed above,
the probable cause is not individual-level constraint but rather some
structural property of the social system that makes interactions
non-random. Two cases should be distinguished here, those in which
diffusion proceeds, respectively, with greater or less speed than the
S-curve predicts. The more usual would be a system in which interactions are stratified according to common levels of education,
income, locale, etc. The characteristic diffusion curve one would
expect under these conditions would be rapid initial acceleration, but
slower-than-expected diffusion later in the curve. A related phenomenon would be sudden jumps in the diffusion curve, which would
occur when the item "broke through" some barrier in the social
structure and reached a new group. Such a pattern was found in the
well-known study of diffusion of a new drug among physicians in a
community; it diffused rapidly within each social clique, but slowly
between cliques (Coleman, Katz and Menzel, 1957).

The other major type of non-random diffusion is that in which the
initial stages of the curve exhibit unexpectedly slow acceleration. In
this case we should expect that constraints are being exercised on
communication by the knowers, or potential sources of information.
This might occur where there is some social or economic advantage
to be gained from being a knower in a system where the majority are
non-knowers, or from having adopted a new practice while most
others are staying with obsolete methods. This kind of "hoarding"

phenomenon is rare in the diffusion research literature, probably because most diffusion studies have been associated with major collective efforts to disseminate—rather than hoard—information and new practices. It is not difficult, however, to think of examples of topics whose diffusion was at least initially retarded by self-imposed constraints on the part of those who were in a position to pass on the information. If this restraining effort is maintained throughout the course of diffusion, it will be hard to detect because its effect will be constant over time; the general S-curve will eventually emerge. Identification of self-restraint among knowers is more likely when it is only temporary, limited to the early stages when there is some advantage to their being part of an informed "elite."

One additional form of constraint is of enough importance to the study of political communication that we should consider it in terms of diffusion theory here. This is *topic-specific constraint,* which consists in prohibitions against communication about certain matters. Examples are not hard to find in interpersonal systems; there are some things that "nice people" simply do not mention, or about which a son would not ask his mother. This means that, in the same system some topics will diffuse quite normally, whereas others will fail to diffuse extensively. The other side of this coin is that some topics are of a character that stimulates communication, so that very rapid and complete diffusion may occur. A good joke tends to travel fast throughout a group of co-workers, and news of some impending calamity (e.g. a hurricane) is likely to be disseminated in a community with great urgency. News of the assassination of President Kennedy, for example, reached almost all Americans within a few hours (Greenberg & Parker, 1965; see also Kraus et al. chapter elsewhere in this volume).

Topic-specific constraints (and stimulated diffusion) comprise a particularly important class of factors in large political systems where the process of communication occurs mainly via formalized channels of communication such as the mass media. There are certain kinds of topics that a given medium will not transmit (e.g. those deemed offensive to its audience), and others that the media make special efforts to diffuse (e.g. "newsworthy" items). Other properties of the mass media tend to foster normal S-curve diffusion patterns. News periodicals (the term is instructive here) disseminate information on a steady schedule, about the same total amount per unit time from one week to the next. Further, the media have the capacity to reach a wider variety of persons with the same information, in comparison with an individual information source whose range of personal con-tacts is likely to be rather constricted. Additionally, the media have assumed the role of news-gatherer, which means that they are mech-anisms for eliciting rate information from persons who hold it–and then in turn reporting it to the broad audience. Finally, the media are professionally engaged in devising new ways of reaching people with their messages, as a means of broadening their audience and base of support in the society.

The introduction of mass media into a political system, then, serves to break down the factors that would foster non-randomness and permit source-imposed or receiver-centered constraints on diffu-sion of information. This leads us to the hypothesis that, the greater the reliance of the system on mass media (which override constraints that operate in interpersonal channels) the more likely diffusion should be to follow the S-curve or null model for a given topic. On the other hand, topic-specific constraints–which imply that some kinds of information will *not* be diffused to any appreciable extent– become *more* likely, the greater the reliance on mass media for communication, because the media exercise much more restrictive constraints over the kinds of content that get transmitted than do informal social channels of communication. Since all social systems employ some combination of interpersonal and mediated communi-cation, in varying proportions, these propositions are potentially empirically testable.

EASTON'S GENERAL MODEL OF A POLITICAL SYSTEM

In order to define categories of communicable content that cor-respond to generalizable components of the political process, it is necessary to work from a general model of political systems. For this purpose, Easton's (1953, 1965a, 1965b) model has been selected here. Because of the importance of the Easton model in the develop-ment of empirical theory within political science, this choice means that research based on the outline being presented in this chapter would be most likely to dovetail with work done in other areas of political behavior. It is eminently conceivable, of course, that alter-native models of a political system might be devised that would serve the internal purpose of organizing this chapter as effectively as does Easton's; the external purpose of stimulating investigations that might contribute to the cumulation of empirical theory regarding political communication is the main reason for selecting this particular model.

The content of political life consists, in Easton's view, of interactions among individuals and groups that involve "the authoritative allocation of values for a society" (1965a: 49-50). This allocation of values may take several forms: depriving someone of something he has, obstructing his attainment of something he wants, or providing access to something that would otherwise be unattainable. These kinds of allocations are *authoritative* if the persons involved consider that they are bound by them. This very broad definition of "political" enables Easton to design an extremely simple model of a political system that is applicable to all sorts of governments, and to subsystems such as business firms, families, churches, etc. Since he is primarily concerned with societal-level political systems, he distinguishes them from smaller subsystems by calling the latter *parapolitical* systems (1965a: 52-56).

Two kinds of persons are identified within a political system; they are the *members* and the *authorities*. The term "member" implies that the person is looked at in terms of "his participation in political life in some shape or form, if only as the passive recipient of the results of the active behavior of others to which he orients himself" (Easton, 1965a: 57). Those "others" are the authorities, who in earlier versions of the model (Easton, 1953, 1957) were identified as "the government." The members provide the system with two types of *inputs,* called "demands" and "support." The system itself, acting through the authorities, continuously performs a "conversion process" that yields *outputs* that are variously called decisions, policies, actions, and services. Because Easton is centrally concerned with the problem of the *persistence* of a given political system, he devotes a great deal of attention to sources of stress on the system; stress can arise, for example, from the input of too many or conflicting demands, or through the erosion of support.

Support for the system is particularly well elaborated in Easton's later writings (Easton, 1965b). Support may be diffuse—attached to the system in general—or it may be specific to a given policy issue. Further, it may be attached to the incumbent governing authorities, or more broadly to the "regime" (i.e. the constitution of the government), or to the "political community" (i.e. the country itself). In parapolitical systems, these levels of support have direct analogies; in a labor union, for example, the organization's officials serve as authorities, there is a set of procedures for election and governance

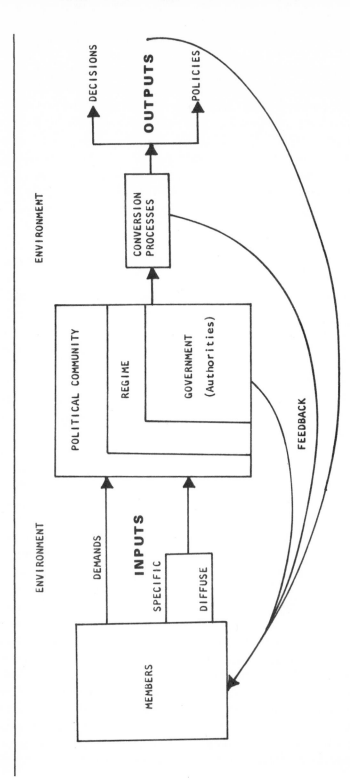

Figure 2: ADAPTATION OF EASTON'S MODEL OF A POLITICAL SYSTEM

that constitutes the regime, and the common work that defines the scope of the union in effect forms the political community. Maintenance of sufficient diffuse support for all levels of the system is essential for the persistence of the system itself. It is perhaps not surprising, then, that Easton views the acquisition of supportive feelings about one's country, regime, and central authority figures as the essence of political socialization (Easton and Dennis, 1969), nor that his concept of "output failure" of a system consists of decisions that cause the erosion of support (Easton, 1965b: 403ff.).

COORIENTATION AND COMMUNICATION SYSTEMS

There are a number of communication problems that can be identified in connection with the Easton model. He puts particular emphasis on "feedback" to the authorities, regarding the reactions of the members to output decisions (What do they support?), and on the flow of demands to authorities from members (What would they support?). This support-oriented and authority-directed view of the communication problems of a political system can be contrasted with diffusion theory—which would imply a member-centered and instrumental conceptualization of communication problems. That is, if we were to concern ourselves with the way in which a system operates from the point of view of its members, rather than with the persistence of a system from the point of view of its authorities, we might begin to ask research questions that would lend themselves to study in diffusionist terms.

An additional distinction is necessary here. In communication analysis, more is at stake than is the case in political analysis. The latter is properly concerned, in Easton's terms, with authoritative allocation of values, based on the conversion of members' demands into outputs that will maintain their support for the system. This affective support ordinarily amounts to no more than acquiescence on the part of members to policy outputs. As indicated schematically in Table 1, the analogous goal in communication is that of achieving agreement on values, through persuasive communication.

Students of communication processes have in recent years, however, called attention to a more direct outcome of communicative interaction, which they have called understanding (Carter, 1965) or accuracy of interpersonal coorientation (McLeod and Chaffee, 1973). This cognitive outcome is simple enough to conceptualize in

TABLE 1
ANALOGIES BETWEEN COMMUNICATION AND POLITICAL SYSTEM PARAMETERS

	Communication system		Political system	
Individual domain	*Goal*	*Mechanism*	*Goal*	*Mechanism*
affective	agreement in values held by members	persuasive communication	outputs that maintain support of members	demand-satisfying conversion processes
cognitive	accuracy of members in perceiving inputs	informational person-person communication	understanding of system functioning	informational person-system communication

the person-person situation; it consists of each person coming to comprehend what the other is thinking, intending, or feeling. Open lines of communication between people should foster this type of outcome—even though the interactants might not come to *agree* on things any more than they had before they began communicating to one another. In a political system, the communicatory relationship at stake is that between the system and its members. As Table 1 indicates, the presumed outcome of communication would be that the members understand what the system is doing—in terms of converting demands and support inputs into policy and decisional outputs. This is a systemic goal that would be of more direct interest to communication analysts than to political analysts, since it is not central to the latter's concern for system persistence. And it is one that lends itself directly to research built on the diffusion model outlined earlier here.

A SYSTEMIC CONCEPT OF POLITICAL INFORMATION

Given this skeletal outline, we are in position to evaluate a communication system within the context of a political system. The core question is that of diffusion of political information to members. Political information can be defined as "knowledge on the part of any member of the system of any changes in the state of the system regarding the authoritative allocation of values." This would include information about demands and support inputs, decisional outputs by the authorities, and the intervening conversion process. As outlined earlier here, diffusion would be expected to follow the normal S-curve throughout the total population of system members unless constraints operate to retard or prevent this. Constraints may be exercised by the sources of information, or they may operate in the receiving members—or they may be imposed by the communication system that transmits such information.

Let us consider the example that is most familiar to most of those who will read this essay. The United States has a well-established political system, and a national system of communications media that are constitutionally guaranteed a wide range of latitude in their activities, under the rubric "freedom of the press." This special guarantee of non-constraint on the part of the regime has been extended to the news media because of their importance in servicing the political system, i.e. because they provide for extensive diffusion of political information. Individuals and interest groups use the media to express a wide variety of demands, and to express (or threaten withdrawal of) their support for the authorities, the Constitution, and the nation as a whole. Constraints are exercised by the news media, both in their selection from among these competing inputs from members (the editing or "gatekeeping" function), and in their choice of topics on which they will generate news information (the reporting or "watchdog" function).

The press closely follows the itinerary of each issue through the governmental machinery, particularly noting such mileposts as the passage of a bill in a legislative body, or its signing into law. There is a great deal of coverage also of the authorities as persons; this is particularly the case with the President and his family, and of serious contenders for the presidency. (While this personality coverage is not expressly *political* communication in terms we have been discussing it here—i.e. it is not directly related to the conversion of demands and support into decisional outputs—we might consider it at least quasi-political in that it is associated with the maintenance of diffuse support for the authorities.) There seems to be less coverage than might be predicted on the basis of their intrinsic importance to the system, of intermediate stages of the conversion process, particularly the preliminary conversion of a set of inputs into a proposed bill. Much of this activity goes on behind closed doors, at the White House and in legislative party caucuses—one clear example of constraints exercised by communication sources. A reverse type of source-controlled constraint consists of the output of public relations offices that are maintained on behalf of almost all governmental authorities today; this content is made easily available by skilled information specialists, and tends to occupy much of the finite space and time slots available in the news media. This in turn tends to crowd out information that might be more enlightening to citizens, but which would require greater reporting effort than the press finds itself willing to expend. The press has taken steps in recent decades to monitor levels of support, particularly diffuse support for the authorities as in the pollster's question, "How would you rate the job X is doing as President?" The sheer cost of monitoring support more extensively—e.g. for other levels such as the regime and the political community, or for other authorities such as the legislative and judicial branches—probably accounts for what might seem to be media-imposed constraints on the provision of this type of information.

More important constraints are exercised by the media through their conventional definition of what is "newsworthy." In the turbulent 1960s, when many new demands were being raised and the withholding of support for the system was widely threatened, a considerable tension surrounded media handling of political news. On the one hand, many activist groups and personalities surfaced and attempted to assert their demands via the press; in response to the anti-war and racial equality movements and a resurgent feminism on the left, there were right-wing movements attempting to register countervailing demands. The turning point for each of these efforts seems to have come when the press ceased labeling it "extremist" and began to treat it as part of the legitimate mainstream of the daily news. This process is poorly understood. The interplay between public opinion and news values remains a chicken-egg puzzle that invites careful longitudinal research. What is needed, in part, is a codification of the cues that induce media personnel to legitimize one cause or issue at the expense of others.

When the Nixon-Agnew administration in turn attacked the press for what it saw as a too-easy admission of leftist demands into this mainstream of public discourse, two different themes of press criticism were pursued. One was a "counterbalancing" principle, which would imply a need for more press coverage of extreme demands from the right. But the more dominant theme was that the press should somehow arrange for more expressions of diffuse support—what President Nixon characterized as the "Silent Majority" who did not oppose his policies but who got no public visibility because they were not sufficiently newsworthy. Vice President Agnew, the most vigorous administration press critic of this era, also put great emphasis on the media's tendency to focus on the campus demonstration or ghetto riot, and to ignore the great bulk of students who were *not* speaking out against the war or the overwhelming numbers of black citizens who were going about their daily lives without overt complaint. Although the media attempted gamely to provide some coverage of such non-events, this genre came to be derided as "the Ag-news." Diffuse support and acquiescence simply don't lend themselves to the journalistic procedures our national media have developed over the past two centuries. Comparative analysis of different political-communication systems is needed to establish the range of viable modes of press functioning in these respects, since the media's response to such criticism has generally been that current editorial criteria are necessary to their maintaining audience and financial support.

The media cannot be characterized as monolithic in this regard, of course. Few indeed are the newspapers that fail to express their own staunch support for the political community ("my country right or wrong"), or for most aspects of the constitutional regime in the United States. And while the national elite press, which includes the TV networks as well as metropolitan daily newspapers and the weekly newsmagazines, give heavy attention to demand inputs, this is not the case with the more parochial local media (see Donohue, Tichenor and Olien, 1972). Demands create stress, and the local community press in most locales strives to control stress on the system by avoiding the communication of demands that might create community conflict. (Janowitz [1952] found an emphasis on community solidarity in urban newspapers that service local neighborhood shopping districts, for example.) This seems to be a conscious pattern of demand-suppression; the closer the editor is to the political authorities in a small community, the less likely his paper is to report stressful demands; in metropolitan communities the reverse is the case (Olien, Donohue and Tichenor, 1968).

MEDIA AS PARAPOLITICAL SYSTEMS

This points up the fact that media organizations, such as newspapers, television newsrooms, wire services and magazine houses, are themselves parapolitical systems subject to the same kind of analysis we have been applying to the national system. Argyris (1974) and Sigal (1973) have analyzed the internal arrangements for the authoritative allocation of values within elite national newspapers, although they did not approach their research in the terms we are using here. Argyris, for example, found a crisis of support that the newspaper's staff described as "the morale problem on the fifth floor", which grew out of competition for the main items of value within a newspaper—salaries, by-lines, status, approval, and the like. The reporters (members) ordinarily accepted the allocations made by the editors (authorities) because of a general pride in the quality of the overall output of their system, which is a nationally honored newspaper. Adjudication among competing demands, such as the rival claims of the national, metropolitan and foreign desks for shares of the limited "news hole" available in the paper, is handled by conferences that bring together the managing editors (authorities) with the sub-editors in charge of these specialties (Sigal, 1973: 15-16). Each news organization is effectively constrained by economic limitations; only so much space in the day's paper, and only a limited number of time slots in the day's broadcasting schedule, are available for news/editorial content. Constraints exercised by "the media" on the diffusion of various kinds of political information, then, are in part the resultant of conversion processes within each medium as a parapolitical system. Lines may be drawn that coincide with the different types of political information implied in the Easton model. For instance, a Washington, D.C. newsbureau has to make space-allocation choices between its urban affairs staff, which would be most likely to communicate demand inputs, and its personnel assigned to cover the Congress—where the process of conversion into outputs is going on much of the time. One influence on the decisions made will be the kinds of demands that the bureau is receiving from the other media, located around the country, that it services. Another will be the input relationships the bureau must maintain with official news sources—many of which would ordinarily wish to regulate the flow of demands, and emphasize support for themselves as authorities. Even this brief discussion here suggests that the analysis of media news organizations as parapolitical systems constraining the diffusion of political information within the national political system is potentially a rich domain for research efforts.

None of this is to suggest, however, that the main constraints on diffusion of political information are to be found in either the sources of demands, support, or decisional outputs of the system, nor in the news media. Practically every extensive review of the research literature on news communication ends up identifying an array of constraints that operate within the individual members of the system (see, e.g., Klapper, 1960; Hyman and Sheatsley, 1947). There is far more information to be found in the news columns and broadcasts of the media than in the minds of the audience. Surveys regularly show that only a fraction of the citizenry can even identify the major authorities beyond the President and a few other chronic newsmakers. Novel demands are widely expressed long before the audience becomes widely aware of them; conversion processes within the governmental machinery attract notoriously low audience interest; decisional outputs, despite heavy converage at the time a bill becomes a law, are cognized by only a small percentage of the members before they become personally affected by these new policies.

It has become conventional in mass communication research to assign the causes of this limited diffusion phenomenon to generalized factors such as "selective exposure" or "perceptual defense", or even simple apathy and lack of interest, on the part of the audience. But we might be able to specify more precisely what is going on—or, more exactly, what is *not* going on—by considering the potential content of political information in terms of the main types of action in the general systems model.

A clue to the problem of non-diffusion can be found in the frequent assertion during the activist '60s of the complaint that much information available lacked "relevance." Although this term became so overused as to be almost meaningless in many situations, there is more than a kernel of sense to the charge if we assume that what was desired on the part of politically active persons was information *relevant to their potential forms of action.* Easton's model suggests what those forms of action might be: the assertion of demands, expressions or withholding of support, and monitoring of the conversion processes and decisional outputs of the authorities. That is, the members of the system who saw themselves as active in these ways wanted information that would help them guide their actions. It is instructive that journalism enrollments in major universities—where much of the activism of the period centered—experienced sharp growth throughout the activist phase; this growth antedated the journalistic heroics of the Watergate scandals by five to ten years (Peterson, 1973). This was also a time in which advocacy journalism—the insertion of political demands directly via the press—flowered, and there was a minor renaissance of the muckraking tradition, with its emphasis on close monitoring of system processes and outputs (see Dennis and Rivers, 1974).

We might hypothesize that active participation by members in the political process begets a heightened relevance of demand and output information. By contrast, times of political quiescence (low demand input) and acquiescence (high diffuse support, regardless of decisional outputs) should be accompanied by a lessened receptivity of the audience to political information that might create stress on the system; instead, the expression of support at various levels should predominate in the press. One of the best-known theories of journalistic history is Siebert's (1952) proposition that governmental constraints on the press increase in times of stress on the total political system (see chapter by Stevens). We may conjecture that these constraints would operate both to stem the flow of demands and to encourage expressions of diffuse support. The nation has in this fashion tended to "pull together" in times of stress even when the vast majority of the papers were politically opposed to the government in power, as in World Wars I and II, and the Great Depression of the 1930s. Still, the 1960s and early 1970s seem to be more than an exception to the Siebert rule. There was certainly stress on the system, which was attempting to prosecute a war in Vietnam and at the same time to meet demands that it redistribute societal values along lines of demographic equality (in terms of race, age, and sex). There were surely attempts to control communication, as governmental "public relations" efforts reached a dubious sort of pinnacle in the Nixon-Agnew years. The general research issue, however, is whether the media responded to these external constraints, or to audience demands for political information, or to self-imposed role conceptions, in determining which kinds of content to diffuse.

The key difference between this era and earlier times of stress might very well be found in the activist orientation of so many members of the system. A government at war ordinarily counts on diffuse support for its efforts, and a suspension of demands for other kinds of values that it might reallocate. But demands continued to flow via the media, and support was held hostage to these demands, throughout the Vietnam war years. Why? Relevance based on activism seems too easy an answer, but it may not be far from the heart of the matter. For the politically active person, all actions relevant to the operation of the political system are personally relevant as well. Media definitions of newsworthiness can be boiled down to a few principles, chief among which is that of audience interest. News organizations survive (as parapolitical systems) by providing information that is likely to be relevant to the activities of their audiences.

LEVELS OF ORIENTATION TO THE POLITICAL SYSTEM

We might conceive of a cumulative typology of four kinds of member orientations to a political system as outlined in Table 2. At the lowest level is the person whose membership is totally passive, and characterized simply by diffuse support for the system. Other than the unavoidable identification of personalities who happen to be in power, there is little political information that will be relevant for this type. Hence, knowledge of governmental outputs or the demand inputs on which they are based will not diffuse through sectors of the citizenry in which this inactive type predominates. A second level is represented by a person whose participation is also supportive in character, but more actively. The image of the "booster" in the American community is roughly analogous. Coupled with active expressions of support on behalf of the system we should expect to find a reluctance to admit stressful new demands to the political process, or to condone the approach of those who would limit their support to specific outputs that satisfy their demands. Relevant political communication from the perspective of this active-support role would tend, then, to be those types of information that would sustain diffuse support and constrain the input of stressful demands. The term "conservative" has often been used to describe this combination of traits (although that label has also been used in so many other ways that much of its meaning may be lost for us).

A third level of orientation toward the political system would include active support *plus* a strong concern with the decisional outputs of the authorities. Members who are involved in policy-oriented activities should find output information highly relevant; supportive communication, in itself, would accordingly become com-

TABLE 2
CUMULATIVE TYPOLOGY OF LEVELS OF ORIENTATION
TO A POLITICAL SYSTEM

Level	General orientation	Relevant parameters of system	Relevant political information	Popular label
I	passive	diffuse support	identification of authorities	"apathetic"
II	active	support input	constraints on demands	"conservative"
III	active	system output	policy decisions	"establishment" "inside-dopester"
IV	active	demand input	all types	"liberal" "radical"

paratively less relevant. In the absence of an active role in policy implementation, a member who nevertheless paid close attention to the political conversion process and resultant decisions might deserve the mildly pejorative label of "inside-dopester" (Riesman, Denney and Glazer, 1950). We should not, however, expect that to be a common case; information about a particular type of political action (support, demand, or output) should be relevant where the person is either involved in that kind of action directly, or has learned to orient himself toward that kind of action through experience in some other parapolitical system. The later case will be discussed below in connection with the topic of political socialization. A fairly accurate term for describing the type whose interest in policy outcomes of the political process is rooted in his direct involvement in either carrying out or reacting to those policies would be "the Establishment." This implies quite strong support for the regime in particular, as the ongoing structure of the system that transcends the incumbency of any single set of authorities.

The final, and most inclusive, level of orientation in this conceptual scheme would be direct involvement with the input of demands. All types of political information are relevant to a member whose inputs are being submitted to competition with other demands, and to the conversion process that will result in policy outcomes. When demands are accompanied by strong support sentiments, they are often described as "liberal", in a somewhat dated usage of that term. When support is withheld, or at least suspended pending satisfaction of one's demand, terms like "radical" and even "outside the system" get applied to them. The heightened relevance of demand information means that support and output information will be *relatively* less important in the eyes of this kind of system member. On the other hand, we should expect all types of political information to diffuse among demand-oriented members of a system, since all are theoretically relevant to them; further, we should expect to find complete diffusion *only* among persons of this orientation.

IMPLICATIONS FOR THE STUDY OF POLITICAL SOCIALIZATION

The foregoing explication of a hypothesized typology of different types of member orientation toward a political system may strike the reader as overly speculative. It has been empirically established, however, that citizens exhibit rather consistent individual differences in their patterns of political participation (Verba and Nie, 1972). And there is a great deal of variation within the media audience in attention to, and absorption of, political information; a conceptual model for organizing the study and explanation of some of this variance is needed. Further, there is some theoretical basis for the presumption that these different forms of political orientation, which could help us account for differential rates of diffusion of political information, can be attributed to action roles that have been learned by parapolitical participation. Specifically, the family communication system in which a child has been raised, and the ways in which that parent-child system has habitually dealt with political information, has proven a reliable predictor of the kinds of political communication behavior the person exhibits in later years (McLeod and Chaffee, 1972; Chaffee, McLeod and Wackman, 1973).

Research on family communication patterns has distinguished four types of parent-child systems, based on the relative presence or absence of two forms of habitual communication. One orientation is socio-oriented constraint on the child, which is manifested by the parents instructing the youngster to defer to his elders, to avoid arguing or antagonizing people, and generally to maintain interpersonal harmony. The second is concept-oriented stimulation, which parents achieve by encouraging the child to inform himself and draw his own conclusions on current issues, or by exposing the child to diverse viewpoints. Families that stress the socio-orientation are called "protective", while that that emphasize concept-orientations are "pluralistic." When both these orientations are stressed in the same family, it is said to be "consensual." And when there is little parental constraint or stimulation of either type, the family is characterized as "laissez-faire."

Children from pluralistic homes tend rather strongly to be more informed and active in public affairs, as measured by a wide variety of indices in many sample surveys in the United States and elsewhere. The children from consensual homes are somewhat less informed, and there is some hint that they are more output-centered in their political knowledge; they are most likely to know their parents' political affiliations, for instance, and yet score quite low on knowledge about current issues. Protective families produce youngsters with rather little inclination toward public affairs media content or toward political activism.

It is tempting to try to equate the four family types with the four levels of political participation and consequent informational relevance that were proposed in the previous section of this paper. The fit between these two typologies is liable to be less than satisfactory; the family communication typology was devised without reference to the family's procedures for allocation of values or the child's role in that process. It is based instead purely on the pattern of communication regarding information about the political system within the parent-child parapolitical system. One might conceive of the family as a microcosm in which the child learns a role (passive, diffuse support, output-oriented, or demand-oriented) *and* acquires information that would be relevant to an analogous role in the larger political system. It would be useful to analyze the kinds of political information that have diffused within the different types of families as described in the previous two paragraphs. We should expect to find support-oriented information in the socially constrained protective family, and all types of information diffusing within the pluralistic home where socio-oriented constraints are lacking and the youngster's demand inputs are encouraged. The consensual family environment, where the child is urged to "take an interest" in the political system, but still experiences socio-oriented constraints against causing interpersonal stress through novel inputs, could lead to an orientation that focuses primarily on outputs—parental decisions within the home, and governmental decisions in the larger society. Still, it would be preferable to develop a more thorough specification of the parapolitical constraints that accompany the purely communicatory elements of these families, and of the different types of political information that would serve as dependent variables in studies of this nature.

IMPLICATIONS FOR THE STUDY OF
PUBLIC OPINION AND POLITICAL KNOWLEDGE

The distinction between opinions and knowledge about public affairs has been a standard theme in public opinion survey research for decades. It has frequently been demonstrated that increased information is associated with more firmly held value judgments on current issues, as indicated by both extremity of opinion and resistance to persuasion. Voters who come to their decisions very late in an election campaign typically have little knowledge about either candidates or issues and are less likely to bother to vote than are the more opinionated citizens (Lazarsfeld, Berelson and Gaudet, 1948;

Berelson, Lazarsfeld and McPhee, 1954). Public information campaigns "fail" to persuade citizens to convert their opinions in a predictable direction, except in occasional cases where the topic is one on which informed persons are unlikely to disagree (Hyman and Sheatsley, 1950; Douglas, Westley and Chaffee, 1970). When offered political information via the media, people appear to learn rather selectively that portion which is consistent with the opinions they already hold (Klapper, 1960).

These findings at the individual level of analysis form the basis for the "limited effects" image of mass communication, i.e. the generalization that media news coverage has only minor powers of political persuasion. From the perspective of the political system as a whole, however, a different interpretation should be made. The dualistic conception of opinions on the one hand and knowledge on the other might be replaced by a homogenization of those two concepts under the single rubric we have been using here, political information. Since the term "political" implies allocation of values, we should assume that only information that carries evaluative meaning belongs in this category. From the point of view of the member of a political system, a distinction between "opinions" and "knowledge" would be irrelevant. Instead the distinction would have to do with political information that relates to his action role within the system. For the member whose orientation is limited to diffuse support for the system, the only information of direct relevance would be that having to do with generalized affective support—and challenges to it, which would trigger his affective reaction. This might be interpreted as "opinion without information" by an investigator whose conception of the research problem was based on the opinion-information dichotomy, but that is a direct product of this particular intellectual definition of the situation. Similarly, demand-oriented members of the system would appear to be "well informed" as well as "very opinionated" in the eyes of the traditional researcher, because so much more of the available political information in the system is relevant to them.

If we were to look on all information about demand and support inputs, political conversion processes, and decisional outputs of the authorities as equally relevant to the system but differentially relevant to individual members, the entire research problem would be cast in a different light. Instead of asking the extent to which an item of political information—whether conventionally describable as an opinion or as a bit of knowledge—diffuses through the entire membership, we should ask the extent to which it is diffused to those members for whom it would be relevant. It appears that such massive constraints operate within individuals because of action-role differentiation that we should never expect more than a few items to diffuse to everyone. Political information that is associated with objects of diffuse support (e.g. the election or assassination of a President) should reach almost everyone via a rapid S-curve process. Information about new and rival demands on the system should be expected to reach only that minority of the members who think of themselves as involved in making or processing demands. If diffusion patterns of these types do not occur, then investigation into other constraints that might have their origins in the media or the source would be in order.

A chapter elsewhere in this book (Kraus et al.) treats at length the problem of studying communication about "critical events." In the context of the political system, a critical event might be described as one that poses a high-stress decision-point. We can draw an analogy from medical terminology; a patient is described as "critical" when his life signs are being closely monitored to see whether he is beginning to get well, or to expire—but before his doctors can determine that judgment. In a political system, where persistence of the system is the central problem, the "life signs" are what Easton calls the "essential variables" of the system. He identified just two: the capacity of the system to make decisions for the society, and the probability that those decisions will be accepted as authoritative (Easton, 1965a: 90-96). Stress on a system occurs when disturbances threaten to displace these essential variables "beyond their normal range and toward some *critical* limit" (italics mine).

A critical event is one, in the view of this chapter, that poses a threat to the interrelationships between a political system and its communication system. This could occur if the event rendered the political system unable to function by making decisions, as in the case of a government so preoccupied with a general strike that it fails to carry out its normal administrative responsibilities. It could also occur, following Easton's analysis, if a significant portion of the members will not accept the authorities' decisions as binding, a situation that was approached in the final days of the Nixon administration when it had lost its legitimacy in the eyes of many citizens because of the Watergate scandals. These essential variables are tests of the capacity of the political system to persist, and threats to them provide excellent opportunities for examining the performance of the communication system *in extremis*. In some cases, the authorities will take steps to flood the communication channels with material that will focus attention on the decisions it must make, as in the case of a government at war that urges cooperation of all channels in that total national effort. The essence of this kind of plea is that the communication system should postpone transmission of demands that might overload the authorities' decision-making capacity temporarily; during World War II this single-minded concentration was achieved to a great extent. In other cases, authorities might attempt to suppress the diffusion of information of their activities, as has been the case with a number of U.S. Cold War military operations in Asia and Latin America.

The general premise underlying governmental attempts to control the press in these kinds of situations is that the political system—to which general allegiance is normally held—might expire if the essential variables are not kept within the normal range. This type of appeal is subject to abuse by authorities, and to too-easy acquiescence by tame media practicioners. When critical events (as defined here) present themselves, they provide an opportunity to assess whether the two interacting systems have achieved an equable balance wherein the media perform their normal diffusion responsibilities fully but do not approach a serious threat to the survival of the system. Authorities in totalitarian systems often invoke system stability as a justification for heavy-handed press controls, as in the 1975 censorship policy imposed in India on behalf of "democracy." In some systems the communication media are operated as an arm of the authorities, e.g. Communist nations, and parapolitical systems like large corporations and military commands with their "kept press" house organs. This is presumably intended to prevent uncontrolled events from becoming critical in the first place. But it is doubtful that any governmental authorities, in any type of political or parapolitical system, would fail to give high priority to the management of diffusion of information they saw as threatening to the persistence of their respective systems. Research dedicated to problems of freedom of communication could profitably focus on comparisons between instances where the media were positively used to rally diffuse support in times of real crisis (e.g. the Kennedy assassination), and those of cynical diversion or suppression by authorities to make life easier for themselves or to thwart their legitimate opponents.

A rather different concept of "critical event" could be developed by focusing on the news media as a parapolitical system. This would be much closer to the usage of the term that is intended by those who specialize in the study of dramatic political events such as Lang and Lang (1960) and Kraus (1962). A news event is critical from the media viewpoint when it poses a novel problem for the system—i.e. the media have no rules to govern the handling of the event—and when it is of sufficient political import that the role of the media within the political system is at stake. These attributes of critical media events can be seen as restatements of Easton's specification of the essential variables of a political system (see preceding paragraphs). The capacity of the media to make a news decision is threatened, and the likelihood that the decision made will be accepted is questionable. The response of the media to a novel and politically important event is conceived in stress on the media as a parapolitical system; the decision that is made (i.e. the way the event is portrayed by the media) in turn determines the form in which this event will be diffused to the members of the larger political system that the media service.

These two conceptions of critical events—one from the perspective of the total political system, and the other in the context of the media as a parapolitical system—invite combination. One of the necessary characteristics of a critical media event is that it be of major importance to the total political system. This condition will be met if it is an event that creates stress by threatening either of the essential variables of the total system, i.e. if it is a news event that poses a challenge to the capacity of the total system to make decisions, or to have them accepted as authoritative. This in turn becomes a threat to the media for analogous reasons. It is small wonder that the news media have developed elaborate plans and procedures that allow them to routinize the handling of almost all news events—even though news by definition consists of events that are to some extent unanticipated.

IMPLICATIONS FOR THE STUDY OF
MEDIA CONTENT AND INTERPERSONAL COMMUNICATION

An early research tradition that has fallen into relatively low estate of late is content analysis. The description and interpretation of media news content is the image the term "mass communications research" is most likely to evoke in persons outside that field; but it has come to be largely a subordinate activity whose principal utility lies in its connection with behavioral effects analysis. There is, to be sure, a continuing interest in questions of "bias" and "balance" in political coverage, particularly regarding opposing candidates in elections. A few decades back, the charge of a one-party (Republican) press could easily be documented, especially in terms of candidate endorsements (e.g. Millspaugh, 1949; Gregg, 1965; Rowse, 1957). But recent studies have generally found coverage in the 50-50 range, at least in major newspapers (Stempel, 1961, 1965; see also Blumberg, 1954; Batlin, 1954), and there is evidence of careful attempts to avoid over-covering incumbents (Repass and Chaffee, 1968). Efron's (1971) claim that network newscasts over-covered Hubert Humphrey's 1968 campaign, the most heavily publicized recent instance of bias research, seems adequately accounted for by vagaries of definition and methodology (Weaver, 1972; Stevenson et al., 1973). Historical research on questions of bias remains viable, as exemplified by Shaw's (1967) study of the impact of introduction of the telegraph on press content (see discussion in chapter by Stevens). But even to the extent that there continues to be imbalanced news coverage of candidates, it can be seen as a narrow and rather superficial research question when we wish to understand the role of communication variables in the political process.

A short-range response to the less-than-satisfying character of evidence of imbalanced coverage is to attempt to demonstrate that it is associated with otherwise unexplainable shifts in public preference for the candidate who receives favorable media treatment. This has not proven an easy research task, although there are several indications that elaborate multivariate surveys calibrating audience and content analyses would demonstrate some effects of biased coverage (see Becker et al. and Siune and Kline chapters).

A more serious departure from the candidate-bias prototype for content analysis would be to conceptualize one's content categories in terms of the model that has been introduced in this paper. The question would no longer revolve around the fate of some set of candidates, or even of political parties, or incumbents vs. challengers. Instead the focus would shift to the media as carriers of messages that inform members of a political system of demands and support inputs, and of decisional outputs of that system. These would become the basic content categories, and subcategories could be elaborated within them as needed to accommodate the variety of forms that these types of information take in the news media.

For the merging of content and audience data, the systemic analog to individual-effects questions would be the problem of diffusion. That is, media content would be monitored for variations in the presentation of demand, support and decisional output information, and surveys of system members would trace the progress of these items through the population. Interpersonal communication, which in traditional analyses at the individual level has been portrayed as countervailing media inputs to the audience, would take on instead the role of either a relay mechanism in the diffusion process or a constraint against diffusion. Individual predispositions of system members would likewise be reconceptualized. Instead of being partisan and ideological in character, a person's orientations would be viewed from the perspective of the model here as focusing differentially on generic elements of the political system, in terms of their perceived relevance. Demand-oriented citizens would be more receptive to media reports of demand inputs to the system than would support-oriented citizens. Interactions between citizens of similar orientation to the system would be more likely to foster diffusion of mutually relevant information (see above) than would interactions between citizens of differing orientations. Further, the kinds of information that would be likely to diffuse interpersonally would be those that both interactants would see as personally relevant. One might hypothesize a principle of "relevance overlap" that would predict that diffusion in interpersonal communication would tend to be most likely on topics of mutual relevance; this means that diffusion would be limited to the lower level of orientation in the cumulative typology outlined earlier here, e.g. to support statements when at least one of the interactants is a member whose orientation to the system is limited to the domain of support.

Research to test hypotheses about interpersonal communication subsystems could be related to descriptions of available media content in several ways. The most obvious would be that the media presumably provide the content that sets the upper limit on what information is available for interpersonal diffusion. But there is a reciprocal loop in this relationship that deserves investigation. If we consider the audience to consist of interacting "molecules" of persons rather than atomized individuals, and if we theorize that the social value of an item of information for a person is at least partly derived from its usefulness to him in personal interaction (see Atkin, 1972; Bybee and Lometti, 1975; Chaffee and McLeod, 1973) then it is possible to consider *audience effects on the media* (see Chaffee,

1972). We should expect media decision-makers to learn, if gradually, what kinds of information their audiences are receptive to; this will be a function, in turn, of the receptiveness of an individual receiver's interaction partners in informal discussion. The hypothesis that lies behind this reasoning is the common charge that the media provide content that serves the "lowest common denominator" in the population. It should be possible to show that where the *most common* level of orientation in an audience is not the *lowest possible* level, media content tends to focus on the most common rather than on the lowest. Media that serve parapolitical systems where higher levels of orientation to the political system are reasonably common should be compared to those that serve audiences that are heterogeneous in terms of orientations toward the political systems, to test this line of theorizing. Although there are "class" as well as "mass" media, the probabilities should normally favor the evolution of the latter since it is the lower level of orientation between two interactants that sets the upper limit of relevance of news content. Demand-oriented content should be the least likely to gain media coverage, while support-oriented content should be most acceptable in media directed toward heterogeneous mass audiences. To test that proposition, it would be necessary to estimate in some objective way what the total corpus of potential demand-oriented and support-oriented information in the system is, and then assess what proportion of it becomes covered as "news" by media that serve audiences with differing system orientations.

METHODOLOGICAL IMPLICATIONS

Translating the abstract sets of inter-relating concepts presented to this point into a program of research is not simply a matter of changing a few elements of a survey questionnaire, or the categories of a coding scheme. Expansion of the scope of research in at least two major dimensions is essential to the kind of study envisioned here. One is expansion in time, to chart the diffusion process. The other is expansion in domains of observation, so that such diverse units as media content, interpersonal discussion, individual orientation and system functioning are examined. It would not be enough to have separate studies of these elements of the total model at the same time; the observations and measurement of parameters of each of them should be organized so that they will be comparable to one another when the stage of data analysis is reached. Each of these expansions on current research procedures deserves some discussion of the pragmatic problems it is likely to present to the investigator.

Studies Over Time

There are two general procedures for tracing changes over time in the state of a system, in terms of the proportion of members who hold a piece of information. One is to draw repeated samples of members at equally spaced time points, sampling without replacement but in such a way that each successive wave provides an unbiased estimate of the total population of system members. The second is to remeasure the same sample of persons at equally spaced time points, assuming that this panel constantly provides an unbiased estimate of the population. Neither of these procedures can be exactly followed in most field situations, and each has its peculiar drawbacks. In addition, there are designs that draw a compromise between the two, such as a study that begins with one group at Time 1, repeats measurement on that group *and* adds a second group that is new to the study at Time 2, etc. The economies of such a combined design should be assessed in light of the weaknesses of each of the two simple designs.

Several methodological problems are common to both the successive-wave and panel designs. Equal spacing of time points is difficult at best—and not always desirable from a substantive standpoint. It requires that a standard between-observations time period be decided upon in advance, or at the least that the time lag between the first two observations be adopted as the standard for all subsequent waves. Unless one knows in advance a good deal about the topic of diffusion that is to be studied, the time period chosen might well fail to match the rhythms of the diffusion process that occurs. For many reasons discussed above, we should not expect diffusion of information within a heterogeneous political system to proceed smoothly over time; interaction is non-random, the media or their information sources can stimulate or constrain diffusion at various stages of the process, and the meaning of a particular item of information can change as events occur that render it more or less relevant. The sensitive researcher should want to design a schedule of measurement time-points that will detect these perturbations from the random model of diffusion. An alternative to the fixed-interval waves approach would be in effect near-continuous measurement, with small random samples of the total sample observed, say, daily or hourly (depending on the anticipated speed of diffusion). This is an extreme version of the successive-waves design; for later data analysis a number of these small subsamples from contiguous time points (e.g. four-day or five-hour blocks) could be aggregated to provide sufficient cases for reliable estimates of the measures. For panel designs, a constant period such as one month between waves could be used for each individual being measured, but different starting dates could be assigned to small subsamples of the panel, so that, for example a few people would be observed on the first day of each month, another few on the second, etc. This too would provide "continuous" monitoring.

Equally spaced observation time-points are not theoretically preferable to randomly sampled time-spaces. Indeed, a random (or systematic random) sample of time spaces has a good deal to recommend it, since it can provide an approximation to continuous monitoring—with some loss of precision—that strikes a compromise among one's desire for continuity, lack of ability to anticipate the course diffusion will follow, and limitations of research resources such as interviewing capacity. The "constructed-week" method of media content monitoring is an example of systematic random sampling of time points with a constant period; specifically, it is typical to measure a newspaper on a starting Sunday, again the following Saturday, then the following Friday, etc. This kind of spacing might be too wide to follow the progress of a single event (see Kraus et al. chapter), but for the kinds of general parameters of political communication outlined in this paper the six-day interval should ordinarily be sufficiently fine-grained. It may be too fine for many studies, in fact, since the investigator must also keep in mind the need to calibrate measures of media content with observations of other units. It would rarely be feasible, for instance, to interview a panel respondent at six-day intervals; some compromise of methods will be dictated by the imperatives of the different components of an integrated study that is attempting to comprehend the course of a diffusion process within a complex political system.

In practice, students of political communication usually know enough about what to expect that they need not resort to continuous monitoring, or approximations to it. For instance, in an election campaign certain time points can be anticipated and observation waves preplanned to coincide with them: primary elections, party conventions, and other standard phases of the campaign scenario. It is also advisable in many situations to remain flexible in the selection of time points, since key events may occur that influence the process of diffusion of one piece or type of information; the "firehouse" model of research organization advocated in the Kraus et al. chapter is based on this premise. The planning of observation waves should flow from one's conception of the central research problem; the study of discrete items of diffusion (e.g. knowledge of a particular event or governmental action) calls for firehouse flexibility, whereas the charting of numerous instances of a general class of information (e.g. statements of support for the authorities, or demands on the system) is better suited to a sampling method that will provide an approximate estimate of continuous monitoring over a long span of time.

Realistically, studies that chart an area of political information over a long time span are not often going to be pre-planned large programatic research projects for which all of the niceties of design can be taken into consideration. The one-shot survey, on a single topic, is the predominant research model and will continue to be so—if for no other reason than that this is the type of project for which funding is usually available. The occasion for extending such a study in time with additional waves of observations often occurs after the original wave of field observation has taken place. Well designed one-wave studies will make provisions for this kind of eventuality, by using repeatable measures and by keeping careful documentation on sampling procedures so that they can be replicated. A good example of this kind of situation was the eruption of the Watergate scandals in the spring and summer of 1973. Several research teams that had conducted election campaign studies in 1972 were able to re-enter the field and convert their designs to longitudinal ones. Robinson (1974) and Sniderman et al. (1975) carried out successive-wave studies of the progress of Watergate perceptions through the electorate, as did O'Keefe and Mendelsohn (1974) and Chaffee and Becker (1975) with panels.

Two problems with panel designs that are avoided by the successive-waves approach bear mention, if only because many readers will be painfully aware of them. One is what Campbell and Stanley (1966) call "reactive" observation, and the other "mortality." Reactive conditions of measurement occur when the individual (or other unit of analysis, such as the newspaper or the legislature) that is being observed is aware of that fact and reacts to it by behaving differently than would otherwise be the case. Mortality consists of attrition from the first-wave sample in later waves; those who remain in the sample after many waves of remeasurement do not necessarily constitute a representative subset of the original population, and as their numbers shrink the estimates based upon them become less reliable.

In comparing the panel and successive-wave designs, one should consider reactive measurement as part of a larger class of threats to validity, which Campbell and Stanley (1966) call "instrument decay." Diffusion can be validly monitored only so long as the same measures are being used at the different time points. Reactive measurement is part of this problem, to the extent that the meaning of, say, an item in a questionnaire changes for the respondent because he has previously answered it and it refers to his behavior. For example, the common questions, "Have you decided how you will vote?" and "Can you name the candidates of the twc parties?" can become downright embarrassing to a person who is asked them in January, April, August and September and the answer is consistently, "No"; by comparison, they are not nearly so threatening to someone who is asked them for the first time in September, which would be the case in a successive-waves design. But the latter method is not free from problems of instrument decay. The meaning of a question that is worded identically over successive waves can nevertheless change, as the political environment in which the question is asked changes. Other kinds of political data, such as media content and legislative roll-call votes, also take on different meanings over time. Instrument decay is not a problem that can be solved simply by adopting unobtrusive measures (see Rothschild chapter) or avoiding the potential contamination of panel reinterviews.

Attrition, or mortality, is an issue that few researchers care to discuss—because there seems to be little they can do to avoid it. Procedures to minimize attrition from panels have not been formalized; it seems to be mostly a matter of hard work. Jennings and Niemi (1975) and Sewell, Haller and Portes (1969) were able to achieve very high rates of retention over several years with panels that were originally high school seniors, by taking advantage of contacts with parents and peers in the young person's community of origin. The successive-waves survey design only seemingly eliminates the need for diligent sampling efforts. Attrition from a panel will obviously tend to consist of losing people who move, are rarely at home, or who do not wish to cooperate with researchers; but those same kinds of persons are also less likely to be included in any single wave of interviewing, as the undercount estimates of the decennial U.S. Census indicate. At least the panel design gives one some idea of who is being lost over time.

If instrument decay, reactivity of measurement and attrition can be held to a minimum, the panel provides some nice advantages over the successive-waves procedure in the richness of data for analysis. If, as in the case of diffusion research, we are interested in parameters that affect *change* in the state of some component of the political system, observation of the *same* unit (person, media outlet, political body) at several points in time is obviously preferable. What changes in other attributes of the unit preceded, accompanied, or followed the acquisition of an item of political information that is critical enough for us to adopt it as the focus of a diffusion study? The answers to such a question provide the stuff dynamic theory is made of.

Unfortunately, the development of modes of analysis appropriate to assess change in a set of variables over time in a panel design has been slow and less than satisfying. Cross-lagged panel correlation (Rozelle and Campbell, 1969) is one promising approach, and many of the methodological difficulties with it have been attacked in recent years by Kenny (1972, 1973). It is applicable only to limited sets of situations, but could probably be used more extensively than it has been in the study of diffusion—at least in those stages of the process where an item is diffusing to a larger proportion of the population with some speed. Path analysis, which was devised (Blalock, 1964; Duncan, 1966; Heise, 1969) as a method of testing hypotheses about processes over time from data that are collected at a single time-point, is also applicable to panel data. Indeed, panel measurement can greatly improve the quality of inferences derived from path analysis, which otherwise must rely on so many untested assumptions that it fails in persuasiveness.

Another method of developing over-time measures is the use of retrospective data, such as by asking a person, "When did you first learn of _____?" For highly salient topics this may be a valid procedure, as in the case of the Kennedy assassination, where it could be rather safely assumed that first knowledge of the event was a vivid enough experience that most people could recall it accurately (Greenberg, 1964b). On the other hand, McLeod and Brown (1975) found that retrospective recall by a voter of his political position (left, liberal, conservative, etc.) greatly overstated the degree of change that had occurred over a two-year span, as determined separately by straight panel measurement (i.e. by asking the same question in both waves). Katz and Lazarsfeld (1955), in the definitive study of the "two-step flow" model, asked their respondents what had been the first source of influential information for them on several topics; the most common response was "don't know." Retrospective data are unreliable and subject to enough biasing effects that they should probably be used only as supplementary measures, for replication of an inference that has initially been established with more trustworthy procedures. Other approximations to over-time measurement include comparative study of systems that have achieved different levels of development at the same time (see Blumler and Gurevitch chapter) and historical use of existing data from the same system at times past (see Stevens chapter).

Achieving Comparability of Data from Different Components

The second major methodological problem in the complex type of research implied in this paper is that of building data sets on different components of a political system—members, authorities, media—that can be combined in a systemic analysis. Comparability in terms of time, coding of observations, and system boundaries, is easy enough to advocate but very difficult to achieve in practice. A similar problem faces the program of cross-national comparative analysis proposed in the chapter by Blumler and Gurevitch. Articulation of observations from one system to another, or from one element of a single system to others, demands ingenuity and not a trivial degree of self-confidence and even courage on the part of the researcher.

Each system, political and parapolitical, has its own "natural" communicatory content, its own schedule of operation, and its own conception of its rightful domain. These have built up over many years of operation and have become institutionalized within each system without much reference to the definitions those same parameters have been receiving in other systems. To achieve comparability for data analysis, then, the researcher will have to impose upon each system or component thereof his own conceptual scheme, and to impose it uniformly across all the units he/she wishes to compare. This kind of procedure is almost certain to arouse complaints from those who study—or participate in—each component, because they will feel (and rightly so) that their particular system is not being analyzed in the terms most appropriate to it. To persist in the face of this altogether reasonable objection, the investigator must confidently assume that the eventual product of his efforts will justify forcing particular subcomponents of the overall system into a conceptual framework that they would not willingly assent to. This chapter is based on the premise that this product will be worth that effort, but the reader should not be unmindful of the potential costs—in terms of misunderstanding, resistance, and outright opposition—that can be incurred by attempting to put together on a common conceptual basis elements of a political system that have not operated on common ground in traditional practice.

Comparability in timing of observations has already been discussed in connection with diffusion methodologies (above). Media other than magazines generally operate on a daily cycle, in that the newspaper comes out each morning or evening, the network television news show must go on each evening, the wire service budget is distributed each morning, etc. Presidents (and most governors) juggle their time frames between the four-year election cycle and the immediate demands of critical events with which they must cope—sometimes within a month, sometimes in minutes. Legislatures function in one- and two-year cycles, their work further segmented in time by the stages of passage of a bill. Judicial institutions typically seem to behave as if time were not a consideration of much importance at all. Demand-generating organizations create their own imperatives of time, ranging in slogans from "freedom now" through "end the war by a date certain" to "wait till next time." These timing characteristics of components of the political system are products of their operating as parapolitical systems. But they must also function vis-a-vis one another. The media allocate their reporting resources differentially over time, for example covering the Congress heavily in the busy summer preceding an election year and then shifting to concentration on presidential candidates in the winter months and the ensuing primary season.

Looked at from the perspective of this chapter's concerns, it would seem wisest to try to avoid organizing a diffusion study to fit the rhythms of any one component of a political system. The focus here is on diffusion of information to the members, and the timing of constraints exercised by various other components on that process should be looked upon as an independent variable whose variation should be assessed as part of the larger process. This implies rather long time periods for an adequate study, with time points selected randomly or by a fixed schedule that will tap the full range of activity of each system component. Only by that sort of procedure can a study escape the charge that it has covered a period that is somehow atypical, and that the findings are therefore not broadly generalizable. For example, if one interviews system members only in the evenings this introduces a time-sampling bias in favor of television news—just as interviewing in the morning would tip things in the direction of the morning newspaper as a source of diffusion. A study of diffusion of generic categories of political information as outlined earlier here would introduce bias in the direction of presidential politics, as opposed to those of other branches of government, if it was restricted to the campaign season of a presidential election year; similarly, a congressional bias is admitted by setting a study in the time-context of an off-year national election.

Pragmatically, the researcher cannot blithely expand the time-scope of a study infinitely, or anywhere near it. Selection of an overall time-span, then, should strive to avoid obvious and gross biases in the sampling of activity of one component or another of the political system. Realizing that such biases cannot be totally avoided, it is well to be aware of those unavoidable biases that are built into a study by the timing decisions that are made. In the long run, the cumulation of comparable inferences from many studies that have used different time-frames should be sufficient to evaluate the seriousness of this type of sampling bias. It becomes even more critical, then, that studies be as comparable as possible in other respects.

The coding of observations into categorical systems is an area in which some major advances have been made in recent years. Research on agenda-setting (see Becker et al. chapter) has forced investigators to use the same coding categories for media content and audience orientations and discussion measures. Flegel and Chaffee (1971) were able to assess the influence on reporting of the perceived opinions of editors, readers, advertisers, and the reporters themselves, by coding by-lined news articles according to the same scheme used in measuring the opinion perceptions. Hesse and Chaffee (1973) compared identical measures in a public opinion survey and in interviews with state senators, to determine which of these legislators were most accurate in estimating the views of their constituents. It should be noted that in all of these studies there are methodological problems associated with the achievement of comparability. Content coders complain that the categories they are given to use miss much of the character of what is actually reported in the press, or the full flavor of individuals' responses to open-ended survey questions. Professionals (e.g. reporters or politicians) often bristle at the simplistic form in which questions are posed to them—questions that in turn sound awfully complicated to many respondents in the general audience. Research following the outline of this chapter can only exacerbate these unhappy situations, by requiring comparability of measurement across more than just two sets of observations on different components of a political system. The researcher must, in most cases, admit the wisdom of respondents' objections to his procedures—and then plunge ahead in spite of them.

Comparability in terms of system boundaries is probably the most difficult of the three factors considered in this section, because it requires of the investigator a very firm definition of the system that he wants to examine. A citizen in the United States, for instance, is a member of a number of political systems—national, state, county, municipal, plus countless districts for mosquito abatement, flood control, judicial administration, schools, etc. The physical boundaries of these various systems often do not coincide with those of the news media; newspapers cover local communities, wire service trunk lines service regions that include several states, and even our national media concentrate their coverage on certain heavily populated or newsworthy portions of the country (e.g. New York, Washington, Los Angeles). The imposition of boundaries on a study must be a unilateral act on the part of the researcher; it will be the rare case where a political system and a media system can be compared directly by using the "natural" boundaries of each and finding that they are happily coterminous.

One solution, in principle at least, would be to predicate one's sampling of political and media systems on the sampling of members. For instance, in 1974 a nationwide study of state and congressional elections was designed by the Center for Political Studies of the University of Michigan (Miller, Miller and Kline, 1974). A multi-stage sampling procedure was used to select adult citizens who would represent a cross-section of the national electorate; these respondents were located in some 65 communities that had first been randomly selected. Media content for analysis was collected by taping local evening television news programs, and archiving local newspapers in those 65 communities. In data analysis, media content was "assigned" to a given respondent only to the extent that the person reported in the interview that he/she read a particular newspaper, or listened to local TV news. (For the most part, national media such as network news and magazines carried too little content on state and congressional races to make it worthwhile incorporating them in this analysis.) The sample of media content, then, was an unbiased estimate of nationwide *exposure to campaign news* across many different contests for important offices, many different kinds of communities, and many different media systems. Since only a dozen or two respondents in any one community were interviewed in the random sampling procedure, this design did not lend itself at all well to the drawing of conclusions about particular elections, communities, or media outlets. It was intended instead to provide data on which generalizations about broad parameters of the political communication process in an election setting could be drawn—preserving the full range of variance in settings that existed within the nation in that year.

Although studies of the scope of the Michigan effort are not going to become commonplace—they require extensive funding and highly skilled personnel—it should be noted that even this massive project was inadequate as a vehicle for examining the kinds of propositions outlined in this chapter. There is almost no provision in the design for tracing the progress of items of political information over time, i.e. for assessing diffusion. Even a two-wave panel would nearly double the cost of some of the most expensive components of the research—such as the audience interviews. A single wave of interviews in a national sample survey takes some weeks to complete, and interviewing teams in some areas simply work faster and on different daily schedules from those in other communities; standardization of observation conditions is very difficult to achieve or even approach, and randomization would be much more so. If we were to add to the Michigan design such requirements as (a) observations of the candidates in the many state and congressional elections; (b) observations of the decision-making of media personnel in these locales; (c) imposition on these observations, and on the audience interviews and media content measurement, of a common system of categories based on the Easton model; (d) with repeated measurement over time to trace the course of diffusion; even the most seasoned research administrator would be likely to conclude that the total task is too immense to be pragmatically possible. And yet that may be precisely the type of interconnected research effort toward which the field will have to work if we are to develop a comprehensive understanding of political communication processes at the level of the national system.

PROGRAMATIC PRIORITIES

The preceding discussion of methodological ideals and pragmatic realities makes it clear that the kind of research outlined in this paper is not going to be conceptualized, proposed, funded, and executed at one fell swoop. It is so far removed from the typical instance of contemporary research on communication and politics as to be all but unrecognizable as part of the same theoretical domain. Some priorities need to be set so that incremental approaches can be made toward realization of a program that will eventually, in retrospect, be seen as aiming toward development and testing of a comprehensive empirical theory of the diffusion of political information.

Two contrasting strategies can be considered. One would hold that the most likely line of research is to build outward from well established bodies of theory and supportive evidence, holding the more speculative aspects of the overall conceptual program in abeyance until the relatively better known portions are thoroughly charted. (This is roughly the incremental strategy that has been followed in the development of the U.S. outer-space exploration program.) At the other extreme it could be argued that it is the most speculative components of the total model that are most in need of immediate exploration and documentation. (This scientific tactic is being pursued in the search for sources of energy that might substitute for fossil fuelds; critical theoretical speculations are tested in limited ways to determine whether they are viable in the least, so that blind alleys can be identified before work on them progresses too far.)

Given the very abstract character of the program of research implied in the conceptual portions of this paper, and the complex and expensive research effort that the methodological sections indicate would be required to carry it out, the latter of the two general strategies seems the more reasonable. That is, the elements of the total outline that have the weakest evidenciary base for assuming their validity should be subjected to empirical scrutiny immediately.

At least two components of the conceptual model of this chapter can lay an absolute claim on research priorities, if we follow the reasoning advanced above. One is the utility of the Easton model as a basis for defining categories of communication content. The other is the proposed cumulative hierarchy of levels of orientation to the political system, as outlined in Figure 3. Since the latter is defined in terms of the former, the order of investigatory battle seems to be clearly indicated. The first question should be whether concepts like support, input, output, and conversion processes of a political system lend themselves to operational definition as categories of political communication; this can be tested for both media and interpersonal communication. If they do not, modifications of the Easton model will need to be devised—or, in the extreme, a different but similarly concise and integrated model will have to be developed as a substitute. Assuming that the Easton concepts survive this first pragmatic test in whole or at least in major part, procedures for identifying them as levels of member orientation to the political system would then become the next research priority.

This would be followed by the most critical test of the point of view that has been taken here, the diffusion approach itself. Previous studies of diffusion have normally taken as their dependent variables rather concrete and singular types of items—either a discrete piece of knowledge, or adoption of a new utilitarian practice (e.g. information of a news event, or use of an agricultural innovation). While some general principles have emerged from this work, there has not developed a widely applicable scheme for categorizing different types of diffusion items according to the type of communication that transmits them, the type of person most receptive to them, nor—most important here—the way in which they are relevant from the perspective of the political system.

Much of the work anticipated in the foregoing two paragraphs can be undertaken without the support of large programatic funding or the efforts of a vast research team under close administrative coordination. If the general goals of this chapter are kept in mind, balkanized research efforts on central parts of the overall conception can contribute in important ways toward the eventual design of a type of research that has not been seen in this field in the past. Such an effort, with its promises of frustrated attempts and at best delayed rewards, would not be proposed here with it not for the conviction that comprehensive systemic inferences are going to be demanded of the field of political communication if it is eventually to have its deserved impact on public policy and professional practice.

REFERENCES

ARGYRIS, C. (1974) Behind the Front Page. San Francisco: Jossey-Bass.

ATKIN, C. K. (1972) "Anticipated communication and mass media information-seeking." Public Opinion Q. 36: 188-199.

BATLIN, R. (1954) "San Francisco newspapers' campaign coverage: 1896-1952." Journalism Q. 31: 297-303.

BERELSON, B. R., P. F. LAZARSFELD and W. N. McPHEE (1954) Voting: A Study of Opinion Formation in a Presidential Campaign. Chicago: University of Chicago Press.

BLALOCK, H. M. (1964) Causal Inferences in Nonexperimental Research. Chapel Hill: University of North Carolina Press.

BLUMBERG, N. B. (1954) One-Party Press? Lincoln: University of Nebraska Press.

BYBEE, C. R. and G. E. LOMETTI (1975) "Information seeking, communication and interpersonal utility," presented to Assn. for Education in Journalism.

[126] Political Communication

CAMPBELL, D. T. and J. C. STANLEY (1966) Experimental and Quasi-Experimental Designs for Research. Chicago: Rand-McNally.

CARTER, R. F. (1965) "Communication and affective relations." Journalism Q. 42 (spring) 203-212.

CHAFFEE, S. H. (1972) "The interpersonal context of mass communication," in F. G. Kline and P. J. Tichenor (eds.) Current Perspectives in Mass Communication Research. Beverly Hills: Sage Pubns.

——— and L. B. BECKER (1975) "Young voters' reactions to early Watergate issues." Amer. Politics Q. (October).

——— and J. M. McLEOD (1973) "Individual vs. social predictors of information seeking." Journalism Q. 50 (summer) 237-245.

———, J. M. McLEOD and D. B. WACKMAN (1973) "Family communication patterns and adolescent political participation," in J. Dennis (ed.) Socialization to Politics: A Reader. New York: Wiley.

COLEMAN, J., E. KATZ and H. MENZEL (1957) "Diffusion of an innovation among physicians." Sociometry 20: 253-270.

DENNIS, E. and W. RIVERS (1974) Other Voices: The New Journalism in America. San Francisco: Canfield Press.

DEUTSCHMANN, P. J. and W. A. DANIELSON (1960) "Diffusion of knowledge of the major news story." Journalism Q. 37 (summer) 345-355.

DONOHUE, G. A., P. J. TICHENOR and C. N. OLIEN (1972) "Gatekeeping: Mass media systems and information control," in F. G. Kline and P. J. Tichenor (eds.) Current Perspectives in Mass Communication Research. Beverly Hills: Sage Pubns.

DOUGLAS, D. F., B. H. WESTLEY and S. H. CHAFFEE (1970) "An information campaign that changed community attitudes." Journalism Q. 47 (autumn) 479-487.

DUNCAN, O. D. (1966) "Path analysis: Sociological examples." Amer. J. Soc. 72 (July) 1-16.

EASTON, D. (1953) The Political System. New York: Knopf.

——— (1957) "An approach to the analysis of political systems." World Politics 9 (April) 383-400.

——— (1965a) A Framework for Political Analysis. Englewood Cliffs, N.J.: Prentice-Hall.

——— (1965b) A Systems Analysis of Political Life. New York: Wiley.

——— and J. DENNIS (1969) Children in the Political System. New York: McGraw-Hill.

EFRON, E. (1971) The News Twisters. Los Angeles: Nash.

FLEGEL, R. C. and S. H. CHAFFEE (1971) "Influences of editors, readers, and personal opinions on reporters." Journalism Q. 48 (winter) 645-651.

GREENBERG, B. S. (1964a) "Person-to-person communication in the diffusion of news events." Journalism Q. 41 (autumn) 489-494.

——— (1964b) "Diffusion of news of the Kennedy assassination." Public Opinion Q. 28 (summer) 225-232.

——— and E. B. PARKER (1965) The Kennedy Assassination and the American Public: Social Communication in Crisis. Stanford, Calif.: Stanford University Press.

GREGG, J. E. (1965) "Newspaper editorial endorsements and California elections, 1948-62." Journalism Q. 42 (autumn) 532-538.

HEISE, D. R. (1969) "Problems in path analysis and causal inference," in E. F. Borgatta (ed.) Sociological Methodology 1969. San Francisco: Jossey-Bass.

HESSE, M. B. and S. H. CHAFFEE (1973) "Coorientation in political communication," presented to International Communication Assn.

HYMAN, H. H. and P. B. SHEATSLEY (1947) "Some reasons why information campaigns fail." Public Opinion Q. 11 (fall) 412-423.

JANOWITZ, M. (1952) The Community Press in an Urban Setting. New York: Free Press.

JENNINGS, M. K. and R. G. NIEMI (1975) "Continuity and change in political orientations: A longitudinal study of two generations." Amer. Political Science Rev. (December).

KATZ, E. and P. F. LAZARSFELD (1955) Personal Influence. New York: Free Press.

KENNY, D. (1972) "Threats to the internal validity of cross-lagged panel correlation," in G. A. Comstock and E. A. Rubinstein (eds.) Television and Social Behavior Vol. III: Television and Adolescent Aggressiveness. Washington: U.S. Government Printing Office.

——— (1973) "Cross-lagged and synchronous common factors in panel data," in A. S. Goldberger and O. D. Duncan (eds.) Structural Equation Models in the Social Sciences. New York: Seminar Press.

KLAPPER, J. T. (1960) The Effects of Mass Communication. New York: Free Press.

KRAUS, S. (1962) The Great Debates. Bloomington: Indiana University Press.

LANG, K. and G. E. LANG (1960) "The unique perspective of television and its effect: A pilot study," in W. Schramm (ed.) Mass Communications. Urbana: University of Illinois Press.

LAZARSFELD, P. F., B. R. BERELSON and H. GAUDET (1948) The People's Choice. New York: Columbia University Press.

McLEOD, J. M. and J. D. BROWN (1975) "Using longitudinal data to identify the political effects of the mass media," presented to World Assn. for Public Opinion Research, Montreux, Switzerland.

——— and S. H. CHAFFEE (1973) "Interpersonal approaches to communication research." Amer. Behavioral Scientist 16 (March/April) 469-500.

——— and ——— (1972) "The construction of social reality," in J. Tedeschi (ed.) The Social Influence Processes. Chicago: Aldine-Atherton.

MILLER, W. E., A. H. MILLER and F. G. KLINE (1974) "A proposal for study of the impact of the mass communications media on political behavior," presented to the Social Science Research Council by the Center for Political Studies, University of Michigan.

MILLSPAUGH, M. (1949) "Baltimore newspapers and the presidential election." Public Opinion Q. 13: 122-123.

O'KEEFE, G. J. and H. MENDELSOHN (1974) "Voter selectivity, partisanship, and the challenge of Watergate." Communication Research 1 (October) 345-367.

OLIEN, C. N., G. A. DONOHUE and P. J. TICHENOR (1968) "The community editor's power and the reporting of conflict." Journalism Q. 45: 243-252.

PETERSON, P. V. (1973) "J-enrollments reach all-time high as some academic disciplines ebb." Journalism Educator (January) 4-5.

REPASS, D. E. and S. H. CHAFFEE (1968) "Administrative vs. campaign coverage of two presidents in eight partisan dailies." Journalism Q. 45 (autumn) 528-531.

RIESMAN, D., R. DENNEY and N. GLAZER (1950) The Lonely Crowd. New Haven: Yale University Press.

ROBINSON, J. P. (1974) "Public opinion during the Watergate crisis." Communication Research 1 (October) 391-405.

ROGERS, E. and F. SHOEMAKER (1971) Communication of Innovations. New York: Free Press.

ROWSE, A. E. (1957) Slanted News: A Case Study of the Nixon and Stevenson Fund Stories. Boston: Beacon Press.

ROZELLE, R. M. and D. T. CAMPBELL (1969) "More plausible rival hypotheses in the cross-lagged panel correlation technique." Psych. Bulletin 71: 74-80.

SEWELL, W. H., A. O. HALLER and A. PORTES (1969) "The educational and early occupational attainment process." Amer. Soc. Rev. 34 (February) 82-92.

SHAW, D. L. (1967) "News bias and the telegraph: A study of historical change."

Journalism Q. 45 (summer) 326-329.
SIEBERT, F. S. (1952) Freedom of the Press in England 1476-1776. Urbana: University of Illinois Press.
SIGAL, L. (1974) Reporters and Officials. Lexington, Mass.: D. C. Heath.
SNIDERMAN, P. M., W. R. NEUMAN, J. CITRIN, H. McCLOSKY and J. M. SHANKS (1975) "Stability of support for the political system: The initial impact of Watergate." Amer. Politics Q. (October).
STEMPEL, G. H. (1961) "The prestige press covers the 1960 presidential campaign." Journalism Q. 38: 157-163.
——— (1965) "The prestige press in two presidential elections." Journalism Q. 42: 15-21.
STEVENSON, R. L., R. A. EISINGER, B. M. FEINBERG and A. B. KOTOK (1973) "Untwisting The News' Twisters: A replication of Efron's study." Journalism Q. 50 (summer) 211-219.
WEAVER, P. H. (1972) "Is television news biased?" The Public Interest No. 26 (winter) 57-74.

POLITICAL CAMPAIGNS AND

MASS COMMUNICATION RESEARCH

Garrett J. O'Keefe

ELECTION CAMPAIGNS have long served as empirical testbeds for the theories of mixed groups of scholars, journalists, social critics, and other citizens trying to make sense out of both political and communicatory processes within society.

The drawing power political campaigns have for those particularly curious about the operations of mass communications will be the main concern here, and why campaigns have such lure is fairly obvious. Chaffee (1974) has noted that campaigns are inherently interesting, even fascinating, events in and of themselves. Further, it can be assumed that most successful contemporary campaigns need mass media inputs, and that media in turn derive sizable proportions of advertising revenue and news content from campaigns. Moreover, campaigns attract social researchers by virtue of having some attributes of experimental research designs (such as a time sequence that "manipulates" audience members) combined with substantial audience numbers and interest under "naturalistic" field research conditions (cf. Campbell and Stanley, 1966).

Of course, precisely because of these elements of experimental design, it is always questionable how generalizable findings derived from political campaign studies are to other social behavior situations

AUTHOR'S NOTE: I am indebted to Dr. Harold Mendelsohn, much of whose thinking and research is reported herein, for his thoughtful reading of the manuscript. The open and unrestrictive support of Columbia Broadcasting System, Inc. in funding the 1972 and 1974 Summit County voting studies is most gratefully acknowledged.

involving communication. That is, individuals may rely on and react to mass communications differently when they know that they need to arrive at a decision and act upon it by a certain time (Election Day) than when, say, they perform in the more flexible roles of product consumers or entertainment seekers vis-a-vis mass media.

An intensive re-examination of the communication orientations and behaviors of potential voters during election campaigns is pres- ently underway in many fields of social research. This is especially true insofar as study of possible "effects" of mass media political content upon cognitions, values and behaviors of voters are con- cerned. Recent studies suggest that media may well have significant effects on potential voters other than overtly persuasive ones, and indeed may exert direct influence on voter decision-making in mea- surable forms (Blumler and McQuail, 1969; McCombs and Shaw, 1972; McCombs, 1972; Chaffee, 1973; Blumler and McLeod, 1974; Mendelsohn and O'Keefe, 1975). While the ensuing discussion will deal primarily with audiences of campaign media, it should be recognized that they comprise only one component of a complex interacting system deserving inquiry during campaigns. Relationships between politicians and the press (e.g. Crouse, 1973; Thompson, 1973); political advertising practices and ethics (e.g. Nimmo, 1970; Alexander, 1972); the rise of the professional campaign consultant (e.g. McGinniss, 1969; Nimmo, 1970); and the impact of communi- cation technologies upon campaign practices (e.g. Bagdikian, 1971; Gabor, 1973; Chisman, 1973) are but a few of the issues often neglected yet essential for fuller understanding of the process of election campaigning.

Presidential campaigns have traditionally been the most popular subjects of study, no doubt because of their interest-generating ability and inherent importance. They will be most extensively examined here, likewise. However, while presidential campaigns maximize probability of both media input and voter involvement, there are issues of relevance to communication researchers, and certainly a great number more of interest to students of politics, which may be better dealt with in lower-key campaigns (see Roths- child chapter). This chapter will proceed with a short overview of earlier research on political campaigns and communication behavior, discuss in some depth more recent research results, and then consider some key research topics and methodological issues that seem profit- able for future research to pursue. For a discussion of substantive theoretical implications of this same body of research, the reader should also consult the Becker et al. chapter.

EARLY CAMPAIGN STUDIES

Studies of the target audiences of political campaigns have traditionally sought observations through survey research methods, or inquiries into "a large number of people, selected by rigorous sampling, conducted in normal life settings by explicit, standardized procedures yielding quantitative measurements" (Hyman, 1973). At least four general modes of survey design are usually identified. These include the cross-sectional or "one-shot" design, typically aimed at assessing characteristics of a given population at one point in time. Undoubtably the most used design, it has been the workhorse of professional and academic political communications investigators for decades. Its limitations are obvious: data-gathering over time is restricted to respondent recall, severely hampering adequate measurement of change, a crucial concern in most communication studies. On the other hand, the design is relatively clean, efficient, and comparatively economical.

Two extensions of the cross-sectional design can be aimed at measurement of change over time, each with varying degrees of success. Trend designs are essentially concerned with examining change within populations over time, and attempt to do so by means of measuring different samples out of a population over different points in time. Professional pollsters have over the last several years begun presenting public opinion data based upon trend analyses, for example in tracing the rise of public support for President Richard Nixon during his landslide re-election year of 1972, and then its dramatic decline a year later.

Cohort designs, on the other hand, assess different samples that fall within the same conditions at different points in time. For example, there is concern with the communication behavior of individuals facing the voting act for the first time, typically between the ages of 18 and 24. A cohort analysis of this group could be carried out by examining persons who fall in that age range every two years during general elections.

Both trend and cohort designs are limited in ability to assess the dynamics of change since the same respondents are not re-interviewed over time. Panel designs make up for that shortcoming by attempting to allow observation of the same samples over time. Panel designs are regarded by many as ideal for political communication research, yet are rarely used due to the effort, expense, problems of attrition, and complexity of analyses required to make full use of the data.

The interjection of modern survey research methods into studies of election campaigns and voter behavior is generally attributed to Paul Lazarsfeld and his colleagues at Columbia University. This group carried out large-scale panel surveys of voter behavior during the 1940 and 1948 presidential election campaigns in the locales of Erie County, Ohio, and Elmira, New York, respectively (Lazarsfeld, Berelson, and Gaudet, 1948; Berelson, Lazarsfeld, and McPhee, 1954). Shortly thereafter, a major series of voter behavior studies based upon national probability samples, using a cross-sectional design, got underway at the University of Michigan with the presidential election of 1952 (Campbell, Gurin, and Miller, 1954; Campbell, Converse, Miller, and Stokes, 1960). These studies are discussed from various perspectives in several other chapters in this volume, and summaries contrasting their conceptual and methodological elements are found in such sources as Rossi (1959), Sears (1968) and Sheingold (1973). Some attention to their investigations of campaign communications behavior is also warranted here.

While the Michigan series is more resplendent in methodological sophistication and sheer volume of data over time, the Columbia studies stand paramount thus far in contributions to knowledge of political communication processes. Data presented in *The People's Choice* (Lazarsfeld, Berelson and Gaudet, 1948) appeared to shatter the initial propositions of the authors that (1) voting decisions were similar to "rational" consumer marketplace decisions, (2) campaigns were times of relatively volatile political change, and (3) the media served significant functions in the direction of activating citizens to vote, reinforcing certain of the voters who had already decided upon a candidate, and converting certain other voters to new candidates. Instead, Lazarsfeld et al. found the prime force behind nearly all vote decisions in 1940 to have been traditional, long-standing ties to either the Democratic or Republican parties, and less directly basic primary and secondary reference group identifications. Only five per cent of the voters could be counted as having been "converted" to the other side during the campaign. Furthermore, campaign media appeared to be of slight importance as source of "influence" during the campaign. The authors suggested *post hoc* that interpersonal communications were a more influential "medium," and that a "two-step flow" of communication functioned within the community whereby more knowledgeable and active "opinion leaders" within social strata processed and passed on campaign information and/or influence to their friends and associates. Berelson, Lazarsfeld and McPhee's report of 1948 election research, *Voting* (1954), reinforced this initial viewpoint, but with little added clarification of the processes. Since the focus of research was upon the voting act, it apparently seemed unimportant to them to pursue variables that looked tangential to that central criterion variable.

However, the data presented in *The People's Choice* and *Voting* leaves the relationship between exposure to mass and interpersonal communications and extent of reinforcement and/or conversion unclear. Nowhere are those voters who stayed with the same candidate, those who became "undecided" for a time, and those converted to another candidate directly compared in terms of their communication behavior. This lack of specific association clouds the common inference from those studies that the media were ineffectual. (See Becker et al. chapter on this point.) Further, the authors did not make efficient use of their multi-wave panel designs, doing little in the way of examining within-voter communication change and possible effects thereof over time.

Unfortunately, no data-gathering studies pertaining to political communication approaching the level of the Columbia attempts were repeated for years thereafter in the United States. The findings of the Lazarsfeld group have tended to be accepted as the final word on the matter, however unintentionally. Many of those early findings were reported in Joseph Klapper's *Effects of Mass Communications* (1960), a widely read and influential summary of research on that topic through the 1950s. While Klapper warned that he was cautiously presenting "tentative" generalizations in proposing a "limited effects model" of mass communication, his propositions, particularly in the realm of politics and the mass media, tended to be taken at face value.

CURRENT RESEARCH PERSPECTIVES

In many ways the study of political campaigns over the years represents a broad yet empirically one-sided competition between two basic approaches to the study of human behavior—the behaviorist stimulus-response learning model rooted in psychology versus the more sociologically based functionalist model. Mendelsohn (1973, 1974) has argued that the stimulus-response model, if pushed to its limits, would equate the effect of a communication upon an individual with that person's simple exposure to that communication, making no allowance for differences between audience members and situational factors, and assuming that audience members are rather helplessly acted upon by political communications. The functionalist model, on the other hand, attempts to take account of the totality of the individual's situation (including communications exposure) as but one element. In terms of voting, account is taken of conditions surrounding a voter both before and during a campaign, and the voting act is viewed as the end-product of many complex and interrelated influences and quasi-decisions. Emphasis is placed upon isolating the unique purposes and functions of mass media within the totality of influences that affect voter decision-making. This is not to say that audiences should be regarded as all-powerful and able to determine for themselves what they will or will not do with any and all messages emanating from the media. Such an assumption may be as unwarranted for mass communications research as the alternative extreme of the omnipotent media. Nonetheless, it is disturbing the extent to which popular criticism of political media content relies upon the behaviorist model alone, as is the extent to which social scientists sometimes fall back upon that model to interpret correlational data lacking in appropriate causal controls.

The Uses-Gratification Approach

More recently, the uses-gratifications paradigm has served as a rallying point for many researchers attempting to get at both potential functions and influences mass communications may provide during political campaigns (Katz, Blumler and Gurevitch, 1974, especially chapters by Kline et al. and McLeod and Becker). For political campaign applications, the underlying assumption of the model is akin to the basic supposition of Blumler and McQuail (1969) that effects on voters of campaign media (in their case, television) depend to a large extent upon motivations of potential voters to follow a particular campaign. In their study of the 1964 British national election, Blumler and McQuail refined the conclusions of the earlier Trenaman and McQuail (1961) examination of the 1959 election in England. Blumler and McQuail credit their reliance upon the uses and gratifications approach for their superior methodology in the 1964 study. It is more likely their own ingenuity in operationalizing the rather vaguely spelled-out model of that time that makes the study an exciting and revealing piece of work. The authors aimed at "emphasizing the gratifications that people derive from consumption of media materials, and the uses to which they put them in the circumstances of their own lives"; and to "determine how (if at all) the persuasiveness of a political message depends upon an individual's motivation for receiving it."

Key findings of that study will be considered later in this chapter, but essentially they showed that interest in the campaign and motivation to follow the campaign determined the extent of attitude change among voters on salient campaign issues (and perhaps candidate decisions) that resulted from exposure and attention to television programming dealing with the campaign.

The 1972 Summit County Study

During the 1972 campaign, a panel study was initiated to investigate the sociopsychological, interpersonal and mass communications-related processes involved in voter decision-making (Mendelsohn and O'Keefe, 1975). The conceptual approach taken was primarily in the uses-gratifications tradition and the method consisted of extensive repeated interviews of voters in Summit County, Ohio, over the course of the campaign.

The study attempted to cast a wide net, encompassing several concepts which had been developed in political communications research between 1940 and 1972. These ranged from opinion leadership, to the dynamics of voting behavior, to selective exposure, to uses and gratifications vis-a-vis political communication behavior. A working assumption was that while the American political scene, particularly as regards mass media, had undergone volatile change over those years, research into voter decision-making and communication behavior had not kept pace. (For example, the Columbia studies were conducted before the era of mass television.) It therefore appeared necessary to attempt to document the voting process both in terms of the earlier work and what numerous smaller-scale studies carried out during the late 1960s had contributed.

The overall design of the study called for a panel survey, with initial interviews conducted with a multi-stage area sample of 1,966 potential voters (age 18 and older) in Summit County during late July, 1972. A panel was drawn from this respondent pool for successive repeated interviews by telephone during August, September, October, and in November following the election. A smaller subgroup of the initial pool was chosen to act as a "control" group primarily to assess repeated interviewing effects; these respondents were interviewed in person only once, following Election Day.

Summit County consists primarily of urban Akron and its immediate suburbs. The Akron area was chosen for a number of geographic, demographic, and media-related reasons. Akron is the heart of a thriving medium-metropolitan industrialized area (with a 1970 metropolitan population of 680,000) with diverse demographic characteristics closely matching those of the United States as a whole. It was served by eight television stations (one locally based, seven from Cleveland, 25 miles away), some two dozen radio stations (nine local), and three major daily newspapers, including the Akron *Beacon-Journal,* (circulation 190,000) and the Cleveland *Plain Dealer* and *Press.* Ohio was highly regarded as a "must" state for George McGovern in 1972, and was allocated close attention by both McGovern and President Nixon in the campaign.

Data were gathered for at least two points in time on 865 persons who voted for a presidential candidate; 618 of these were interviewed all five times. Examination of those 865 continued in interviews beyond 1972. In 1973, nearly 600 of them were successfully re-interviewed by telephone following the summer Senate Watergate hearings. Those interviews revolved around the early Watergate disclosures (O'Keefe and Mendelsohn, 1974). Following the general elections in November 1974, an effort was made to re-interview by telephone as many of the 865 1972 voters as could be contacted; 70 per cent of the interviews were completed. The demographic and political profile of the 1974 cohort is remarkably similar to that of the 1972 voting group; the 1974 sample's vote declarations for governor of Ohio and U.S. Senator matched the outcomes of those two races in Summit County within two percentage points.

It was assumed for the study that when confronted with an election, voters are faced with two distinct decisions: (1) whether to vote or not; and (2) which of several candidates to vote for. Those individuals deciding not to vote before the campaign or relatively early in the campaign generally fall out beyond the parameters of the campaign "audience" and remain unexposed and hence immune to the various propaganda messages. They are generally either uninterested in politics overall, or in a given election, or both. Another (much smaller) group is comprised of persons who more-or-less intend to vote but end up not doing so as a result of lack of opportunity (forgetting to register, illness on election day, etc.) or become discouraged from doing so by the nature of the candidates, distaste with campaign methods, etc.

For those who do decide to vote, two fundamental variables appear to affect the roles that exposure to campaign-related media will play in ultimately influencing or not influencing their vote decisions. These variables are time of decision and the difficulty of decision. If voters decide early in the campaign, their exposure to campaign-related media will be primarily limited to searching out and reacting to materials that will be supportive of, or that will justify, their earlier decisions. Rather than open-mindedly weighing the positive and negative attributes of all contenders, the majority of early deciders appear quite dogmatic about their choices and remain so throughout the campaign. They also tend to report their decisions to have been "not at all difficult" to make. Although these voters may be exposed to counter-propaganda during the campaign and even learn new things about all candidates, their early committed loyalties seem untouched by the media and other information services—at least as far as the possibility of conversion goes. In the 1972 study, three-fourths of all voters fell into this immutable early-decider category. On the other hand, one-tenth of the voters in that study indicated early intentions to vote for a particular candidate but switched to the opposition side at some point during the campaign. These same voters tended to report disproportionately low political interest, moderate attention to the campaign, moderate to low campaign media exposure, high anticipation of media influence prior to the campaign, and high actual media influence on their vote decisions throughout the campaign.

Voters initially undecided early in the campaign, comprising over 14 per cent of the Ohio panel, generally were likely to find it more difficult to decide for one candidate or another, and appeared to have more of a propensity to use whatever sources of influence were available to them during the campaign—including the media—to help them arrive at their decision. These late deciders resembled the "switchers" described above, except that they were less prone to anticipate influence from the media prior to the campaign.

By themselves, time of decision and difficulty of decision do not determine media influence. More importantly, voters' pre-campaign attitudes toward the media, uses of the media, and anticipations regarding media influences, all affect exposure to campaign-related media content and impacts on vote decisions. In turn, the presentiments relating to the media are influenced by a host of voter dispositions including demographic characteristics, life styles, political and communicative socialization experiences, ideological stances, political partisanship, and previous experiences with the media and other forms of communication. As a political campaign begins to unfold, it would seem that all these variables come together in determining what might be considered to be voters' communication behaviors. In particular, three such behaviors affect the influence media may have on voters' decisions. These are interest in and attentiveness to the campaign-related media, the amount and frequency of exposure to campaign-related media, and the amount and frequency of interpersonal discussion about the campaign.

In the functionalist paradigm the focus is primarily on the voting act itself—including the often difficult decision of whether to vote or not, and the usually more trying decision of whom to vote for. As a dependent variable the voting act is impinged upon by numerous independent variables, many of which are closely interrelated. Indeed, certain of these variables appear more "independent" than others. Not to be overlooked are the all-important intervening variables which may be associated with both operative independent variables and the dependent voting act. Here, it should be noted that analytically, intervening factors such as attitudes on political issues, images of candidates, and aspects of media behavior may also be regarded as dependent variables vis-a-vis demographic and personality characteristics, and as independent variables vis-a-vis the voting act.

The guiding model in the Ohio research can be seen in the context of the uses-gratifications approach. One main concern has been with attempting to trace identifiable patterns of political communication behavior during campaigns to functional antecedents or presentiments that existed prior to the start of the campaign, and then attempting to determine the extent to which antecedent-communication behavior sequences have consequences in the form of communication effects. Analytically, the process becomes one of seeking contingent conditions under which specific communication use patterns are most likely to result in specific consequences (Chaffee, 1973). For example, evidence has been found that the strength of the relationship between campaign media exposure/attention levels and reported influence on vote decisions was contingent upon voters' pre-campaign expectations of being influenced by communications during the campaign. The greatest reported influence occurred under high anticipation and attention/exposure conditions, and the lowest under relatively low anticipation and exposure/attention conditions.

TOPICS FOR FUTURE RESEARCH

During the last three decades of research focusing upon communication processes in political campaigns, it is apparent that several key topic areas recur. The topics to be discussed within the remainder of this presentation are by no means inclusive of all that could be profitably studied within the framework of a political campaign, but they exemplify the state of the art. They are topics which have been at least touched upon in the past, remain unresolved today, yet propose the possibility of being empirically resolvable if greater effort is expended in the future.

The subjects to be discussed include the nature of political influence, attributes of voter decision-making, voter uses of the mass media during campaigns, campaign media content, cognitive effects of campaign communications, voter perceptions of campaign issues and candidate images, the role of interpersonal communication in political campaigns, voter typologies and communication behavior, political parties and communication, political socialization and communication behavior, variation in election campaigns as a variable affecting communication, community composition and media environment as variables affecting communication; there is a closing note on methodological problems in political communication research during campaigns.

The Nature of Political Influence

The concept of political influence has been floating around in political behavior and social psychological research for decades, with few attempts at clear explication. Even in the classic work *Personal Influence,* it is difficult to tell from Katz and Lazarsfeld's (1955) presentation whether it is "influence" or "information" hypothetically flowing between opinion leaders and followers. Dahl (1957) has referred to influence as "a shift in the probability outcome"; Gamson (1968) suggests that influence occurs when person "A is at least partially determining B's behavior, altering it from what it would have been in A's absence"; and Easton (1953) has argued that "to give (influence) any differentiated meaning we must view it as a relationship in which one person or group is able to determine the actions of another in the direction of the former's own ends."

In any case, it seemed appropriate in the 1972 Ohio study at least to try to ascertain what voters perceived influence as meaning, by asking them whether particular events depicted via the media had "influenced" their vote decision and, if so, how and/or why they had been influenced (or not). It did not seem reasonable to prescribe fixed dimensions of influence from the social interaction literature and impose what could have been artificial categories upon the respondents. Through that procedure, it was found that more than 20 per cent of the sampled voters claimed they had been rather consistently influenced by various events (e.g. the Eagleton matter, Kissinger's "peace is at hand" statement) presented through various communication sources during the campaign. Through intensive open-ended analysis, it became clear that one sizable segment of voters interpreted influence in terms of justification, or rationale-building, for decisions already made (similar to the standard but still unspecified "reinforcement" inference). Another group reported being influenced in terms of receiving help in making up their minds whom to vote for, or in switching from one candidate to another. Research is currently underway to delineate the net effects of many possible influence sources upon this voter decision-making. Degree of reported influence also needs to be empirically associated with changes in respondents' positions on issues, perceptions of candidates' positions on issues, and perceptions of candidates' images. This should ideally be conducted by measuring perceived influence, issue and image change, and communication behavior at a minimum of three points in time with use of appropriate causal modeling techniques.

If it is assumed that voters can be said to have had their decisions influenced when there is a measurable change, the switching of a vote choice per se is an oversimplified criterion of change. Use of a strength-of-commitment (to a candidate) measure was quite revealing for many analyses of Ohio voters in 1972. Consideration should be given to examining net changes in voters' orientations toward all candidates over the campaign. For example, respondents might be asked for the probability they would vote for each of the candidates running prior to the conventions, and thereafter the probabilities that they would vote for the actual nominees. Shifts in probabilities associated with candidates could be examined in the context of campaign events, political advertising, speeches, etc. Such shifts should give a fuller picture of the nature and impact of different forms of influence upon voter decision-making.

Further, it needs to be examined if influence in this case refers more to "information" in the sense of content that aids voters in discriminating between candidates, so that the voter can choose based upon his own perceptions of what the more important attributes are; or whether it refers more to content telling the voter which attributes are the most important as well as ranking candidates on those attributes. Or, perhaps some voters simply wish to be told whom to vote for without much cognitive deliberation.

Earlier, an antecedents-communication-consequences model was discussed in terms of data from the 1972 study. It was found that campaign interest, difficulty of decision and age were the three main independent predictors of reported influence. That is, voters who were more interested, voters who had a harder time making up their minds, and younger voters were likelier to report being influenced. And, the more influence had been anticipated prior to the start of the campaign, the likelier influence was to be reported later, particularly when campaign exposure and attention levels were high. Furthermore, exposure and attention were best predicted by previous political interest and concern over the election victor, while anticipatory influence was best predicted by level of education (closely followed by occupation). The higher the education and occupation levels, the greater anticipatory influence tended to be. Such relationships should be clarified with more explicit measures. To what extent do potential voters actively seek out influence, versus passively assuming they will be "reached" during the campaign? What factors is anticipatory influence, still a vague concept, dependent upon? Do certain previous political communication behaviors lead to such anticipation? Is anticipation the product of a socialization process? To what extent might individual communication patterns, such as the kinds of family communication patterns categorized by Chaffee, McLeod and Wackman (1972), be associated with such anticipations?

Factors in Voter Decision-Making

Despite the wealth of data on voting, little attention has been paid directly to relationships between decisional processes of voters and corresponding communication behavior. While concepts rooted in the psychology of cognition have been making their way more and more into the political communication literature, few attempts have been made to apply such thinking to the specific realm of voter decision-making (Carter, 1965; Chaffee, Stamm, Guerrero and Tipton, 1969; Atkin, 1973; Edelstein, 1973; Edelstein, 1975). One such variable, difficulty of decision, is probably dependent upon several variables, and in turn may affect many others. Among the components of difficulty may be included the number of alternatives facing the decision-maker, number of discriminating attributes between alternatives, lack or excess of information, felt importance of the decision in terms of its consequences, and publicness of the decision.

In the 1972 study, it was thought useful to begin inquiry into difficulty of voting decisions by directly asking voters how difficult it was for them to decide to vote for either McGovern or Nixon, rather than attempting to set up a more complex index or scale based upon theoretical preconceptions. Voters responding that the choice had been either very or somewhat difficult were then asked what particular things had made it difficult for them. Their answers by and large suggested that while these voters had been able to formulate judgments about each candidate, they did not have the ability in most cases to make meaningful discriminations between the candidates. Fifty-four per cent of the panel voters reporting difficulty traced it to their holding negative orientations toward both candidates. Only four per cent indicated their difficulties arose from positive attitudes toward both men. The remainder of the reasons included misgivings about having to vote against one's party, being confused by the campaign, and specific campaign events (Eagleton, Watergate, etc.). It is especially interesting that 65 per cent of the reasons given were classifiable as pertaining exclusively to personality attributes of McGovern and Nixon, while only 11 per cent exclusively concerned campaign issue attributes; another 22 per cent combined both personality and issue-related reasons.

While most of these voters appeared to be saying that their difficulty was based upon inability to discriminate, in some cases they had made meaningful discriminations but the candidate they wanted to vote for, or perhaps the only candidate they thought they could vote for, had negative qualities which were very hard to overlook. Study has yet to be made of those individuals who, try as they might, were unable to make a discrimination or to overlook flaws in their preferred choice, and ended up not voting.

Strong differences in difficulty of decision were found between 1972 and 1974. In 1972, the "difficult" voter tended to be less educated and less politically involved—especially Democrats "reluctantly" voting for McGovern. In the 1974 election, many of those reporting difficulty were more highly educated Republicans who had voted for Nixon in 1972; Watergate apparently had taken its toll. However, both the 1972 and 1974 groups expressing difficulty were likely to score lower in attention to campaign media, suggesting that while difficulty appears very much a characteristic of given campaign situations, campaign communication behavior is likewise. Constructs such as difficulty appear more predictive of communication behavior than traditional demographic or political disposition indicators.

When does a voter "decide" upon a candidate? This would seem to depend upon many factors important to communication, few of which have been explored. Traditional "early deciders" do not become so by writ, but by deciding earlier than other voters. For at least some of them, the decision process appears quite difficult and the role of communications media may be very important. However, these voters tend to be overlooked in studies of campaigns because they are viewed as constants. Interviews following the primary election could hopefully shed some light on these earlier stages of voter decision-making. What is the role of the primary election process in this? Do reasons for voting in primaries differ from those for voting in general elections? Do media use patterns differ in primaries from those found in general elections?

Political Uses of Media During Campaigns

As discussed earlier, Blumler and McQuail (1969) applied a uses-gratifications paradigm to their study of the 1964 British national elections. Since that effort, numerous smaller scale studies have been carried out focusing upon various functions the media may serve in election campaigns (Atkin, 1972; Katz, Gurevitch and Haas, 1973; McCombs and Weaver, 1973; McLeod, Becker and Byrnes, 1974; McLeod and Becker, 1974). The 1972 Ohio data indicate that the uses voters made of mass communications, including kinds of information sought about candidates, and agenda setting and cueing, varied with attention paid to the campaign, time of decision, and difficulty of decision. Subsequent research would benefit from more penetrating measures of these concepts.

The extent to which early-sought gratifications are fulfilled by media and other communication sources over the campaign should be investigated. For example, does anticipation of using the media for surveillance yield greater learning over the course of the campaign? The key concept of the Blumler and McQuail study was said to be *motivation* on the part of voters to follow the campaign over television. Motivation was operationalized as the ratio of "reasons for watching" over "reasons for avoiding." A resurrection of this most interesting (if troublesome) variable would be valuable. It could be measured by a ratio taking into account the relative *weight* of gratification items as well as simple scoring. It should, of course, be applied over all campaign sources. This "drive" component of campaign attendance has been all too neglected thus far. What kinds of individuals are the most motivated to follow a campaign? For what reasons? What media best serve these varying degrees of motivation?

Are there patterns of motivations dependent upon gratifications sought, such as decisional assistance or post-decision justification?

Blumler and McQuail found that older and more experienced voters were more likely to have their interest aroused by the approach of the campaign, as were those who eventually switched support from one party to another. To what extent do such conditions build anticipation of influence? To what extent is campaign media exposure actively sought, as opposed to being incidentally obtained? In the 1974 Summit County study, it was found that nearly one out of five voters said they had made a special effort to find out more than they already knew about the candidates, and that nearly half of these voters had turned to *non*-media sources (campaign workers, pamphlets, friends, etc.) for that purpose, with another 40 per cent naming newspapers. Moreover, a third were "completely" satisfied in their search, with nearly all the rest reporting "partial" satisfaction. This dimension needs further pursuit. It should also be noted that only ten per cent of the 1974 voters said they had learned something after deciding upon a candidate that made them even more convinced they had made the right choice; three per cent said they had learned something that made them uncertain they had made the right choice. Perhaps while "reinforcement" appears the dominant mode here, voters' consciousness of being reinforced seems decidedly limited.

The assessment of exposure to the mass media in 1972 utilized typical indices largely aimed at replicating earlier measures. In some ways these were beneficial; in too many other ways they were severely limiting. While charting voters' reliance upon one medium over another yields some interesting data, much narrower aim should be taken at specific media contents. Which campaign events, as presented to voters through what kinds of media contents, have what kinds of impacts upon voters? Individual major news events, advertisements and the like need to be identified by voters in terms of their relative impacts.

Campaign Media Content

The bulk of recent research in the uses-gratifications context has been concerned with political news; one could reasonably assume that political advertising deserves equally close attention. Political communication content categories need greater specification, based upon how they are perceived by audiences. More presentation to the respondents of specific media materials, including news and political advertisements, should be conducted, along with free respondent recall of particular messages and reactions to them. Content analyses may divulge more insights into voter communication orientations if they are directed at themes other than simple bias in direction of one candidate or another. Graber (1971a, 1971b) has shown that in coverage of the 1968 presidential election, 20 major U.S. newspapers studied were quite uniform in the aspects of candidates they chose to report; personality-image attributes received wider play than issue-related attributes. Contrarily, Bowers (1972) analyzed political advertising in major daily newspapers in 23 states, and found that 46 per cent of the ads dealt with issues, versus 36 per cent dealing with personalities. Differences are almost certain to occur depending upon particular elections and candidates, and may affect the agenda of attributes upon which voters base (or justify) their decisions. Content analysis could also examine the "information content" of campaign news and advertising, for example in terms of how well the content provides voters with information explicitly drawing discriminations between candidates on relevant attributes, thus perhaps easing in one sense difficulty of voter decision-making.

There is a long research tradition of content analyses of political campaign materials aimed at various aspects of the campaign theater, much of it directed at detection of overt content bias (e.g. Danielson and Adams, 1961; Stempel, 1961; Stempel, 1965; Stempel, 1969; Russo, 1971; Lowry, 1971). The tradition continues to flourish, usually taking little account of audience perceptions of bias. For example, while Efron (1973) claimed a distinctive "liberal" bias on the part of the three major television networks in their coverage of the 1968 presidential campaign, Stevenson et al. (1973) were unable to replicate Efron's results using her same procedures over the same content. Evarts and Stempel (1974) found news magazine content leaning somewhat toward the Republican Party, while television network news programming and major newspapers appeared oriented more toward Democratic candidates. And, Meadow (1973) found that the three major television networks and the New York *Times* devoted greater length and space to McGovern than to Nixon in 1972. The great caution required in the building of content categories is discussed in such texts as Holsti (1969).

Robinson (1974) presents data to the point that newspaper endorsements of presidential candidates in 1972 were associated with differentials of about 3 per cent in voting behavior on the part of voters presumably exposed to the endorsements. The associations held even when such traditional explanatory variables of vote as party identification, political interest, education and region were controlled for by Multiple Classification Analysis. Robinson utilized a University of Michigan Center for Political Studies 1972 national probability sample of 1,119 adults, and focused on 501 respondents who reported having voted for a presidential candidate *and* having followed the campaign in a newspaper. Candidate choice was compared against the candidate endorsed by the newspaper read by the respondent, a good example of research combining specific content analysis with audience attention data.

Cognitive Effects of Campaign Media

Campaigns are likely to influence agendas of political issues both from the point of view of the candidate and that of the voter. The candidate is forced to find out the main issues of concern to constituents, and at minimum pay lip service to the fulfillment of constituents' needs. In turn, the candidate wields some power in being able to direct voter attention to those issues he emphasizes. Of course, in the long run campaigns can be claimed to have a strong reinforcement effect in that they "reinforce" citizens' attitudes toward their own political system, regardless of partisan dispositions. It is paramount that campaigns serve to prompt the act of voting every so often, regardless of whom or what is voted for.

In the first chapter of this volume, Becker et al. describe some of the less-obvious cognitive effects of campaign communications, focusing upon increments in general political information gain, perceived importance of campaign-related (agenda-setting) media functions, and more general cognitive changes in perceptions of the political system, community consensus, etc. It seems certain that campaign media have other effects than persuasive ones, and more attention needs to be devoted to these.

Even if one's goal is an analysis of campaign media as an instrument of propaganda or persuasion, it is possible to use a relatively simple paradigm of the persuasion process, such as the one McGuire (1969) employs in his explication of attitudes and attitude change, to delineate other aspects of the persuasion process which can be studied apart from the end result of change in behavior itself. Loosely following McGuire's model, one can examine as dependent variables the *awareness* of various political communication contents during a political campaign, *comprehension* of the intended meaning within those messages, attitude *change* in the direction intended (or unintended) by the message, *retention* of that attitude change at least until a time when a behavioral manifestation of that attitude change may be possible, and *motivation to behave* in the intended direction. The bulk of research directed at political communication over the years, however, has dealt almost exclusively with the final outcome of change in behavior (whom is voted for in the end result), and has found little variance to explore. "Conversion" from one candidate to another regularly appears to afflict only three to five per cent of voters studied. To be sure, attention has been given to "awareness" through measurement of simple exposure to political communications, but most of that effort has been expended under the assumption of exposure as an independent (with "effect" dependent) rather than dependent variable. In line with motivational factors, Atkin, Bowen, and Sheinkopf (1973) report data suggesting that perceived attention to televised political commercials is more related to learning than is degree of exposure to the commercials. Also, the perceived entertainment value of the commercials was associated with increases in knowledge.

Perceptions of Campaign Issues and Candidates' Images

Coupled with the decline in party identification as an explainer of voter candidate preferences has been a rise in the importance of campaign issues and candidates' images. Recent research indicates that while it no doubt helps a candidate gain support from a voter if they are both of the same party, it is at least equally important that they share opinions on what voters regard as salient issues (Campbell and Stokes, 1959; Campbell, Converse, Miller, and Stokes, 1960; Converse, Clausen and Miller, 1965; Key, 1966; Converse, Miller, Rusk, and Wolfe, 1969; Flanigan, 1972; Miller, Miller, Raine, and Brown, 1973; Sears and Whitney, 1973). Or, more to the point, it is important that the voter perceives such agreement, whether accurately or inaccurately (Sherrod, 1971; Mendelsohn and O'Keefe, 1975).

Similarly, many authors have suggested a rise in the importance of candidate images or personality attributes, in recent years, particularly in light of the emphasis television coverage appears to give to that attribute (Carter, 1962; Tannenbaum, Greenberg, and Silverman, 1962). Again, recent studies suggest that voters' perceptions of candidate image are at least as predictive of vote as is party identification, and probably more so in most elections (Weisberg and Rusk, 1970; Mendelsohn and O'Keefe, 1975).

Data from the 1972 Summit County study strongly indicate that the frequently drawn party-versus-issue-versus-image trichotomy does little justice to the complexity of attributes used by voters in candidate selection. Voters' party identification, perceived agreement with candidates on five fundamental campaign issues, and images of candidates on six dimensions were inserted into a regression analysis to determine their ability to explain variance in presidential vote. While Nixon's image of trustworthiness and McGovern's image of "safeness" explained the most variance, close behind was voters' perceived agreement with both candidates on economic issues, followed by other image and issue groupings—and quite distantly by party. The picture was one of mixes of attributes being used by voters, highly intercorrelated with and interdependent upon one another. Democrats, for example, tended to register a different mix of issue and image rankings than Republicans or independents. Curiously, party explained more variance in vote for late than for early deciders; issue and image perceptions explained more variance among early deciders.

The Summit County voting panel was asked in 1972 and 1974 which attribute they thought they had based their decision upon— the candidates' party, stand on issues, or personal qualities. Stand on issues was the most mentioned in both the 1972 presidential election and the 1974 Ohio gubernatorial and senatorial elections; party and personal qualities were more frequently mentioned in the 1974 statewide elections than in 1972.

Blumler and McQuail (1969) reported change in issue and image perceptions over the campaign within their panel, associated with differences in media exposure and motivation. Patterson and McClure (1974) have found changes in issue perceptions of candidates among voters more frequently exposed to prime-time television during the 1972 presidential campaign. Closer inspection of relationships between change in issue and image perceptions, and exposure and attention to broadcast versus print media, needs to be carried out. Are changes in images more associated with television news and commercial exposure than with newspaper content exposure, as many writers have assumed? Such a linkage has yet to be established empirically.

Interpersonal Communication and Political Campaigns

The "two-step flow" model is clearly inadequate to the task of describing and explaining relationships between interpersonal and mass communications uses and consequences during political campaigns, and is sorely in need of comprehensive revision (cf. Chaffee, 1972). In the Summit County studies, interpersonal communication sources ranked far below television or newspapers on numerous dimensions as preferred sources of political campaign information and influence. While the traditional opinion leadership items were used (with slight modification) in that study, it appeared more useful to derive a four-fold typology of political information and opinion giving and seeking, distinguishing between political guidance givers (14 per cent of the sample), guidance seekers (18 per cent), those who tend to do both (guidance exchangers, 32 per cent), and those tending to do neither (non-participants, 37 per cent). These categories are similar to television content gratifications listed by Blumler and McQuail (1969). Guidance *exchangers* tended to be the group exhibiting greater levels of political interest, knowledge and media use typically associated with "opinion leaders." Guidance givers, along with seekers, actually fell below non-participants on those attributes. At best, guidance exchangers may include an opinion leader cohort in which political communication is primarily directed at other such leaders. In somewhat the same vein, Chaffee and McLeod (1973) found that respondents' amount of political discussion predicted political information seeking more than other factors, regardless of selective exposure, particularly when respondents' political interest level matched that of their friends.

Voter Typologies and Communication Behavior

Rossi (1959) suggested stratification of panel samples in campaign surveys to over-represent specific groups of voters who might be more prone to show change in candidate preferences over the course of a campaign. These groups could be studied more efficiently and in larger numbers once they were identified. One such group surfaced in the Summit County study, and had been less directly pointed to in the earlier panel studies. Low-to-middle income high school graduates proved noteworthy in that they tended to express greater difficulty in deciding whom to vote for, were likelier to be late deciders, were less interested in politics and the campaign, attended to campaign media less, but disproportionately indicated anticipating influence and being influenced over the campaign. Of particular interest was the emergence in the sample of an apparently well-educated, yet politically uninterested, younger, less cynical group of voters who admitted to seeking political guidance in general, and who anticipated influence from that input. Examination of such groups should be carried out over other campaigns, as should research into more natural cohorts as political activists, black and other ethnic minority voters, blue-collar voters, and first-time voters.

Much of what has been reported and discussed above is congruent with the "floating voter" hypothesis advanced by Converse (1966), that those voters least exposed to mediated campaign messages are the most likely to shift candidate preferences within campaigns. However, the fact that the "switchers" in the 1972 sample reported disproportionately higher anticipation of influence despite lower campaign media exposure puts the issue into a new perspective. Moreover, the proposition that low-exposure floating voters are more likely to change parties between campaigns could be put to a clear test within a longitudinal sample (Dreyer, 1971). Related to this issue is research conducted by Krugman (1965) and Ray (1973) among others, suggesting that persuasive media content may in some cases be most effective with low involvement audiences. (See Rothschild chapter.) That is, individuals who have not concerned themselves as much with the topic being dealt with may be more open to persuasive appeals on that topic. Ray has evidence that voters less involved in an election campaign may be somewhat more open to persuasive media appeals on behalf of candidates. Also, greater public affairs media exposure levels have been reported for those more highly involved voters likely to split vote tickets between parties (DeVries and Tarrance, 1972).

More careful examination of the values and behaviors of the nonvoting respondents should be carried out. The problem of nonvoting is obviously becoming more pertinent in contemporary American society (Lang and Lang, 1968). What factors enter into the "vote or not vote" decision? To what extent is difficulty of decision a factor here? It is a long-standing assumption that the mass media serve as "activators" during campaigns in terms of helping get out the vote. Empirical data supporting this contention is sparse, however; little investigation has been made as to the role of the media and other communication sources as a behaviorally motivating agent, except to some extent in the violence-aggression area. Blumler and

McLeod (1974) have recently presented data suggesting rather strong implications for the role of communication in voting turnout. Mass and interpersonal communication among nonvoters should be examined and compared to communication among voters for further examination of this issue.

Political Parties and Communication Behavior

The early Lazarsfeld work became strongly concerned with party affiliation as a variable, and indeed there often seemed to be more concentration upon the effects of other variables on partisanship than on actual votes for candidates. It had been established that in 1940 and 1948 affiliated voters tended very much to vote for their party's choice. Since then, research bearing upon political communication has focused more and more upon the candidate, at the expense of examining variables that go into selection of a party, and possible later change in party affiliations. Given national poll trends showing that the Republican Party has been for some time losing affiliates to both Democratic and Independent ranks, and indeed lags behind "independents" in numbers, perhaps the potential role of political communication in this movement bears closer study. The Republican Party of late has spent sizable amounts of money for a media "public image" campaign. Toward what end? Can the media attract voters toward or from party identifications? The fact that party identification has become much less associated with candidate voting in recent years does not necessarily mean that it has become an attribute of lesser concern in political campaign research. Rather, the movement in party affiliation patterns over the years deserves even closer scrutiny. Mendelsohn and Crespi (1970) have suggested that one of the more subtle long-range effects of television upon political life in our society has been to lessen the import of the party machineries in getting candidates elected. The immediacy and range of television has decreased potential impact of the strong local party organization upon vote choices, in their view. If so, it would seem to follow that television has also reduced the salience of parties as a political force within our society overall.

In a Gallup Poll taken during March 1975, a quarter of the national sample said they would be "likely to" support a new political party in the 1976 presidential race which would "support policies that are more conservative—that is, more to the right—than those of the Republican Party today." Interestingly, equal proportions of Republicans and Democrats (24 per cent each) reported their support was likely, as did 29 per cent of the independents.

Glenn (1973) has presented trend data over recent years suggesting that traditional relationships between party and social class have declined considerably outside of the South. In a cohort analysis, Glenn and Hefner (1972) found no evidence that the process of aging leads to Republican Party identification. However, older voters appeared to include greater proportions of Republicans, perhaps due to the political climate that prevailed at the time they were socialized to the electorate. Using similar techniques, Glenn (1969) and Glenn and Grimes (1969) have indicated that the often-assumed lessening of political participation among the aged is at least in part a function of socio-economic patterns particular to the aged in our society. Knoke and Hout (1974), in a study of change in party affiliations between 1952 and 1972, report father's party affiliation to have the largest effect on a voter's party affiliation, with age and demographic composition explaining relatively small proportions of variance.

Political Socialization and Communication Behavior

Major political campaigns have obvious potential as circumstances under which the socialization of young individuals into the "realities" of political behavior in our society may be accelerated. Campaigns are times of heightened political communication among politically involved parents, and the import of that communication is likely to rub off, on, or in some cases be directed at, the child. Schools likewise contribute to the dissemination of information about the role of campaigns in the political system during pre-election periods. And, the child, adolescent or young adult regularly in tune with mass communications almost cannot escape the imprint of a major campaign upon both news and entertainment media content. While earlier political socialization research by-and-large ignored mass media as a potential socializing agent (Hyman, 1959; Greenstein, 1965; Hess and Torney, 1967; Easton and Dennis, 1969; Langton, 1969), more recent work has acknowledged that media may make some contribution to the formation of cognitions and values concerning the political system. These studies are reviewed in the Becker et al. chapter, and include panel studies by Jennings and Niemi (1973) and Chaffee, Ward and Tipton (1973); the latter and Chaffee, McLeod and Wackman (1972) used the 1968 campaign as a setting.

The young adult voting for the first time is at a critical juncture of his political life cycle, perhaps the most critical of all in terms of impact upon his subsequent political behavior. It is a time when some 15 to 20 years of political learning, interest-building, value formation and ancillary behavior are transformed into the first of a series of political acts. Although youngsters are sometimes involved in campaign activity (Chaffee et al., 1970), voting has been termed "the main form of political participation for most citizens . . ." and the act which "the most dramatic changes in America" derive from (Sears, 1969). Evidence indicates that behavior surrounding the first vote of an individual, particularly in a highly salient presidential election, is also likely to set the stage for later behavior in subsequent election campaigns (Campbell et al., 1960). However, rather sparse data exist concerning the kinds of political orientations the young adult brings into this first voting situation. The political socialization literature of the last decade has almost exclusively concerned itself with the development of political orientations of children and early adolescents. Little is available on the translation of these orientations into effective political participation in the form of voting.[1] Sears's (1969) exhaustive review of political behavior studies led him to conclude that "late adolescents and young adults would seem to enter the electorate with relatively few family-based political pre-dispositions. At that age, the number who do not clearly share even a party preference with their parents is almost as great as the number who do, and on more esoteric matters the continuity is even slighter. This would suggest relative openness of mind . . ." (p. 387). This "openness" is also traditionally coupled with lower voting rates, lower interest and attention, and lower mass media use (Berelson et al., 1954; Campbell et al., 1960).

The study of political socialization need not and should not stop with the first voting act. As voters move through different life cycle stages, their political inclinations almost surely transform to a degree (McLeod and O'Keefe, 1972). Campaigns may be seen as opportunities for solidifying these gradual changes over time. While no doubt what happens between campaigns is of extreme import to voter decisions (Lang and Lang, 1968), the campaigns are nonetheless times at which action must be taken, and which should leave something of an impact upon later political orientations. While the voter may react in an election to what was experienced over the period since the last election, the vote cast likewise leaves its mark on how the next between-election period is going to be interpreted. The individual who voted for Richard Nixon in 1972 doubtless read the early, and perhaps even the later, signs of Watergate in a different perspective from the person not voting for Nixon (Chaffee and Becker, 1975).

VARIATION IN ELECTION CAMPAIGNS

There may well be political times when mass media play more important roles, and when communications in general may function in more salient ways. For example, for the vast majority of voters in the 1968 presidential election, Hubert Humphrey and Richard Nixon were tried, true, or at least well-known characters. For most citizens, it was not necessary to use communications media to find out about these candidates as personal entities. Indeed, it was for most citizens not necessary to use campaign information channels to find out where these men stood on issues—one could easily extrapolate from their past stands to discern their policy preferences. On the other hand, many potential voters in 1972 found themselves faced with an unknown; national polls suggest that George McGovern was recognized as a political entity by perhaps five per cent of the adult U.S. population as late as January 1972. The 1972 Ohio data strongly suggest that indeed voter attention was much more directed at McGovern as an "unknown" in terms of exposure to the Democratic Convention, open-ended responses describing things "learned" from the media during the campaign, etc. In many crucial respects, the 1972 presidential campaign was atypical, on a par in recent decades only with the lopsided 1964 contest between Johnson and Goldwater. Shulman and Pomper (1975) have developed a causal modeling pattern that strongly suggests that 1964 and 1972 were unique at least in terms of voters' positions on issues being stronger independent predictors of presidential candidate choice than party; the impact of standard demographic predictors and family political traditions was less than is usual, as demonstrated by contrasting findings for 1956, 1960, and 1968.

While trend studies such as Schulman and Pomper's can do much to describe such long-range differentiations in campaigns, longitudinal panel analysis is still preferred for its ability to discern changes in the ways in which the same voters respond to different campaign situations. Communication-related variables that may be most profitably examined vis-a-vis variation across election campaigns include degree of information-seeking about candidates and issues, degree of agenda setting and agenda cueing, information gain, anticipatory influence, difficulty of decision, and reported influence.

Some insight may be gained from mathematical simulations of voting behavior across campaigns. Tullock (1967), for example, has attempted to impose an economic model onto the voting process, in which the voting act is regarded in terms of its "payoff" for the individual. Payoff in turn becomes a positive function of benefit expected to be derived from the success of one's candidate, the likelihood that one's own vote will make a difference, and one's estimate of the accuracy of one's judgment; it is a negative function of one's perception of the cost of voting. It appears that at minimum the voter's perception of potential benefits and whether one's own vote makes a difference are likely to be derived from political media content. Researchers applying computerized simulation techniques to communications behaviors in campaign situations include McPhee (1963) and Shaffer (1972).

Examination of trends over elections and political districts may also serve a useful purpose in specifying baseline data for future comparison purposes. McLeod and O'Keefe (1969) traced county-by-county returns over six previous primary elections in Wisconsin in order to establish a baseline to estimate voter turnout and party cross-over in the 1968 presidential primary, and relate those variables to the vote in that election. It was found, for example, that at least some of the support George Wallace gained in that election resulted from relatively low turnout among registered Democrats and a tendency for some Republicans to cross party lines (legal in Wisconsin) and vote for Democratic candidate Wallace in the primary.

Community Context and Media Environment

It seems imperative that a more comprehensive view of the nature and impact upon voting behavior of community history, aggregate demographics, political structure, and mass communications structure be taken into account in campaign studies. Likewise, detailed analyses of the conduct of campaigns within communities, particularly vis-a-vis mass media, is often lacking. This is a major argument against national sample studies of political communication in campaigns, unless at least some communities can be isolated and oversampled enough to allow partialing on significant community variables.

Suggestions have recently been made of cross-community studies aimed at manipulating extent of media availability as a variable. This approach has strong possibilities, provided that enough variance can be found. It is obvious that small communities vary significantly on several dimensions of available television entertainment content (over one dozen channels in Los Angeles versus one in some Nebraska communities, for example), and during political campaigns some states and regions receive much greater attention than others, depending upon such factors as numerical concentration of voters, primary elections, and histories of "swing" voting.

Comparisons might also be considered between campaigns for Congressional or statehouse districts, comparing districts in urban areas where use of major newspapers and television channels as campaign inputs is often more efficient and economical, against rural districts where use of media does not generate commensurate payoff at least in terms of target audience size.

Some Recurring Methodological Issues

Blumer (1959) dealt with many methodological issues that remain unresolved today, in his critique of political communication research of the 1940s and 1950s. Blumer argued that the study of mass communications as a variable was plagued from the start because media content was neither homogeneous nor constant, two key attributes he deemed necessary for the analysis of a phenomenon as an independent variable. Blumer said that research pretending that mass media content possessed these qualities was likely to yield spurious results. For example, he compared the study of mass communications "collectively" as an independent variable and attempting to measure "effects" of this variable on voting behavior, as being as fruitless as trying to find out the effects of conversation on voting. More cogently,

> ... presentations made through the mass media are likely to evolve and change to meet newly developing conditions. Thus, to treat the media as a single, homogeneous and constant factor is to ignore their real character....

> ... Obviously, the same difficulty exists in selecting any single-medium as an independent variable, as in recent trend studies designed to determine the effects of television on voting. (p. 200)

Blumer specifically criticized the Elmira and Erie County studies on these grounds, and it must be admitted that were his piece written fifteen years later most of the same criticisms would hold up. Only very recently has attention been paid to multiple measures of exposure to different media contents. Even so, simply breaking down exposure to say, newspapers, into news versus entertainment content areas, or even general news versus campaign news, is not going far enough. Until specific examinations of precisely what was presented and attended to by the receiver within those content areas, and under what kinds of dispositions and situations the content was attended to, are conducted movement cannot begin out of this quandary. To be sure, uses-gratifications research paradigms have done much to alleviate the problem by turning the question around and investigating needs potentially serviceable by mass communications as a key dependent variable. It is clear from the beginning that "needs" are not homogeneous and constant within audiences. While Blumer did not conclude with clear-cut suggestions for research design, he did specify that the answer obviously did not lie in more free-form naturalistic studies nor in more constrained laboratory experiments.

While panel surveys are highly regarded instruments of campaign research, the literature on use of the panel method in the study of social behavior is not an overly developed one. Since Lazarsfeld's (1940) presentation on the procedure, other literature has mainly been concerned with statistical control of the data and re-statements of Lazarsfeld's 16-fold table technique of panel analysis. Sobol (1959) and Morrison, Frank and Massey (1966) were concerned with analytic problems inherent in panel mortality and resulting bias; Lehnen and Koch (1974) present a model applicable to correcting for respondent attrition under some circumstances. Little has been done on effects of repeated testing on respondents in panel designs, although the potential for contamination is widely recognized. Initial indications are that interviewing may build interest, but very few respondents (four per cent) in the five-wave Summit County panel suggested it increased the likelihood of their voting. On the other hand, Clausen (1968) and Kraut and McConahay (1973) present data suggesting that being interviewed by a public opinion pollster increases the likelihood an individual will vote in a subsequent election. Kraut and McConahay propose that being interviewed serves to reduce feelings of political alienation and isolation, common barriers to voting. Being interviewed in a poll, the results of which may be immediately publicized and have import for policy in some way, may be differently perceived by respondents than being interviewed in an academic survey.

Jennings and Niemi (1973) in their longitudinal study attribute their approximately 70 per cent response rate after eight years in part to having two opportunities to contact each respondent—via either the parent or child in each pairing as an informant. The problem of respondent attrition in longitudinal studies is more directly addressed by McAllister, Goe and Butler (1973), who emphasize getting extensive tracking data in the first wave of a projected longitudinal study. Recent applications of causal modeling approaches (Blalock, 1971) have done much to increase the productivity of the panel design. Chaffee, Ward and Tipton (1970) and Atkin (1973) have exhibited the power of such a model combined with cross-lagged correlation even in a two-wave panel situation. The applicability of path analysis to such designs is attested to by Blumler and McLeod (1974).

Still lacking in resolution are some of the key issues surrounding attribution of both sampling error and measurement error in survey research centering on political campaigns, particularly research employing panel designs. For instance, the more panel designs are relied upon in the future, the more the chronically low reliability in standard political and communication behavior survey measures needs to be coped with. Unfortunately, researchers in this area have been slow to attempt to resolve the problem, no doubt because their interests for the most part lie with the large-scale issues involved. Nonetheless, it becomes extremely difficult to speak of inferring change over interview waves in panel studies when one-item measures with undetermined reliability levels are used. Indeed, the validity of many such measures appears to stem primarily from the fact that they have been used before and have produced explanable variance. The more the study of political campaigns moves away from simple description toward explanation and causal inference building, the more crucial this issue of measurement becomes. Measurement devices have simply not kept pace with the race toward sophistication in designing analytic models such as path analysis, discriminant analysis, and the like. The matter will not be resolved by haphazardly building more items into indices, or arbitrarily adding more levels of response into single-item measures of opinion or whatever. Clearly, more attempts at validation are needed along the lines of McLeod and Becker's (1974) cross-validation study of the gratification concept as used in political communication research. Equally important, along with developing research aimed at within-voter change over time estimates, item reliability must be taken into account. The field as a whole has done little over the years to answer, or even address, points such as these raised in such sources as Maccoby and Hyman's (1959) critique of *Voting,* and in the debates of Selvin (1958) and McGinnis (1958) over the proper application of statistical tests of significance in survey research.

In some ways, it may be of immense help to have the kind of deeply interrogative examination characterized by Lane's (1959) *Political Life* to get a firm handle upon the uses and effects of political communication within our society. Probably many scholars working in this area have had the experience of reading a detailed questionnaire, rich in open-ended data, and have found themselves begging to go back to the respondent for more answers as to "why." No doubt greater attention to people around them who are unlike themselves politically and in terms of communication habits would assist the researchers. On another level, when one sees the depth of insight and revelation in such popular studies as Studs Terkel's best-seller *Working* (and the numerous folk inferences about communication behavior therein) even less satisfaction is derived from data gathered by standard survey techniques. The survey instrument may be the most sophisticated, and certainly the most efficient, device of the moment for the assessment of citizen behavior during political campaigns, but it must not be regarded as an end unto itself.

NOTE

1. Currently a longitudinal study of young adults who voted for the first time in the 1972 election is underway at the Mass Communications Research Center of the University of Wisconsin (Madison). It is directed by Jack McLeod, and funded by the John and Mary R. Markle Foundation. Reports to date from this work include McLeod, Brown and Becker (1975) and Chaffee and Becker (1975).

REFERENCES

ALEXANDER, H. E. (1972) "Broadcasting and politics," in M . K. Jennings and L. H. Ziegler (eds.) The Electoral Process. Englewood Cliffs: Prentice-Hall.
ATKIN, C. K. (1972) "Anticipated communication and mass media information seeking." Public Opinion Q. 35: 188-189.
––– (1973) "Instrumental utilities and information seeking," in P. Clarke (ed.) New Models for Mass Communication Research. Beverly Hills: Sage Pubns.
–––, L. BOWEN and K. G. SHEINKOPF (1973) "Quality versus quantity in televised political ads." Public Opinion Q. 37: 209-224.
BAGDIKIAN, B. (1971) The Information Machines. New York: Harper.
BERELSON, B., P. LAZARSFELD and W. MCPHEE (1954) Voting. Chicago: University of Chicago Press.
BLALOCK, H. M. (1972) Social Statistics. New York: McGraw-Hill.
BLUMER, H. (1959) "Suggestions for the study of mass media effects," in E. Burdick and A. J. Brodbeck (eds.) American Voting Behavior. Glencoe: Free Press.

BLUMLER, J. G. and J. M. MCLEOD (1974) "Communication and voter turnout in Britain," in T. Leggatt (ed.) Sociological Theory and Survey Research. Beverly Hills: Sage Pubns.

——— and D. MCQUAIL (1969) Television in Politics: Its Uses and Influence. Chicago: University of Chicago Press.

BOWERS, T. A. (1973) "Issue and personality information in newspaper political advertising." Journalism Q. 49: 446-452.

CAMPBELL, A., P. E. CONVERSE, W. E. MILLER, and D. E. STOKES (1960) The American Voter. New York: Wiley.

——— and D. E. STOKES (1959) "Partisan attitudes and the presidential vote," in E. Burdick and A. J. Brodbeck (eds.) American Voting Behavior. Glencoe: Free Press.

———, G. GURIN and W. E. MILLER (1954) The Voter Decides. Evanston: Row, Peterson.

CAMPBELL, D. T. and J. C. STANLEY (1966) Experimental and Quasi-Experimental Designs for Research. Chicago: Rand-McNally.

CARTER, R. F. (1962) "Some effects of the debates," in S. Kraus (ed.) The Great Debates. Bloomington: Indiana University Press.

——— (1965) "Communication and affective relations." Journalism Q. 42: 203-212.

CHAFFEE, S. H. (1972) "The interpersonal context of mass communication," in F. G. Kline and P. J. Tichenor (eds.) Current Perspectives in Mass Communication Research. Beverly Hills: Sage Pubns.

——— (1973) "Contingent orientations and the effects of political communication," presented to Speech Communication Association, New York, N.Y.

——— (1974) "National election campaigns as a vehicle for testing major hypotheses about communication." Mass Communications Research Center, University of Wisconsin (Madison).

——— and L. B. BECKER (1975) "Young voters' reactions to early Watergate issues." Amer. Politics Q. (October).

——— and J. M. MCLEOD (1973) "Individual vs. social predictors of information seeking." Journalism Q. 50: 237-245.

———, J. M. MCLEOD and D. WACKMAN (1972) "Family communication patterns and political socialization," in J. Dennis (ed.) Socialization to Politics. New York: Wiley.

———, K. R. STAMM, J. L. GUERRERO and L. P. TIPTON (1969) Experiments on Cognitive Discrepancies and Communication. Journalism Monographs No. 14.

———, L. S. WARD and L. P. TIPTON (1970) "Mass Communication and political socialization." Journalism Q. 47: 647-659.

CHISMAN, F. P. (1973) "Politics and the new mass communications," in G. Gerbner, L. P. Gross and W. H. Melody (eds.) Communications Technology and Social Policy. New York: Wiley.

CLAUSEN, A. R. (1968) "Response validity: Voter report." Public Opinion Q. 32: 588-606.

CONVERSE, P. E. (1966) "Information flow and the stability of partisan attitudes," in E. Dreyer and W. Rosenbaum (eds.) Political Opinion and Electoral Behavior. Belmont, Cal.: Wadsworth.

———, A. R. CLAUSEN and W. E. MILLER (1965) "Electoral myth and reality: The 1964 election." Amer. Political Science Rev. 59: 321-336.

———, W. MILLER, J. RUSK and A. WOLFE (1969) "Continuity and change in American politics: Parties and issues in the 1968 election." Amer. Political Science Rev. 63: 1083-1105.

CROUSE, T. (1973) The Boys on the Bus. New York: Random House.

DAHL, R. A. (1957) "The concept of power." Behavioral Science 2: 201-218.

DANIELSON, W. A. and J. B. ADAMS (1961) "Completeness of press coverage in the 1960 election." Journalism Q. 38: 441-452.

DEVRIES, W. and V. L. TARRANCE (1972) The Ticket-Splitters. Grand Rapids, Mich.: W. B. Eerdmans.

DREYER, E. C. (1971) "Media use and electoral choices: Some political consequences of information exposure." Public Opinion Q. 35: 544-553.

EASTON, D. (1953) The Political System. New York: Knopf.

――― and J. DENNIS (1969) Children in the Political System: Origins of Political Legitimacy. New York: McGraw-Hill.

EDELSTEIN, A. (1973) "Decision-making and mass communication: A conceptual and methodological approach to public opinion," in P. Clarke (ed.) New Models for Mass Communication Research. Beverly Hills: Sage Pubns.

――― (1975) The Uses of Communication in Decision-Making. New York: Praeger.

EFRON, E. (1973) The News Twisters. Los Angeles: Nash.

EVARTS, D. and G. H. STEMPEL (1974) "Coverage of the 1972 campaign by TV, news magazines and major newspapers." Journalism Q. 51: 645-648.

FLANIGAN, W. H. (1972) The Political Behavior of the Electorate. Boston: Allyn and Bacon.

GABOR, D. (1973) "Social control through communications," in G. Gerbner, L. P. Gross and W. H. Melody (eds.) Communications Technology and Social Policy. New York: Wiley.

GAMSON, W. A. (1968) Power and Discontent. Homewood, Ill.: Dorsey.

GLENN, N. D. (1969) "Aging, disengagement, and opinionation." Public Opinion Q. 33: 17-33.

――― (1973) "Class and party support in the United States: Recent and emerging trends." Public Opinion Q. 37: 1-20.

――― and M. GRIMES (1969) "Aging, voting and political interest." Amer. Soc. Rev. 33: 563-575.

――― and T. HEFNER (1972) "Further evidence on aging and party identification." Public Opinion Q. 36: 176-187.

GRABER, D. A. (1971a) "Press coverage patterns of campaign news: The 1968 presidential race." Journalism Q. 48: 502-512.

――― (1971b) "The press as opinion resource during the 1968 presidential campaign." Public Opinion Q. 35: 168-182.

GREENSTEIN, F. I. (1965) Children and Politics. New Haven: Yale University Press.

HESS, R. D. and J. V. TORNEY (1967) The Development of Political Attitudes in Children. Chicago: Aldine.

HOLSTI, O. (1969) Content Analysis in the Social Sciences and Humanities. Reading, Mass.: Addison-Wesley.

HYMAN, H. (1959) Political Socialization. New York: Free Press.

――― (1973) "Surveys in the study of political psychology," in J. N. Knutson (ed.) Handbook of Political Psychology. San Francisco: Jossey-Bass.

JENNINGS, M. K. and R. G. NIEMI (1968) "The transmission of political values from parent to child." Amer. Political Science Rev. 62: 169-184.

――― and R. G. NIEMI (1973) "Continuity and change in political orientations: A longitudinal study of two generations," presented to American Political Science Association, New Orleans, La.

KATZ, E., J. G. BLUMLER and M. GUREVITCH (1973) "Uses and gratifications research." Public Opinion Q. 37: 509-523.

―――, M. GUREVITCH, and H. HAAS (1973) "On the use of mass media for important things." Amer. Soc. Rev. 38: 164-181.

――― and P. LAZARSFELD (1955) Personal Influence. Chicago: University of Chicago Press.

KEY, V. O. (1966) The Responsible Electorate. Cambridge, Mass.: Harvard University Press.

KLAPPER, J. T. (1960) The Effects of Mass Communications. New York: Free Press.

KLECKA, W. R. (1970) "Applying political generations to the study of political behavior: A cohort analysis." Public Opinion Q. 35: 358-373.

KRUGMAN, H. E. (1965) "The impact of television advertising: Learning without involvement." Public Opinion Q. 29: 349-365.

KNOKE D. and M. HOUT (1974) "Social and demographic factors in American political party affiliations, 1952-1972." Amer. Soc. Rev. 39: 700-713.

KRAUT, R. E. and J. B. McCONAHAY (1973) "How being interviewed affects voting: An experiment." Public Opinion Q. 37: 398-406.

LANE, R. (1959) Political Life. New York: Free Press.

LANG, K. and G. E. LANG (1968) Politics and Television. Chicago: University of Chicago Press.

LANGTON, K. P. (1969) Political Socialization. New York: Oxford.

LAZARSFELD, P. F. (1940) "Panel studies." Public Opinion Q. 4: 122-128.

———, B. BERELSON, and H. GAUDET (1948) The People's Choice. New York: Columbia University Press.

LEHNEN, R. G. and G. G. KOCH (1974) "Analyzing panel data with uncontrolled attrition." Public Opinion Q. 38: 40-56.

LOWRY, D. T. (1971) "Agnew and the network TV news: A before-after content analysis." Journalism Q. 48: 205-210.

MACCOBY, E. E. and R. HYMAN (1959) "Measurement problems in panel studies," in E. Burdick and A. J. Brodbeck (eds.) American Voting Behavior. Glencoe: Free Press.

McCALLISTER, R. J., S. J. GOE and E. W. BUTLER (1973) "Tracking respondents in longitudinal surveys: Some preliminary considerations." Public Opinion Q. 37: 413-416.

McCOMBS, M. E. (1972) "Mass communication in political campaigns: Information, gratification and persuasion," in F. G. Kline and P. J. Tichenor (eds.) Current Perspectives in Mass Communications Research. Beverly Hills: Sage Pubns.

——— and D. SHAW (1972) "The agenda-setting function of the mass media." Public Opinion Q. 36: 176-187.

——— and D. WEAVER (1973) "Voters' need for orientation and use of mass media," presented to the International Communication Association, Montreal, Canada.

McGINNIS, R. (1958) "Randomization and inference in sociological research." Amer. Soc. Rev. 22: 408-414.

McGINNISS, J. (1969) The Selling of the President, 1968. New York: Trident.

McGUIRE, W. J. (1969) "The nature of attitudes and attitude change, in G. Lindzey and E. Aronson (eds.) Handbook of Social Psychology, Vol. 3. Reading, Mass.: Addison-Wesley.

McLEOD, J. M. and L. B. BECKER (1974) "Testing the validity of gratification measures through political effects analysis," in J. G. Blumler and E. Katz (eds.) The Uses of Mass Communications. Beverly Hills: Sage Pubns.

——— and G. J. O'KEEFE (1969) "The use of aggregate data in analyzing primary elections." Journalism Q. 46: 287-293.

——— and G. J. O'KEEFE (1972) "The socialization perspective and communication behavior," in F. G. Kline and P. J. Tichenor (eds.) Current Perspectives in Mass Communication Research. Beverly Hills: Sage Pubns.

———, L. B. BECKER and J. E. BYRNES (1974) "Another look at the agenda setting function of the press." Communication Research 1: 131-166.

———, J. BROWN and L. B. BECKER (1975) "Watergate and the voter: A Panel study of communication in the 1972 and 1974 elections," presented to American Assn. for Public Opinion Research, Itasca, Ill.

McPHEE. W (1963) Formal Theories of Mass Behavior. New York: Free Press.

MEADOW, R. G. (1973) "Cross-media comparison of coverage of the 1972 presidential campaign." Journalism Q. 50: 482-488.

MENDELSOHN, H. (1973) "When voters decide: The influences of the mass media," presented to American Sociological Association, New York.

––– (1974) "Behaviorism, functionalism and mass communications policy." Public Opinion Q. 38: 379-389.

––– and I. CRESPI (1970) Polls, Television and the New Politics. Scranton: Chandler.

––– and G. J. O'KEEFE (1975) The People Choose a President: A Study of Vote Decisions in the Making. Dept. of Mass Communications, University of Denver.

MILLER, A., W. MILLER, A. RAINE and T. BROWN (1973) "A majority party in disarray: Policy polarization in the 1972 election." Ann Arbor: University of Michigan Center for Political Studies.

MORRISON, D. G., R. E. FRANK and W. F. MASSEY (1966) "A note on panel bias." J. of Marketing Research 3: 85-88.

NIMMO, D. (1970) The Political Persuaders. Englewood Cliffs: Prentice-Hall.

O'KEEFE, G. J. and H. MENDELSOHN (1974) "Voter selectivity, partisanship and the challenge of Watergate." Communication Research 1: 345-367.

PATTERSON, T. and R. McCLURE (1974) "Political advertising: Voter reaction to televised political commercials." Study No. 23, Citizens' Research Foundation, Princeton, N.J.

RAY, M. L. (1973) "Marketing communication and the hierarchy of effects," in P. Clark (ed.) New Models for Mass Communication Research. Beverly Hills: Sage Pubns.

ROBINSON, J. P. (1974) "The press as kingmaker: What surveys from the last five election campaigns show." Journalism Q. 51: 587-594.

ROSSI, P. H. (1959) "Four landmarks in voting research," in E. Burdick and A. J. Brodbeck (eds.) American Voting Behavior. Glencoe: Free Press.

RUSSO, F. D. (1971) "A study of bias in TV coverage of the Vietnam War: 1969 and 1970." Public Opinion Q. 35: 539-543.

SEARS, D. (1968) "The paradox of de facto selective exposure without preference for supportive information," in R. Abelson et al. (eds.) Theories of Cognitive Consistency. Chicago: Rand-McNally.

––– (1969) "Political behavior," in G. Lindzey and E. Aronson (eds.) Handbook of Social Psychology, Vol. 5. Reading: Addison-Wesley.

––– and R. WHITNEY (1973) "Political persuasion," in I. de Sola Pool et al., Handbook of Communication. Chicago: Rand-McNally.

SELVIN, H. C. (1958) "A critique of tests of significance in survey research." Amer. Soc. Rev. 23: 519-527.

SHAFFER, W. B. (1972) Computer Simulations of Voting Behavior. New York: Oxford.

SHEINGOLD, C. A. (1973) "Social networks and voting: The resurrection of a research agenda." Amer. Soc. Rev. 38: 712-721.

SHERROD, D. (1971) "Selective perception of political candidates." Public Opinion Q. 35: 554-562.

SHULMAN, M. and G. POMPER (1975) "Variability in election behavior: Longitudinal perspective from causal modeling." Amer. J. of Political Science 19: 1-18.

SOBOL, M. G. (1959) "Panel mortality and panel bias." J. of the Amer. Statistical Association. 54: 52-68.

STEMPEL, G. H. (1961) "The prestige press covers the 1960 presidential campaign." Journalism Q. 38: 157-163.

––– (1965) "The prestige press in two presidential elections." Journalism Q. 42: 15-21.

––– (1969) "The prestige press meets the third party challenge." Journalism Q. 46: 699-706.

STEVENSON, R. L., R. A. EISINGER, B. M. FEINBERG and A. B. KOTOK (1973) "Untwisting The News Twisters: A replication of Efron's study." Journalism Q. 50: 211-219.

TANNENBAUM, P., B. GREENBERG and F. SILVERMAN (1962) "Candidate Images," in S. Kraus (ed.) The Great Debates. Bloomington: Indiana University Press.

THOMPSON, H. T. (1973) Fear and Loathing On the Campaign Trail '72. San Francisco: Straight Arrow.

TRENAMAN, J. and D. McQUAIL (1961) Television and the Political Image. London: Methuen.

TULLOCK, G. (1967) Toward a Mathematics of Politics. Ann Arbor: University of Michigan Press.

WEISBERG, W. F. and H. F. RUSK (1970) "Dimensions of candidate evaluation." Amer. Political Science Rev. 64: 615-628.

Chapter 5

TOWARDS A COMPARATIVE FRAMEWORK FOR

POLITICAL COMMUNICATION RESEARCH

Jay G. Blumler and Michael Gurevitch

WRITING IN 1975, nobody could claim to be able to paint an assured portrait of the field of investigation to be discussed in this chapter. It is not merely that few political communication studies have yet been mounted with a comparative focus. More to the point, there is neither a settled view of what such studies should be concerned with, nor even a firmly crystallized set of alternative options for research between which scholars of diverse philosophic persuasions could choose. In fact comparative political communication research must be the least advanced topic dealt with in this volume. If, following Socrates then, awareness of ignorance is the first step to wisdom, a second may be taken by attempting a diagnosis of the main barriers holding back the evolution of a coherent and sustained comparative approach in this field.

OBSTACLES TO COMPARATIVE RESEARCH

Some of the obstacles impeding such a development reflect imperfections to some extent endemic in all branches of social science: poor measurement; primitive theory. The main measurement lack frustrating comparative work at present is a dearth of politically illuminating indicators of the communication structures found in various countries. It is true that certain aggregate measures of communication growth have enabled investigators to compare levels of media development and their correlates throughout the world. The standard examples include: daily newspaper circulation per 1,000 population; percentages of households possessing radio receivers and television sets; numbers of cinema seats per 1,000 population; the diffusion of telephones; items per capita of domestic and foreign mail; domestic telegrams per capita, etc. (Lerner, 1957; Fagen, 1964; Schramm, 1964; UNESCO, 1964; Farace and Donohew, 1965; Frey, 1973). Two weaknesses are immediately evident when such a list of commonly deployed aggregate indicators is compiled. They measure merely the *volume* of communication capacities and transactions; and they are not specifically *political.* An outstanding exception on both counts is Nixon's index of press freedom (1965), which was based, however, not on 'hard' verifiable data but on informed experts' subjective judgments of the amount of government control exerted over newspapers in diverse states. It is also true that a richer store of individual-level data about especially the election communication behavior of citizens resides in public opinion survey archives scattered throughout the world. Yet the items used by survey researchers to measure political message exposure are so unstandardized at present as virtually to defy comparison across national boundaries. That is why comparative perspectives cannot be significantly promoted by undertaking secondary analyses of existing survey data; they are typically too disparate for manipulation within a common framework. Clearly, then, any viable strategy of comparative research advance must accord a high and early priority to enrichment of our sparse measurement resources.

The difficulties to be faced in implementing such a prescription should not be minimized. Information about political communication arrangements touches on areas of high sensitivity to many regimes. In some societies essential data may be sparse, in others widely dispersed. Definitions of more subtle phenomena may be incorrigibly variable. Nevertheless, these handicaps, however acute, are more secondary than primary. In principle, at least, measurement problems could be tackled with an expectation of success if scholars in different societies could reach some agreement over the topics and relationships they wished to examine in concert. Theoretical clarification is logically prior.

That is why the lack of sustained discussion of theoretical issues in comparative political communication study is even more deplorable. The resulting vacuum has tended to be filled by both ad-hoc-ery ("I did thus and so in my own country with interesting results, so will someone elsewhere please replicate my work") and rag-bag-ery

("Let's see what turns up when 39 predictor variables are regressed onto four mass communication variables in 115 countries"). Unfortunately, work of this kind is inimical to progressive continuity. It trades in no pre-defined problems, the resolution of which would open up yet other issues for scrutiny. It lights no torch that can be handed on from one investigator to the next. At this point, however, two sources of possible misunderstanding of our position should be cleared out of the way at once. First, we do *not* suppose that prior hypothesis formation followed by testing is a "universally valid description of scientific enquiry and discovery" (Friedrich, 1966). In addition to "the use of data for testing existing theory" there is an equally respectable "use of data as an active element in the process of theory building" (Russett et al., 1965). Yet both models of social science activity do presuppose the existence of a body of theoretical propositions that can somehow be augmented as well as tested. Secondly, it would be inexact to imply that all comparative political communication research conducted to date has been theoretically virginal. Unfortunately, such perspectives as have emerged so far, however, have often been applied to a rather limited, perhaps even ideologically biased, set of concerns. It is almost as if in order to engage in cross-national research you must be interested in either the determinants of press freedom attained in different societies (Nixon, 1965; Farace and Donohew, 1965) or in the role of communication in modernization and national development (Lerner, 1957; Deutsch, 1961; Pye, 1963; Fagen, 1964; Schramm, 1964; Alker, 1966; McNelly, 1966; McCrone and Cnudde, 1967; Cutright and Wiley, 1969; Winham, 1970; Frey, 1973).

Other difficulties arise from the *diffuse* yet *problematic* place of communication in politics. On the one hand, all political life implies some form of communication activity. As Pye (1963) has pointed out, there is a "peculiarly intimate relationship between the political process and the communication process." If politics is about power, the holder's possession of and readiness to exercise it must in some manner be conveyed to those expected to respond to it. If politics is about participation, this consists in itself of "the means by which the interests, desires and demands of the ordinary citizen are communicated to rulers" (Verba, Nie and Kim, 1971). If politics is about the legitimation of supreme authority, then the values and procedural norms of regimes have to be symbolically expressed, and the acts of government have to be justified in broad popular terms. And if politics is about choice, then information flows clarifying alternative policy options must circulate to those concerned with decisions, whether as their shapers or as consumers of their consequences. Communication, then, is so ubiquitously embedded in politics that a bewildering embarrassment of riches confronts the would-be cross-national enquiry team. Objects of investigation must somehow be selected, and the principle of parsimony requires an economical yet productive choice (LaPalombara, 1970). But what exactly would it repay researchers to concentrate their comparative attention *on?*

On the other hand, empirical work has repeatedly shown that any defined set of communication factors typically accounts at best for only a limited proportion of the variance in any political phenomenon being studied. Even statistically significant indications of mass media effects on political attitudes usually consist of only low- to modest-sized correlations. This suggests that any attempt to identify political consequences attributable to the diverse communication arrangements operative in different societies could be bedeviled by the intrusion of many analytically extraneous forces. Although there can be no perfect solution to such a problem, the need to face up to it has both substantive and methodological implications. Substantively, it demands a selection for study of those areas of political outlook and behavior where consequences of communication arrangements are most likely to be found. Even so, extraneous forces will still be at work, which can be coped with methodologically in only one of two ways: (1) controlling them by conducting research in countries that are so far as possible similar politically, ideologically, economically and technologically; or (2) building them overtly into the research design so that their intervention, along with that of communication factors, can itself be compared in different polities. We are still a long way, however, from knowing how in practical detail to handle any such difficulty when it arises.

A PROPOSED POINT OF DEPARTURE

In fact, the obstacles outlined above seem so formidable as to be virtually off-putting. Is the game really worth the candle? Perhaps before canvassing various ways of organizing a comparative effort, we should ask the most prior question of all: why bother to study political communication cross-nationally? What has this line of research to offer that no other approach could provide?

Not only is there a clear answer to this question (at last!), but its terms also provide a point of departure for generating a conceptual framework in which a series of comparative political communication studies could be anchored. In a sense many political communication processes can be most fruitfully studied in all their concrete detail in single-country research—whether they be processes of communicator socialization, gate-keeping, campaigning, mobilization and participation, voting behavior effects, information diffusion, etc. It is true that the projection of any such work across national lines might dramatically expand "the range of variation in the national setting from which the . . . researcher draws his cases" (Frey, 1970), thereby providing "a population sample, for testing hypotheses, that offers greater extremes on relevant variables, and broader variation among irrelevant variables, than can be attained within a single culture" (Sears, 1961). But thus conceived, comparative research would pose no new questions for investigators to answer, only extend the data base for tackling old ones. Yet there *is* one highly important question on which single-country research, however comprehensive or sophisticated, can shed virtually no illumination at all: *how does the articulation of a country's mass media institutions to its political institutions affect the processing of political communication content and the impact of such content on the orientations to politics of audience members?*

Let us pause for clarification at this stage since such a formulation of a supposedly key issue has few precursors in the literature. Clearly the relationship of mass media institutions to political institutions is assumed in all states to have consequences of major import and is never left to chance. All political systems must one way or another regulate the performance of media institutions in the political field. In part this is because the mass media, through their relations with the audience, have access to a potentially independent power base in society (Gurevitch and Blumler, forthcoming). Partly it is because newspapers and broadcasting services do not merely supply a set of consumer goods but also "play a constitutional and political role in society" (Hirsch and Gordon, 1975). That is, they set much of the agenda of political debate. They help to determine which political demands will be aired, and consequently have a chance of being satisfied, and which others will be relatively muted. They affect the chances of governments and other political actors to secure essential supports (cf. Chaffee's chapter for a similar view). And they present a broader or narrower band of opinion about how the issues of the day should be tackled, structuring the options between which voters may choose. Consequently, care is taken in all states to identify those political agencies to which the media will be accountable and to specify the terms of their brief; to clarify the rights and obligations falling on both political and media personnel in the communication sphere; and to define and safeguard whatever freedoms are thought to belong to it. The universality of the assumption of a public stake in how the media operate politically is demonstrated by the fact that even regimes rooted in the most liberal traditions have found it necessary in recent years to set up commissions charged to enquire into the adequacy of press performance and to recommend remedies for any identified shortcomings.

Yet the consequences that flow from the regulatory arrangements made on the interface of political organization and media organization cannot be measured without introducing some comparative element. This is because in a single country at a given moment there can be *no variation* at this high structural level. It is true that such a comparison can be effected longitudinally over time within one country's borders where changes in the linkages of the media to politics have occurred during a particular historical period. On the other hand, as Frey (1973) has observed, "the big drawback to national time-series analysis is the problem of generalization," since it "usually deals with one or just a few nations." In addition, historical research in a single country is unlikely to encounter the same range of variation that can be found by cutting across national boundaries. In Britain, for example, there has been no significant change in the relationship of broadcasting to the state since the formation of the BBC in 1927. Thus, cross-national comparisons are essential to any attempt to probe and understand the effects of different ways of controlling the mass media politically; and a central ingredient in any framework for comparative political communication analysis must be a set of dimensions specifying how the linkages between political and mass media organizations may vary in different societies.

The recent work of Seymour-Ure (1974) and Hoyer et al. (1975) has already yielded many penetrating insights into one such linkage: the relationship between press systems and party systems. However, these investigators have been mainly interested in the societal conditions that favor a closer or more remote party involvement in press structures. For instance, Seymour-Ure shows how features of political culture and party organization have given rise to different degrees of what he terms "press-party parallelism"; and Hoyer et al. have carefully traced the impact of market conditions on the alignment of newspaper and party interests. A more fully-fledged comparative framework would strive to extend these ideas in two directions. First, what are the main *varieties of linkage* by which political and media institutions and personnel may be connected? Although press-party ties are undoubtedly one major form, we should not neglect other linkages that may be equally crucial. Second, what *consequences* are likely to flow from variations in how the mass media are politically regulated? Although Seymour-Ure and Hoyer et al. appear to assume that certain political functions of the media will co-vary with differences in press-party connections (Hoyer et al. perceive a party press as "conflict provoking", for example, as distinct from a more detached newspaper system which goes in for "conflict management and consensus building"), they do not try to spell out the full range of consequences that cross-national investigators might look for. On the whole, then, they treat the political attachments of the media in the manner of a dependent variable, responsive to prior historical circumstances, instead of treating them as an independent variable, capable of prompting measurable developments at other levels of communication and political systems.

POLITICAL AND MEDIA STRUCTURES:
FOUR DIMENSIONS OF LINKAGE

Our first theoretical task is to conceive a set of dimensions along which the connections between media institutions and political institutions may vary. Since the purpose of such a scheme is to facilitate and guide cross-national research, its elements should a) together cover the most important features of any country's political communication structure and b) be such as to tap and explain differences in the political performance of media systems under highly varying structural conditions. Accordingly, we propose a framework, consisting of four dimensions, by reference to which the political communication arrangements of different states could be profiled, and their further consequences for the production, reception and wider repercussions of political messages could be hypothetically specified:

(1) Degree of state control over mass media organizations; (2) Degree of mass media partisanship; (3) Degree of media-political elite integration; (4) The nature of the legitimizing creed of media institutions.

Degree of State Control

Despite the seeming familiarity of the dimension of degree of state control over media organization, its conceptualization bristles with many awkward difficulties. First, although Nixon (1965) has shown that media systems can be subjectively characterized as more or less subordinate to government control, even informed judges may be guided by different criteria or be misled by appearances. Are there any manifestations of media subordination, then, that could be translated into a more objectively compiled set of indicators? Second, the notion of "state control" itself is quite wide-ranging: its expressions are legion and its targets myriad. What specific forms of control, then, most merit inclusion in a measure of media subjection to (or autonomy from) the state? Third, we need to avoid the trap of conceptualizing freedom of communication in exclusively dichotomous terms—as if it prevailed in certain societies and was absent in others without susceptibility to significant gradation in either camp. Such a distinction is not entirely false, as Siebert et al. (1956) realized when differentiating liberal from authoritarian "theories of the press." Communication will certainly assume a different role in those societies where (a) political organization is essentially monopolistic, (b) political truth is believed to inhere in the tenets of some authoritative doctrine as interpreted by a ruling party and (c) the mass media are primarily expected to uphold such a unitary conception of political truth, from those societies in which (a) diverse political organizations compete with each other for popular support, (b) the legitimating creed of the state transcends all existing political formations (none is assumed perfectly to embody it) and (c) the mass media are expected, individually or in concert, to transmit a variety of political standpoints. In the first case political control of the media will seem natural and legitimate, and in the second its imposition will always require a special justification (Franklin, 1973). Nevertheless, even in the first situation professional communicators may enjoy more or less latitude to cover political affairs according to their own lights, while in the second freedom of communication may be limited by a more tightly or loosely woven web of restrictions. Politicians and media men in both camps certainly do behave as if crucial consequences did in fact flow from these distinctions.

Some of these difficulties may be eased by dimensionalizing in terms of the *commonly exercised rights*[1] *of governments (or agencies responsive to their wills)*[2] *to intervene in the affairs of the mass media*[3] *so as to regulate their communication performance.* [4] This formulation directs attention to certain concrete areas where such rights of intervention may exist and where the resulting degree of state control could be fairly readily measured as if at high, intermediate or low levels. In particular three such areas may be singled out on the grounds (1) that when rulers strive to bend the media to their wills their efforts are most commonly directed to these fields and (2) that in less controlled systems media men jealously guard their independence in precisely these respects. They are: control over the appointment of media personnel; control over the financing of media enterprises; and control over media content.

Control over appointments can be a powerful instrument of subordination by ensuring a stationing of politically reliable individuals inside the media instead of obliging rulers to depend on the problematic impact of external pressures and sanctions on the behavior of communication staffs. This form of control mixes two elements: a right of political appointment; and a belief that political criteria are relevant to the selection of media personnel. At one extreme all appointments could be based on the political credentials of the candidates. Or recruitment might be restricted to candidates who had first undergone approved training and socialization procedures including some element of political indoctrination. Or media personnel might have to be licensed, thereby giving the licensing authority a power to grant or withhold permission to work in the communication sector. Such comprehensive devices are unlikely to be found in systems sensitive to the creed of freedom of expression, where a more limited political control may focus on appointments to top positions in media organizations. A good example of low control of this kind may be found in the British system of public service broadcasting, where the Prime Minister merely appoints the governors of the BBC and the members of the Independent Broadcasting Authority, and where no stipulation reserves these posts for politically affiliated individuals.[5] In contrast, there is a stronger right of state intervention in certain continental systems, either because the government may appoint to executive posts (e.g. Directors-General) as well as to supervisory boards, or because many board places are specifically set aside for politicians.

On the principle that he who pays the piper calls the tune—or at any rate is less likely to have to listen to uncongenial and discordant tunes—*control over media finance* may also be a powerful vehicle of state subordination. Such a form of control will function differently according to the sources from which media organizations draw their revenues. Those organizations which depend entirely or in great part on directly provided government funds are clearly most open to direct political control. Even where the media derive their income from their own clientele, however, whether on the basis of sales (as in the press), of a license fee (as in some broadcasting systems) or of advertising (both press and broadcasting), governments may institutionalize their rights of intervention either by subjecting these sources of income to government approval (e.g. when license fees are raised) or by special taxes (e.g. a levy on advertising revenue). Media operating in such conditions usually prefer them to the tighter financial controls perceived to inhere in government funding per se. In Britain, for example, the BBC is at this writing waging a determined campaign to preserve the license fee system, arguing that its present freedom would be jeopardized if radio and television services had to depend directly on government grants. In some countries a spate of actual and threatened newspaper closures has recently spurred state provision of supplementary financial aid in many forms. The press has been variously helped by newsprint subsidies, reduced postal charges, and grants intended to shore up papers in secondary market positions. The degree of financial subordination involved in these arrangements may depend less on the size of the funds available for subsidy, however, than on how they are allocated—whether by discretionary decision, enabling administrators to discriminate between different media outlets, or by more automatically applicable objective criteria. Thus, media systems in different countries may be placed on a continuum according to the proximity of their revenue sources to the government, the degree to which governments maintain legal holds over non-governmental sources of revenue, and the degree of discretion enjoyed by a political authority in allocating the funds at its disposal.

The existence of political *control over media content* may be more important for its indirect repercussions on the work of professional communicators than for instances of its direct exercise. For one thing a need to apply the control by censoring some media article in advance of its appearance, or by subsequently punishing its authors and publishers, is a sign that the system has in a sense failed. For another, no theoretical order could possibly be superimposed on the many discrete and variable grounds by which content regulation may be justified in different regimes.[6] Content control, then, is theoretically interesting primarily in its role as a sanction, capable through its background presence of influencing the behavior and attitudes of communicators in advance of, or while preparing, media output. If so, what might matter in placing political communication systems on a continuum from high to low control of this kind would be (a) the overall range of content that may be subject to regulation, (b) the degree of specificity inherent in such regulation (more specific injunctions entailing less latitude) and (c) how far the control system is operated directly by the political authorities themselves or by intermediary bodies, such as quasi-judicial regulatory agencies or communication councils.

Degree of Mass Media Partisanship

The mass media may be tied to political parties as well as to government agencies. Accordingly, our second main dimension of political communication structure focuses on the *degree of partisan commitment* exhibited by mass media outlets. Although the manifestations of media partisanship are not so complex as in the case of state control, they are also not quite so straightforward as might seem at first sight to be the case. Seymour-Ure's (1974) notion of "press-party parallelism" rests on three criteria: party involvement in mass media ownership and management; the editorial policies of newspapers; and the party affiliations of readers. We would eliminate the last criterion from a structurally-focused definition of media partisanship, however, since it is an important empirical question how far party linkages of an organizational and editorial kind give rise to selective audience patronage patterns along party lines.

Nevertheless, the determinants of media partisanship are indeed multiple. They include any organizational connections to political parties, the stability and intensity of editorial commitments and presence or absence of legal restraints on the rights of the media to back individual parties. In combination these would allow for five levels of media partisanship. The highest degree of partisan involvement exists when the parties are directly associated with the running of media enterprises via ownership, provision of financial subsidy or membership on management and editorial boards. Some examples of highly partisan systems in this sense may be found in Scandinavia, where there is a strong party press, and in Holland, where TV and radio programing are to some extent the responsibility of separate, politically affiliated broadcasting bodies. Next, there is a condition of voluntary fixed partisanship, where, short of any structural connection of the parties to the media, a party may count on the unconditional and unswerving loyalty of a particular organ—as in the support invariably given the Conservatives by the Daily Telegraph in Britain or that given the Republicans by the Chicago Tribune in the United States. A third level reflects a more qualified brand of partisanship, where a medium may usually back a favored party but where the support tends to be conditioned by the expression of numerous qualifications, hesitations and references to party short-comings as well as by a readiness to see some merit in the policies of opposing parties (including even an occasional refusal to proffer the customary election endorsement). Some observers judge that one consequence of the growing importance of political television in many countries has been a shift by newspapers from the second to the third of these levels of partisan identification (Thoveron and Nobre-Correia, 1974; Seymour-Ure, 1974; Butler and Stokes, 1974). Fourthly, there is an ad hoc and in a sense unpredictable form of partisanship, where the political stance of a medium is determined afresh according to the merits of the case perceived as decisive each time a need to declare a preference arises. Finally, there is a condi-tion of non-partisanship in which a communication outlet may not take sides and strives at all cost to maintain its political neutrality, as exemplified by those broadcasting organizations that are obliged by law or charter to refrain from openly supporting any political position.

Degree of Media-Political Elite Integration

The two dimensions outlined so far apply mainly to certain *formal* arrangements through which political influence over the media may be channeled. However, much of the mutual responsiveness to each other of the personnel working in these spheres may be due to less formal aspects of the relationship between them. Hence, there is a need for an additional dimension, focusing on the degree of integra-tion between media elites and political elites, and serving to identify and highlight some of the *informal* mechanisms through which influence flows, in both directions, may be managed.

The hub of concern here is the degree of political affinity and social-cultural proximity that obtains between these two sets of structurally differentiated elites. Clearly in most political systems media organizations are to some degree structurally differentiated from political institutions. This structural gap may nevertheless be bridged in various ways. First, members of media elites may be recruited from or socialized into the same social and cultural back-grounds that characterize members of political elites and thus come to share similar interests and uphold similar values. Second, there may be an overlap of personnel. Many media elite members may either support particular parties and even undertake activity on their behalf or alternatively think of themselves as lukewarm adherents or as "independents." Contrariwise some legislators may be drawn from the ranks of ex-journalists. Moreover, as the persuasion process becomes more intense and specialized, "boundary" agencies may be formed both in political institutions (press officers) and the media (public relations or liaison officers), staffed by individuals with experience in the "other" domain. Finally, outside the specifically vocational contexts where politicians and professional communicators meet, members of media and political elites may engage in more or less informal interaction with each other, perhaps belonging to the same clubs, mixing in the same circles and generally seeing each other more or less often for diffuse social purposes. Such contacts may promote a growth of mutual understanding among individuals in these different elites, rendering them more responsive to each other's views and problems.

The Nature of the Legitimizing Creed of Media Institutions

A central mechanism that may act as a check against the formal and informal tendencies to subordinate media performance to politicians' goals may be found in the occupational creeds embraced by members of media professions. Essentially media professionalism implies a "distancing" of the reporter, commentator, producer or media executive from the pressures of "external" interests and a fidelity to the internally generated norms of the profession itself. Creeds promoting such an insulation may be compounded in varying mixes of such elements as: belief in the primacy of service to the audience member (over and above any duties owed to organized political authority); emphasis on the need to master certain specialist communication skills before audiences can be addressed effectively; belief in the watchdog function of journalism and the need for media personnel to adopt an adversary stance in their relations with politicians; and commitment to such universalistic criteria of political truth as impartiality and objectivity, at the expense of tenets of party doctrine.[7] In short, communication systems may be classified according to the degree to which the legitimizing creed underlying them expects media personnel to pay allegiance and give service to some hegemonic or party-determined ideology or conversely gives pride of place to "professional rationality" and requires media professionals to behave as if above the political battle.

POLITICAL COMMUNICATION STRUCTURES
AND THEIR CONSEQUENCES: THREE AREAS OF EFFECT

How exactly do the political communication arrangements outlined in the foregoing pages matter? Where should we look for
evidence of their impact on media reporting of political events and
how citizens react to such coverage? The literature is surprisingly
void of systematically framed attempts to answer such questions.
Perhaps observers have been so fascinated by the tensions inherent in
the struggle of politicians to control communication organs in the
teeth of professional resistance that speculation about *outcomes*
traceable to differences in this relationship has been in short supply.
Our next theoretical task, then, is to elucidate some of the consequences that might flow from variations in the structural linkages
between the mass media and politics. At this stage theoretical order
would not be much advanced if we simply laid out an assorted
scatter of postulated effects. Therefore we have striven to define
below a limited set of dimensions capable in each case of accom-
modating a large number of related consequences. In conceiving
them we have focused on phenomena that (a) should be sensitive to
structurally-derived influences, (b) might be amenable to cross-
national comparison and (c) would represent some of the most
deep-seated perspectives likely to underlie the political outlook and
behavior of citizens when responding to political communication
flows.

In sum three dimensions of the effects of political communication
arrangements seem to meet these conditions. They are: (1) the
valuation of politics as such; (2) degree of partisan commitment; (3)
degree of consensus over society's agenda of political issues. Each of
these dimensions has been so conceived as to embrace consequences
at both the medium level and the audience level. At medium level
they will be visible in both the ground-rules that professionals are
expected to comply with when processing political outputs, as well
as in the amount and direction of media contents that are devoted to
political affairs. At audience level these consequences will be manifested in the orientations of individuals to political communication
and in their attitudes to closely related features of the political
system. Thus, our overall theoretical framework proceeds from the
structural linkages of media institutions to the political system, via
the performance of media institutions as reflected in ground-rules of
political output processing and consequential variations of content

patterning, to the attitudinal and behavioral linkages of individual citizens to the political systems in which they live.

The Valuation of Politics as Such

Politics is a field of activity that can attract or repel, engage people or turn them off, be thought worthy of respect or be treated with indifference and contempt. The precariousness of its attraction renders it vulnerable to various influences, among them some that stem from the perceptions that people form of the connections between communication sources and political institutions.

This dimension of politicization runs like a vertical thread through all the ranks and levels of the political communication system. Media personnel may enthuse about their political duties or approach them in a perfunctory spirit. Media organizations may employ a larger or smaller team of specialist political correspondents. Their ground-rules may reflect either a "sacerdotal" or a "pragmatic" attitude to the claims of political items, in the former case regarding political coverage as an intrinsically important service that must be provided as of right, and in the latter insisting that political material should fight its way into print and programs on its news value merits alone (Blumler, 1969). Media organs may devote a larger or smaller proportion of their space and time to the airing of political questions. The content they do provide may concentrate on explaining and interpreting the substantive issues of politics, or treat them instead as mere counters in a power game to be followed for the drama and spectacle that its ups and downs afford (Weaver, 1973). Similarly, audience members may be more or less politicized. They may be more or less interested in political affairs, find political decisions more or less relevant to their personal lives, be better or less well informed, feel a keener or lesser sense of duty to be involved, and be prepared to participate more or less actively in their country's political processes. They may also assume different roles in the political communication system, adopting that of a "monitor", for example, if looking primarily for cognitive insights into developments, or that of a "spectator", if interested more in the affective "thrills and spills" connected with the fluctuating fortunes of the leading actors performing in the political arena (Blumler, 1973). Finally, people may repose a higher or lower degree of trust in the authenticity of political messages and in the integrity of their sources.

But how might structural differences in the linkages of the media to political institutions affect some of these manifestations of valuations placed on politics as such? Different answers to this question may be generated in the form of opposed hypotheses, which reflect in turn their origins in contrasts of function, role and perspective that inhere in the differentiation of political from media personnel.

On the one hand, there is a *subordination-promotes-politicization hypothesis*. This reflects the outlook of politicians who are suspicious of the incorrigibly "trivializing" tendencies of independent media professionals when presenting political news and views (Crossman, 1969). In their eyes subordination (in all its forms) should serve to check these tendencies and help to bring political communication processing, content provision and audience outlook in line with the high regard and respectful attention that this supremely important sphere of life deserves. According to this standpoint, then, more subordination will yield more political content of an essentially serious kind that will be followed more avidly, with a monitor's concern to become well-informed, by members of the audience.

On the other hand, there is an *autonomy-promotes-politicization hypothesis*. Reflecting the outlook of professional communicators who stress the need for their own intermediary intervention before messages will be meaningful and credible to audiences, this view regards subordination in all its forms (especially state-linked) as counter-productive to politicization. The subordination hypothesis (above) is dismissed especially for failing to take account of the critical and prior role of trust. In subordinate systems political intervention will be seen by media personnel and audience members alike as mechanisms designed to control and limit comment on behalf of "external" elements. Politics may be perceived as a closed game, limited to a small number of powerful, remote and inaccessible players who produce messages that merely voice their own interests. Consequently trust will be impaired, leading to a loss of attention and a reduction of respect for what goes on in the political arena. Conversely, less restrictive arrangements may encourage media personnel to exercise independence and initiative in covering political affairs, and audience members to show more interest in politics and to pay more attention to materials about it.

One feature of both positions as stated is their global character. Subordination on all axes generates, as it were, more (or less) politicization according to one's philosophic taste. This may highlight an advantage of our own insistence on breaking down the linkages of the mass media to the political system into a multiplicity of dimensions and subsidiary forms. For politicization could conceivably be responsive to different combinations of influences stemming from different dimensions of subordination. Thus, our framework could be drawn on to frame *interaction hypotheses* about the structural sources of high or low politicization. Consider two contrasting examples. One refers to those systems that are already marked by a quite high development among professional communicators of an ideology of political independence and accountability to the audience. In such circumstances increments of extra subordination along the other three structural dimensions might well act as a counter-weight against sensational and mistrustful styles of reporting, and so promote and facilitate a growth of politicization at other levels. Contrariwise, in systems that are already marked by a high degree of state subordination, trust and its other politicizing concomitants might well increase as media elites distance themselves from political elites and develop a more self-conscious view of the independent political function they should be serving.

Degree of Partisan Commitment

A second major area of structurally-derived effects focuses on identifications with the main contestants in the political arena. This does not concern the *particular* sides that people may decide to support but rather their readiness to back *any* of the available power-competitors. The converse of such partisan commitment is not political apathy, or dismissal of all politics as uninteresting and political communication as untrustworthy, but rather an attitude of political open-mindedness and a disposition to accord an equal hearing to all viewpoints. The hypothetical derivation of consequences in this area from linkages of the mass media to the political system is more straight-forward than was the case with "politics as such." We may primarily postulate a hand-in-glove relationship between the range and intensity of party ties to the media at the structural level, and degree of partisan commitment at other levels. This association may be intensified or leavened, however, by parallel linkages along the dimensions of media-political elite integration and media professionalism.

Manifestations of media partisanship may be found, first of all, in the various ground-rules for processing political material that obtain in different media outlets. For example, those which are committed to non-partisanship may operate ground-rules that lean over backwards to guarantee a balanced coverage of all political parties. An example may be found in Blumler's (1969) account of how BBC producers covered the British General Election campaign of 1966 on television:

> When the last *Election Forum* was being prepared, for example, the reporters spent much time looking for a suitable final question to put to Mr. Wilson. They sought one that would give to the Labour Leader the same opportunity that Mr. Heath had enjoyed on the previous night to wind up with a positive and broad-ranging summary of his party's election case. When preparing an item on floating voters for *Campaign Report,* many filmed interviews were inspected before the producers were satisfied that the reason given by a Labour leaner for supporting the Government would seem as convincing as the material they intended to present from a pro-Conservative leaner. And during a *24 Hours* debate on housing, instructions were passed on to the interviewer to steer the discussion into an area of presumed Labour strength (rents and local authority housing), so that it would not be dominated by challenges to other aspects of the Government's record in this field.

Alternatively, in media under more partisan influences, the ground-rules may include formulas intended to justify a favored treatment of certain positions. An example is Cayrol's (1974) finding, from a study of broadcasting coverage of the French Parliamentary elections of 1973, that ORTF staff deemed it "quite normal for the Government to have special access to television" over and above the rights of non-ruling parties. Next, structural differences may be reflected in patterns of media content itself—for example, in the inclusion of varying amounts of committed editorial comment; in the provision of a one-sided or more balanced platform for the statements and views of different party spokesmen; and in the headlining and angling of news reports themselves. At the audience level, we may or may not find that party-linked media attract followings that are predominantly determined by the party affiliations of readers, listeners and viewers.[8] And, more subtly, individual audience members may either follow politics in an open-minded, non-committed fashion, looking for materials that may help them provisionally to make up their own minds on the points at issue between the competing parties, adopting the role, then, of "vote-guidance seekers"; or they may be aiming more single-mindedly to bolster and strengthen a partisan commitment already entered into, taking up the role, so to speak, of "reinforcement seekers" (Blumler, 1973).

The dimension underlying these various ramifications is reminiscent of Parsons and Shils' (1951) pattern variable of universalism-particularism. People and institutions may be oriented to political conflict either in terms of their affiliations to particular parties, in which case the key values being upheld would include loyalty, a forthright readiness to take sides and steadfastness of commitment; or with reference to such more abstract, universal and, in a sense, disembodied principles as impartiality, fairness, objectivity and measured choice. It is intriguing to note here the possible bearing of this distinction on the rising tide of electoral volatility that has recently been observed in a number of western countries. It is not all that fanciful to suspect that some part of this development may be traceable to the increasing intervention in politics of the essentially non-partisan and highly universalistic medium of television (Blumler, 1974; Butler and Stokes, 1974; Thomsen and Sauerberg, 1975). This underlines the urgency of mounting research that is capable of clarifying the part played by the universalistic or particularistic orientations of different communication outlets, in steering audience members towards one or the other of these polar attitudes.

The Structure of the Political Agenda

A third area where the political connections of the mass media might have measurable consequences concerns the main issues forming the political agenda of a society at a particular time. What we have in mind here is related to, but not identical with, the numerous "agenda-setting" studies that have played such an important part in the recent revival of scholarly interest in studying political communication effects (see Becker, McCombs and McLeod chapter) but which might at first sight seem unsuited to cross-national comparisons. After all, the individual issue items featuring in such work inevitably tend to be colored by unique national circumstances—e.g. the honesty-in-government theme following the Watergate disclosures in the United States and the balance-of-payments issue in Britain. By shifting the focus of attention away from the determination of *individual* issue concerns and towards the *overall shape* of the agenda placed before the public, however, the area becomes more amenable to comparative research and also opens up facets of agenda-setting that have received little attention so far.

Questions can be raised about the main sources of issue inputs. Are they dictated chiefly by political leaders or do they stem from the perspectives of media professionals? In more autonomous systems, media ground-rules may encourage journalists to inject their own view of the issues that count into the political debate; in more subordinate systems, professional self-restraint may be more the order of the day. Turning to media content, the political affiliations of media outlets may affect the degree of consensus they reach in terms of the issues that are emphasized most frequently and prominently. Here we can postulate the emergence of a high degree of consensus in situations where the media tend to give play to various issues on the basis of standardized and widely shared criteria of news value. Hence, in relatively autonomous systems, unencumbered by external controls, the application of professional criteria to the selection and presentation of political issues would result in a consensual view of the political agenda.[9] In single-party systems this might lead to a high degree of consensus among the different media, albeit based on political rather than news-value judgments. In party-linked multi-party systems we might expect the media to put forward more divergent views about the items that belong on the national agenda. Finally, at the audience level, we would expect a reproduction of these same patterns—citizen consensus over issues being higher in both autonomous and single-party subordinate systems, and lower in highly partisan systems with low state control.

SOME PRIORITIES OF PRACTICAL ACTION

By pegging out a far-flung conceptual terrain, asserting numerous propositions about associations among phenomena to be found in it, and raising controversial issues of philosophy and definition, the authors hope that the foregoing pages will have made some contribution to that revival of theoretical speculation which must precede any empirical advance on the comparative political communication front. Once one leaves the exhilarating realm of theory, however, to enter the more workaday world of practical implementation, it becomes obvious that no part of the scheme that has been outlined could be carried out overnight. Before any attempt can be made to validate, modify or discard the various hypothetical statements propounded above about the consequences that flow from national variations of political communication structure, a long program of instrument-fashioning must be initiated. Because of the large number and extreme diversity of the variables that jostle each other in one complex page, this could be a formidable and demanding process. That is why it is essential to think in terms of *priorities* of advance: What are the steps that most urgently need to be taken if the theoretical framework presented here is to become more practically operational and testable?

Inventory Extension and Country Classification

One line of attack would strive to increase the number of communication measures on which as many societies as possible (ideally all societies) could be compared. The main thrust of this effort should be directed toward preparing a set of measures for as many countries as possible of the structural subordination of media institutions to political institutions along both the state-control and party-linkage dimensions. It will be no easy task to generate the required categories and to classify countries in terms of them. It will require a painstaking search through masses of variegated documentary material—statutes, media charters, and other instruments of media organization and finance—ascertaining what data are available for different countries and trying out different ways of bringing them within common analysis frames. This will involve a struggle to standardize definitions of variables and procedures for placing political units along the continua they reflect. It will call for ingenuity in constructing composite indices out of multiple subsidiary criteria. On a task of such magnitude and complexity, significant progress cannot be made by solitary investigators or even by a research team based in a single country. Resources would need to be pooled on a cross-national scale. For inventory extension, probably only a fully international body with near-universal membership, such as UNESCO, could muster the resources for the necessary effort.

A Build-Up of Other Critical Instruments

A different approach would be required to deal with the other variables that are critical to the theoretical framework—especially the degree of integration between media and political elites, and the nature of the legitimizing creed that defines the role of media professionals in the political communication process. Measurement of the roles adopted by audience members when following political affairs could also profit from such exploratory attention. Clearly, the adequate measurement of these variables would necessitate much prior pilot fieldwork, conducted in a range of carefully selected multi-national sites, and aimed at (a) identifying empirically the main components of the multi-dimensional fields they cover and (b) ensuring the cross-national equivalence of whatever measuring instruments are developed. It is not supposed that such an effort would need to start entirely from scratch; in each case there is a fund of past theoretical and empirical work that could be drawn upon. Even so, its products might have to be substantially modified, so as to meet the conceptual demands of our scheme and to be subjected to some tests of cross-national validation.

The previous discussion of degree of media-political elite integration has suggested that this might be measured along at least three dimensions. Similarities of socio-cultural background between members of the two elites would require collection of those items of information that are deemed relevant for describing and identifying the location of individuals within the stratification systems of different societies. Thus, although in many societies information about level and type of education would be central to this exercise, in other settings, other variables, such as ethnic origin, regional origins, personal wealth, religious affiliation, or even less ascriptive data, such as information about military service or membership of diverse clubs and associations, could tap different facets of the attributes that matter in comparing different elite sectors. In the case of exchange of personnel between the two domains, information would be needed about the occupational histories of members of the media and political elites. Finally, more direct measures of the frequency and type of contacts linking members of media elites with those of political elites would be required. This could involve an adaptation of the techniques of "network analysis", designed to measure the degree to which the universes of acquaintanceships and contacts of different individuals are confined to members of their own occupational domain or extend to members of other elite circles as well (Barton et al., 1973; Boissevain, 1974; Mitchell, 1969).

In the case of *professionals' legitimizing ideologies,* the published work on mass media professionalization is only indirectly relevant as it stands. For example, the eleven criteria of professionalism used by McLeod and Rush (1969) to compare journalists' attitudes in the United States and Latin America—including emphases on special skills and training, a concern for career advancement, respect for colleagues, freedom from internal supervision, etc.—could be applied to the members of any profession; they refer only obliquely to the specifically political functions of journalism. Even the work of Johnstone et al. (1972-73) on newsmen's values takes for granted the socialization of journalists to norms of neutrality and objectivity. We still need to devise a measure that focuses more directly on attitudes promoting or inhibiting a distancing of journalists from the goals of political authorities.

In the case of *audience roles* in the political communication system, past work is more securely established so far as face applicability is concerned. Blumler (1973) claims to have detected four types of audience members in terms of motivations to follow mass media coverage of political events: the "monitor", looking for information about political developments relevant to his own circumstances; the "spectator", looking for excitement and other affective gratifications; the "liberal citizen", looking for help in making up his mind between posited alternatives; and the "partisan", seeking a reinforcement of his existing beliefs and loyalties. However, the empirical independence of these dimensions has not yet been confirmed, and their cross-national equivalence has certainly not been tested.

How might serviceable measures of such critical variables be developed? An indispensable precondition would be the organization of a cross-national collaborative team whose members would jointly attempt to construct and validate a set of appropriate instruments in each case. A sequence of three steps might then be followed. First, pilot work should be undertaken in countries chosen to maximize cultural difference so that the measures that eventually emerge can be applied with greater confidence in a variety of settings. Second, a sizable battery of items that are assumed to reflect different facets of the outlook in question should be administered to samples in each of the participating countries. Third, endorsements of the items should be subjected to multi-dimensional analysis to ascertain whether their dimensional structure is sufficiently common to make cross-national measurement and comparison meaningful and to establish just what the key dimensions are.

Observation Studies Inside Media Institutions

A third line of advance is more limited in focus than the preceding suggestions, but is potentially rich in the insights to be gained; its pursuit could help to fill what might otherwise be a glaring gap in our stock of cross-national political communication measures. The strategy proposed here is prompted by the fact that although a number of observational studies have been conducted by academics stationed in media enterprises at crucial political periods in recent years (Blumler, 1969; Cayrol, 1974; Gans, 1971; Kumar, 1975; Waltzer, 1966; Warner, 1969) the results are disparate, difficult to compare and have not gravitated toward any common analytical core. This situation could be immeasurably improved by the adoption of three guidelines. First, investigators given facilities to observe the political workings of a mass media organization should sensitize themselves to the concept of "ground-rules of political output processing." That is, they should aim to formulate at least some of their findings in terms of the kinds of ground-rules that were explicated by media personnel under questioning or were regarded by the observers as implicit in the procedures they followed. Next, these formulations should be collected from as many situations as possible and sifted with the aim of producing a number of items couched as statements about mass media policies of political coverage. Finally, such a battery of statements would be administered in surveys of media personnel, working on political materials in different countries, for evaluation as accurate or inaccurate reflections of the policies adopted in their own organizations.

Testing the Model

Only after some of these prior tasks of instrumentation have been completed will it be feasible to try to test the model as a whole.[10] This implies a comparative in-depth study of the media in politics in a few selected countries, organized perhaps through regionally-based political science, public opinion, or related disciplinary associations. Participating countries should be chosen so as to minimize differences of technological, economic, political and cultural development, and hence to maximize the chance of detecting significant associations of communication variations. A strategy for this approach would need to deploy more or less simultaneously a range of measures of different kinds—i.e. of structural linkage, media ground-rules, content variation, and audience outlook—straddling the different levels of analysis implied by the conceptual framework. It is mainly through such a design that hypotheses generated from theoretical speculation can be profitably tested. Although it is true that the findings of such a study would strictly speaking be applicable only to the settings from which they were drawn, they would nevertheless have a wider relevance in two respects. First, by stimulating theory modification, they could influence the design of studies subsequently mounted in other regions and cultural settings. Secondly, even findings from a limited subset of societies can provide a basis for informed guesses (or hypotheses) about their application to other countries, particularly if we know how the latter are placed (via inventory extension, for example) along the structural dimensions that provide the central pillars of the comparative framework outlined in this chapter.

RIVAL PERSPECTIVES

The philosophical orientation underlying this chapter should by now be clear. It treats seriously certain distinctions that adherents of other philosophic positions tend to dismiss as relatively insignificant. It supposes that media systems may be classified as more or less subordinate to, or autonomous from, the political institutions of society; that such structural differences give rise to a differential processing of political material and manner of presenting political ideas, issues and events to the public; and that political communication processes in different societies, as initiated or mediated by more-or-less autonomous media, will have differential consequences for the linkages between individual citizens and their political systems.

Disagreement with this viewpoint comes in several shapes and sizes. Some analysts have maintained that the media in all societies play an essentially passive role, and hence are bound to be subservient to the political order:

> Essentially the mass media do not produce anything original; their normal function is to transmit news. At certain moments of history the mass media may be able to influence the timing of political events, but in the long run the media must adapt to the institutions which are its information sources; they are thus likely to reproduce certain features of the political order (Hoyer et al., 1975).

Others regard the mass media as transmitters of a hegemonically-shaped consensus of social and political values:

> The mass media cannot ensure complete conservative attunement; nothing can. But they can and do contribute to the fostering of a climate of conformity, not by the total suppression of dissent, but by the presentation of views which fall outside the consensus as curious heresies, or, even more effectively, by treating them as irrelevant eccentricities, which serious and reasonable people may dismiss as of no consequence (Miliband, 1969).

Yet others suspect that we have concentrated our attention on a merely "formal autonomy" of media institutions "from the state and government" (Hall, 1974) and indeed that media production is always and everywhere subject to control:

> There is no such thing as unmanipulated writing, filming or broadcasting. The question is, therefore, not whether the media are manipulated but who manipulates them (Garnham, 1973).

The essence of our response to these rival perspectives takes two forms. First, they pay less than sufficient regard to the relationship that the mass media can enter into with their *audiences*—a relationship of dependence and trust that provides them with a potentially independent power base in society, which explains in turn the insistent but varying attempts of many political authorities to control their operations. We have therefore treated the extent to which variations in such forms of control are productive of major consequences at other levels as an empirical question, to be settled by implementing suitably devised research designs. The answers, of course, are not pre-determined. When they emerge, they might even support the scepticism expressed in the rival perspectives quoted above.

Secondly, we are aware of a failure of many members of these other camps to suggest how the accuracy of their picture of the place of the media in politics might be tested. If the focus of analysis is shifted towards the inescapably political character of the mass media and their inevitable dependence on the distribution of external power forces, then we must apparently view the media as if in a *fixed and unvarying* relationship to the world of politics. It is difficult to see how such a perspective could be effectively substituted for our own as a methodological corner-stone of comparative political communication analysis.

NOTES

1. The phrase, "commonly exercised rights" is intended to exclude from consideration sweeping legal powers over communication that are only rarely or never applied in practice.

2. The identification of these agencies must be settled empirically for each regime. In certain systems, for example, one might wish to exclude or give less weight to common law restrictions enforced by an independent judiciary.

3. We are more interested here in controls over mass media performance than in laws applying to the utterances and conduct of private individuals (e.g., communication behavior in demonstrations).

4. We exclude governmental regulations applying generally to all industries such as industrial relations and taxation laws, as distinct from those which are aimed at communication control as such.

5. Some observers regarded it as in breach of traditional practice when for a time the chariman of the BBC was an ex-Conservative minister and that of the IBA was a former Labour Minister; relief was expressed when both individuals were eventually replaced by top educators.

6. These may include, for example, breaches of the peace, defamation, slander and libel, invasions of privacy, reporting inimical to a fair trial or in contempt of court, publishing of obscene or other indecent and corrupting articles, safeguarding official secrets and security-sensitive information, and, in the case of many broadcasting systems, doctrines

prescribing fairness and impartiality in presenting opposing views on controversial issues and bans on editorializing. See chapter by Gillmor and Dennis on legal research.

7. Ij is interesting to try to relate these observations to the distinction drawn by Johnstone et al. (1972-73) between advocates of a neutral and restrained, as opposed to a more challenging and participant, press in the debate raging in the United States at present "over the definition of responsible journalistic practice." The former views the journalist as someone who transmits news to the public that has emerged naturally from events, while the latter endows him with a more creative part to play in cultivating public understanding of what is newsworthy; but both positions share common ground in shunning particularistic commitments and a taking of sides. Thus the more passive view insists on "the observer's neutrality vis-a-vis information" while the more active one demands detachment from other political actors: "sources provide leads but the reporter must sift them for the real story." Beyond the United States, however, this nub of journalistic consensus may crumble, and some newsmen may aim overtly to throw their weight behind one side or the other in a political conflict. Of Portuguese journalists, for example, it has recently been said (The Guardian, June 9, 1975) that, lacking a "tradition of independent professionalism" after 48 years of dictatorship, they "could be defined as party politicians who have taken to writing."

8. Despite the keen interest of political communication scholars in selective exposure patterns, this seemingly elementary source of a party-biased audience structure has not yet been subjected to a sustained empirical analysis. The problem is confounded, of course, by a confusion of party-based selectivity with other social-background determinants of media use that may also be associated with party allegiance. Controls for educational attainment and prior political interest would also be needed in any study designed to examine how far the structural ties of individual media to individual parties give rise to audience patronage along party lines.

9. It is perhaps in this interpretive context that the McCombs and Shaw (1972) findings of "a high degree of consensus among the news media about the significant issues" of the 1968 presidential campaign in the United States should be placed.

10. Of course the studies proposed for the prior task of instrumentation need not be viewed only as services to be performed in the cause of testing this particular model. In many cases their execution would be inherently worthwhile, adding substantially to our knowledge of how the political communication process works in different countries.

REFERENCES

ALKER, H. (1966) "Causal influence and political analysis," in J. Bernd (ed.) Mathematical Applications in Political Science. Dallas: Southern Methodist University Press.
BARTON, A., B. DENITCH and C. KADUSHIN (eds.) (1973) Opinion-Making Elites in Yugoslavia. New York: Praeger.
BLUMLER, J. G. (1969) "Producers' attitudes towards television coverage of an election campaign: A case study." Sociological Rev. Monographs 13: 85-115.
——— (1973) "Audience roles in political communication: Their antecedents, structure and consequences," presented to International Political Science Assn.
——— (1974) "Mass media reactions and roles in the February election," in H. R. Penniman (ed.) Britain at the Polls: The Parliamentary Election of February 1974. Washington, D.C.: American Enterprise Institute for Policy Research.
BOISSEVAIN, J. (1974) Friends of Friends. Oxford: Basil Blackwell.
BUTLER, D. and D. STOKES (1974) Political Change in Britain. London: Macmillan.
CAYROL, R. (1974) "The ORTF and the March 1973 elections," presented to workshop on the political role of the mass media of the European Consortium for Political Research.

CROSSMAN, R. (1969) The Politics of Television. London: Panther.

CUTRIGHT, P. and J. WILEY (1969) "Modernization and political representation: 1927-1966." Studies in Comparative International Development 5: 23-41.

DEUTSCH, K. (1961) "Social mobilization and political development." Amer. Political Science Rev. 55: 493-514.

FAGEN, R. (1964) "Relation of communication growth to national political systems in the less developed countries." Journalism Q. 41: 87-94.

FARACE, V. and L. DONOHEW (1965) "Mass communication in national social systems: A study of 43 variables in 115 countries." Journalism Q. 42: 253-261.

FRANKLIN, M. (1973) "Freedom and control of communication," in I. Pool and W. Schramm (eds.) Handbook of Communication. Chicago: Rand McNally.

FREY, F. (1970) "Cross-cultural survey research in political science," in R. Holt and J. Turner (eds.) The Methodology of Comparative Research. New York: Free Press.

——— (1973) "Communication and development," in I. Pool and W. Schramm (eds.) Handbook of Communication. Chicago: Rand McNally.

FRIEDRICH, C. J. (1966) "Some general theoretical reflections on the problems of political data," in R. L. Merritt and S. Rokkan (eds.) Comparing Nations: The Use of Quantitative Data in Cross-National Research. New Haven: Yale University Press.

GANS, H. (1971) "The sociologist and the television journalist: Observations on studying television news," in J. Halloran and M. Gurevitch (eds.) Broadcaster/Researcher Cooperation in Mass Communication Research. Leicester: Centre for Mass Communication Research.

GARNHAM, N. (1973) Structures of Television. London: British Film Institute.

GUREVITCH, M. and J. G. BLUMLER (forthcoming) "Linkages between the mass media and politics: A model for the analysis of political communication systems," in G. Gerbner (ed.) Current Trends in Mass Communication. The Hague: Mouton.

HALL, S. (1974) "Media power: The double bind." J. of Communication 24(4): 19-26.

HIRSCH, F. and D. GORDON (1975) Newspaper Money. London: Hutchinson.

HOYER, S., S. HADENIUS and L. WEIBULL (1975) The Politics and Economics of the Press: A Developmental Perspective. London: Sage Pubns.

JOHNSTONE, J., E. SLAWSKI and W. BOWMAN (1972-73) "The professional values of American newsmen." Public Opinion Q. 36: 522-540.

KUMAR, K. (1975) "Holding the middle ground: The BBC, the public and the professional broadcaster." Sociology 9: 66-88.

LaPALOMBARA, J. (1970) "Parsimony and empiricism in comparative politics: an antischolastic view," in R. Holt and J. Turner (eds.) The Methodology of Comparative Research. New York: Free Press.

LERNER, D. (1957) "Communication systems and social systems: A statistical exploration in history and policy." Behavioral Science 2: 266-275.

McCOMBS, M. E. and D. SHAW (1972) "The agenda-setting function of the mass media." Public Opinion Q. 36: 176-187.

McCRONE, D. and C. CNUDDE (1967) "Toward a communications theory of democratic political development: A causal model." Amer. Political Science Rev. 61: 72-79.

McLEOD, J. M. and R. R. RUSH (1969) "Professionalization of Latin American and U.S. journalists." Journalism Q. 46: 583-590 and 784-789.

McNELLY, J. (1966) "Mass communication and the climate for modernization in Latin America." J. of Inter-American Studies 8: 345-357.

MILIBAND, R. (1969) The State of Capitalist Society. London: Weidenfeld and Nicolson.

MITCHELL, J. C. [ed.] (1969) Social Networks in Urban Situations. Manchester: Manchester University Press.

NIXON, R. (1965) "Freedom in the world's press: A fresh appraisal with new data." Journalism Q. 42: 3-14, 118-119.

PARSONS, T. and E. SHILS [eds.] (1951) Toward a General Theory of Action. Cambridge, Mass.: Harvard University Press.

PYE, L. [ed.] (1963) Communication and Political Development. Princeton, N.J.: Princeton University Press.

RUSSETT, B., H. ALKER, Jr., K. DEUTSCH and H. LASSWELL (1965) World Handbook of Political and Social Indicators. New Haven: Yale University Press.

SCHRAMM, W. (1964) Mass Media and National Development. Paris: UNESCO; Stanford, Cal.: Stanford University Press.

SEARS, R. (1961) "Trans-cultural variables and conceptual equivalence," in B. Kaplan (ed.) Studying Personality Cross-Culturally. Evanston, Ill.: Row, Peterson.

SEYMOUR-URE, C. (1974) The Political Impact of Mass Media. London: Constable and Beverly Hills: Sage Pubns.

SIEBERT, F., T. PETERSON and W. SCHRAMM (1956) Four Theories of the Press. Urbana, Ill.: University of Illinois Press.

THOMSEN, N. and S. SAUERBERG (1975) "The political role of mass communication," presented to American Enterprise Institute seminar on recent Scandinavian political development.

THOVERON, G. and J. NOBRE-CORREIA (1974) "Press concentration in French-speaking Belgium and its implications for the political content of newspapers." Presented to workshop on the political role of the mass media of the European Consortium for Political Research.

UNESCO (1964) "World communications: Press, radio, television, film." Paris: UNESCO.

VERBA, S., N. NIE and J. KIM (1971) "The modes of democratic participation: a cross-national comparison." Beverly Hills, Cal.: Sage Pubns.

WALTZER, H. (1966) "In the magic lantern: Television coverage of the 1964 national conventions." Public Opinion Q. 30: 33-53.

WARNER, M. (1969) "Decision-making in American TV political news." Sociological Rev. Monographs 13: 169-179.

WEAVER, P. (1973) "Is television news biased?" The Public Interest 26: 75-74.

WINHAM, G. (1970) "Political development and Lerner's theory: Further test of a causal model." Amer. Political Science Rev. 64: 810-818.

Chapter 6

CRITICAL EVENTS ANALYSIS

Sidney Kraus, Dennis Davis,
Gladys Engel Lang and Kurt Lang

SOCIAL SCIENTISTS have sought to assess the impact of events upon individuals and societies from the inception of the various social research disciplines. Early work in history and political science often consisted of descriptions of events and the links between them, particularly events purported to be turning points in history. An entire political era could be described in terms of anecdoted reports of events, and events were frequently used to explain social changes.[1]

Event-based explanations of social change often emphasized the influence that individuals (great men) had in controlling and using certain situations. Significant social dramas (events) enabled individuals to consolidate their power over others. A leader like Napoleon was viewed as rising to power through his ability to use situations to gain the loyalty of others. (When loyalty could not be gained by peaceful means, it was elicited by force of arms.) Thus, the ability of man to control his own destiny lay in his power to dominate situations. This view is non-deterministic in that every individual has some potential for becoming a great man no matter what his social origin.[2]

This interpretation of events was subjected to intense criticism.

AUTHORS' NOTE: This chapter has been prepared by the first two authors, under a grant from the John and Mary R. Markle Foundation. The second half of paper is based on a collaborative proposal with the third and fourth authors, which was presented to the Social Science Research Council in connection with its planning for studies of the 1976 national election campaign.

Critics did not deny that events may be influential, rather they argued that every observer will have his own subjective views of the impact of events. These views cannot be subjected to empirical test. One historian will construct a plausible causal ordering of a set of events while another historian can construct an equally plausible, but very different ordering of the same set. Different great men may consequently be found. Neither version can be proved correct.

Rather than use events as a basis for explaining social change, some empirically oriented social scientists sought to isolate general social variables that determine other variables. Using models of how social variables should interrelate, they attempted to predict how society would change. These models were deterministic in that once the most useful set of independent variables had been defined and measured, researchers assumed that precise predictions could be made about conditions that would create social change in the future. In contrast with event-based explanations, these deterministic models in effect discounted the ability of isolated individuals to introduce any significant social change.[3]

Critical events analysis as we introduce it in this chapter can be regarded as falling between the two social science approaches de-scribed above.[4] Like the great man approach, we consider it vital to analyze certain events and their consequences as a means of exploiting and predicting social change. We accept the assumption that men can control history by dominating events. But we have added what we believe is an important caveat to this assumption. Events have impact only when certain social conditions are present. Thus, we share with the deterministic model approach the view that it is necessary to measure certain social variables to predict social change. Critical events analysis seeks to identify those events which will produce the most useful explanations and predictions of social change. In doing this, the social conditions which reinforce or nullify the impact of events must be specified.

Another distinction can be made between the great man approach and the deterministic model approach, in relation to the research role which we have assigned to critical events analysis. The great man approach typically used data collected at the individual level of analysis. The actions of individuals in specific situations were ana-lyzed to determine how they were able to be influential. While this information may be quite accurate, it is difficult to use such data to explain or predict relationships between variables at other levels of analysis.[5] For example, one can accumulate detailed information concerning the actions of a President, but it is difficult to work from that data to explain why unemployment and education are negatively correlated in the U.S. There may be no demonstrable links connecting these phenomena. Researchers using the great man approach were often very willing to speculate on the existence of such links and to generalize far beyond the level at which they collected their data.

On the other hand, the deterministic model approach most often leads to data aggregated at the societal level of analysis. For example, the level of unemployment, the level of religiosity, or the suicide rate for an entire social system could be measured. These measures could be intercorrelated and a causal model linking them would be hypothesized for the future. One prediction might be that as unemployment increases and religiosity declines, the suicide rate will increase. But the aggregate statistical data cannot be used to make predictions about the behavior of a specific individual. If a particular person ceases to attend church and loses his job, he will not necessarily commit suicide or even be more likely to commit suicide.

Critical events analysis attempts to integrate data collected at the individual and societal levels of analysis. Our contention is that such data can permit more useful models of social processes to be constructed and evaluated. We have tried to describe below the nature of the models that might emerge from critical events analysis. While our attempts in this regard here are admittedly highly speculative, we believe there is a need for such models. It is important to try to understand how the actions of societal leaders in specific situations impinge upon social processes and are in turn influenced by these processes. Commonsense analyses of events (i.e., news reports) are often filled with speculative models that assume certain kinds of links between elite actions and social changes.[6] In our view such links do exist but they are probably very different and much more complex than the analyses offered by journalists. In fact, the commonsense analyses of journalists may themselves need to be incorporated into adequate models.

To understand the need for the approach we have outlined below, it is useful to examine the role that commonsense analyses of events play in our society. Every day, most of us read news reports which speculate on the social consequences of certain events. Critical events analysis is sometimes confused with such commonsense analyses. Below, we have discussed commonsense analyses and have differentiated them from critical events analysis.

COMMONSENSE STUDY OF EVENTS

Ours is an event-conscious society. We subject current events to constant, frequently elaborate scrutiny. We have structured highly specialized bureaucracies to provide detailed, accurate and objective reports of thousands of events each day. We label our past by references to signal events that aroused widespread public concern, such as the Vietnam War era or the Watergate era. We judge our public officials by their ability to act effectively in certain critical situations, such as President Kennedy's handling of the Cuban missile crisis or President Ford's response to the Mayaguez incident.

While it is not difficult to get evidence of the attention people give to events, and while our tendency to continuously reanalyze the significance of events can be documented by even a superficial content analysis of newspapers or news magazines, the role that this activity plays in the development of our society is uncertain. While immense resources are devoted to commonsense description, we have long neglected to examine the significance of this effort to report and analyze events.

Commonsense Assumptions Concerning the Study of Events

As a society we act on the assumption that it is necessary for certain events to be reported and that everyone should have equal access to these event reports. We have traditionally rationalized our actions with a variety of platitudes. For example, it has been widely argued that equal access to event reports provides a basis for informed, responsible participation in society. Freedom of the press as developed in the U.S. Constitution was derived from the libertarian notion that democracy will flourish when everyone can gain access to competing ideas, opinions and reports in a free marketplace of ideas.[7]

We can summarize many of the traditional notions used to explain the role of event reports with a simple model of the social process that is inherent in these rationales. While the model is our creation, we believe it adequately synthesizes most of the assumptions of causality in libertarian and social responsibility conceptions of press functions. The model contains four causal links. First, objective reports of significant events (surveillance) produce citizens who are alert and informed about the most salient aspects of their environment. When a sufficient number of persons are alerted, through interpersonal discussion they consider alternate ways of responding to events. Such discussion necessarily results in the democratic choice of the most reasonable course of action. (This stage may be short circuited when one individual in the group is recognized as an opinion leader and his action recommendations are accepted without much discussion.) Finally, group agreement results in actions that are socially responsible and useful not just for the group but for the society as a whole. We will call this the surveillance model in recognition of the central role which it gives to media surveillance of the environment.

The surveillance model provides a logically consistent justification for developing mass media industries devoted to the communication of event reports to everyone. To the extent that this model is tenable, these industries provide an important service for our society. But is the model valid? Do event reports actually play the role indicated by this model?

Commonsense Study of Events and Critical Event Analysis

There is evidence that under certain conditions the surveillance model does hold. For example, Tichenor et al. (1973) found that when a controversial issue arises in a small community, media surveillance serves to inform most people in the community equally well on a set of basic set of facts related to the issue. But the same research group (Tichenor et al., 1970) earlier reported that, in general, media may have the opposite effect. On most public affairs issues media reports serve to increase the knowledge of those persons who already know the most. That is, routinely media news serves to widen the "knowledge gap" between the informed and uninformed — creating a situation that does not seem conducive to broadly democratic decision making.

We need to assess the social conditions that affect how people attend to and subsequently use news reports about salient events. It will be necessary to create more than a single model to explain the social consequences of various types of reports. In some cases the traditional surveillance model may be useful, but it is likely that other models will prove at least as powerful in explaining social change. News event reports are created for and assumed to be used in a particular social process with particular consequences. Critical event analysis seeks to ascertain the nature of this social process and examine the consequences of event reports. Are event reports used as media professionals intend them to be used? What role do these reports play in the social processes which they serve? The ultimate purpose of critical event analysis is to provide a scientific explanation of how elite actions have social consequences and how certain social processes constrain elite actions or negate their intended impact. Crucial links in these explanations will be found by tracing how event reports are created, received and used.

PREVIOUS EVENT-RELATED RESEARCH

A body of research exists that partially fits the needs we have defined. As we indicated above, social scientists have studied the impact of events almost from the inception of the various social science disciplines. Frequently, these studies bore much resemblance to the commonsense study of events conducted by journalists. However, social science based studies typically were more concerned with social effects while media reports tended to focus on the details surrounding events. We can illustrate the strengths and limitations of previous research by considering several important studies. We summarize below what we consider the critical attributes of these studies, and what these characteristics tell us about the research approaches that generated them. Then, in the next section, we will suggest how more useful research can be designed.

Choice of Provocative Events

One immediately apparent characteristic of previous event studies is that they are largely focused on events which researchers considered significant or provocative. Events studied include bombings (Lever, 1969), assassinations (Greenberg and Parker, 1965; Meyer, 1969; Hofstetter, 1969), kidnappings (Sorrentino and Vidman, 1974), parades (Lang and Lang, 1970), political conventions (Lang and Lang, 1970), presidential candidate debates (Kraus, 1962), and the famous Orson Welles dramatized invasion from Mars (Cantril, 1958). However, the reasons researchers had for believing their events to be significant appear to vary greatly. Some researchers may have been impressed by evidence of massive social impact. For example, Cantril (1958: 291-293) confessed to having been intrigued by the widespread panic that followed the War of the Worlds broadcast. In the case of the Langs' (1970) research on the effects of televised political conventions, one motivation was a concern for understanding how a new communication medium might alter the electoral process.

The multiplicity of purposes that have motivated studies of events has meant that researchers collected data on quite different variables using differing measures and diverse data analysis techniques. The lack of a common rationale for conducting studies of events renders them collectively less useful. The findings of one study cannot be easily compared to those of another when variables, measurement procedures, and data analysis techniques all differ.

Ad Hoc Design of Event Studies

The typical event study is a field observation in which the event itself constitutes a quasi-experimental manipulation. Ideally, the most useful data set would include measures taken immediately before and immediately after the event occurs, with concurrent measurement in a "control" site that was not visited with the event.[8] If only a small amount of time has elapsed between measures and if one can assume that only the occurrence of the event has intervened, then the researcher can have more confidence in attributing measured changes to the event.

Unfortunately, most critical event studies do not use this ideal design, though most researchers would acknowledge its usefulness and attempt at least partially to follow it. Most salient events cannot be manipulated by the researcher. They are beyond his control. He can at best anticipate their occurrence, not influence it. (Of course, one could conceive of a world in which social scientists stage elaborate events to gauge their impact. But this would raise serious ethical and legal questions.)

Events vary in the degree to which they can be anticipated. Some are scheduled months in advance, such as the national political party conventions; others occur with no warning (e.g. the assassination of a President). Many events vary between these two extremes, being unscheduled but foreshadowed by a strong possibility that they might occur. For example, during the Apollo moon missions, the chance of a fatal accident existed. In any particular presidential primary race, at least one candidate is likely to make a statement that receives widespread public attention. By planning for an event of this type, the researcher can develop measurement instruments and even organize a field staff well in advance of the event. Preliminary baseline measures can be taken on an appropriate sample of respondents. Typically, though, even this level of preparation for an event study is not undertaken; most event studies collect data only after the event has occurred. To illustrate this point we should examine event studies on a continuum with two time dimensions— when the event occurred and when the research response to the event began.

The New York newspaper strike (Berelson, 1962) was entering its second week when Columbia University's Bureau of Applied Social Research went into the field. As it turned out, data were gathered when the strike was less than half over. This event could have been anticipated—the probability that a strike would occur had been relatively high—but the research team did not act in anticipation of the event. Recalling it thirty years later, Dr. Berelson said, "We decided after the first two or three days [of the strike] to get support and do the research."[9] The Langs' decision to conduct research came some time after the warning, but before it occurred. A MacArthur Day parade in Chicago was scheduled ten days in advance. The research idea, however, emerged some three days before the event (Lang and Lang, 1970: 39). Much public information was available which enabled these researchers to prepare for their work. Some events may be scheduled but still offer no forewarning of their potential significance. Even if Cantril knew of the Welles broadcast, could he or anyone have predicted the panic-reaction to it on that October night in 1938? Such events do not permit baseline data to be collected.

Extent of Elite Planning

There is an increased effort by elites responsible for staging events to structure them so that certain effects will be achieved. McGinniss (1969) has described the effort made by the 1968 Nixon campaign planners to create televised settings in which the candidate would appear calm, candid and responsive. Advertising and public relations professionals are engaged to build images of leaders by instructing them on how to behave in public. If events are correctly staged, all parts should be consistent. If the leader is to convey the image of "just folks", he will dress casually, use colloquial language in conversations, tell a few homely stories, hug his wife, etc. When an event is artificially constrained for the media in this manner, it may tend to elicit a more homogeneous public response. For critical events analysis, an assessment of the degree to which an event is staged can aid in the design of the event study. One prime focus of any study of a structured event will be to examine whether the event elicited intended responses. Another concern will be to determine which segments of the public perceived the event as staged.

Study of structured events can lead to conclusions concerning one set of links between elites and social action. How do staged elite actions serve to elicit responses from the public? For example, in the fall of 1974 President Ford's effort to get the public to Whip Inflation Now was poorly received despite a carefully staged effort. Clearly, the structuring of events in certain ways does not always (or perhaps even very often) translate into desired public action. The White House Watergate transcripts indicate that many schemes to manipulate the public fail. President Nixon and his advisors planned many events that went unnoticed. In some cases, the press failed to give the events coverage; in others, the events were simply ignored in the flood of daily news reports to which the public is exposed every day. This does not mean that the public is invulnerable to manipulation, but the process linking elite actions to public responses is far more complex than the intuitive models of even the most skilled promotional communication experts would suggest.

Most event studies have not been concerned with staged events. Rather the focus is on dramatic, unplanned events such as assassinations and disasters. While useful, it is unlikely that these will contribute greatly to an understanding of typical links between elites and the public. In times of crisis, elites may be able to command conformity from the public or widespread acceptance of elite action that will not extend to more normal situations. Sorrentino and Vidman (1974) found that two political kidnappings resulted in public acceptance of implementation of a war measures act that curtailed civil rights in Canada. It would be important to ascertain the consequences of elite actions that occur in less unsettled settings. The Langs (1970) provide examples of studies of staged events. Their work provides insight into how televised political convention coverage and political campaign efforts may translate into certain public responses. Much more research is necessary to understand the social processes involved here.

Journalistic Coverage of Events

The extent to which event reports serve to emphasize only certain aspects of events affects study design. Just as elite staging can result in homogeneous public response, reporting that concentrates on certain parts of events can also limit the range of public response. For example a racially inspired clash between members of a city council can be reported as a minor argument that stems from personal antagonism between the combatants. In this case, the reporter may be motivated by a desire to avoid increasing racial tension in a city; or may be using a standard formula of his paper for characterizing city council arguments; if he wrote his story any other way it would inevitably be rewritten by editors.

Thus, event studies must consider how event reports are structured by media professionals to achieve certain desired effects. Most mass media in the U.S. survive in their present form only because large numbers of people use them every day. News media must make their content attractive and interesting to thousands or even millions of readers or viewers. The formulas used to convert events into news may necessitate some distortion. It has been argued that TV coverage of events is systematically distorted because events are almost always visually represented by 30 seconds of seemingly dramatic action even when the event itself was quite undramatic (Wax, 1970).

In addition to determining whether elites have the impact they intend, event studies should consider whether journalists have the impact they seek. Just as elites use common sense and intuition to guide their staging of events, journalists tend to rely on institution-alized professional formulas for event reports. Just as elites probably can be very poor predictors of their impact on the public, there is no reason to assume that journalists are much wiser.

Crouse (1972) tells of how news organizations consistently warned reporters covering the Muskie presidential campaign in 1972 not to submit stories that analyzed Muskie's personality. References to Muskie's personality inadvertently included in stories were deleted by editors. Thus, early reports of Muskie crying in New Hampshire tended to be terse statements of fact. However, when one paper chose to print a report that considered personality, it stirred much public interest and soon editors for most major papers demanded similar material from their reporters.

Very few examples exist of events research that have considered the intentions of journalists. Yet these intentions can affect the way the event report is received even when the impact is very different from that which the reporter intends. For example, research may find that systematic attempts to describe events in a highly dramatic fashion produce certain consistent consequences. Perhaps some segment of the TV news audience is only interested in being entertained by dramatic descriptions. News is as real (or unreal) as a contiguous situation comedy or crime drama. If a group of persons exists whose use of news falls into this pattern, certain consequences may follow. Research might show that such people are only stirred to action by the most highly dramatic reports. Reports may need to be very unusual to be heard above the din of sensationalism that attends even minor events.

Most studies that have considered the intentions of journalists do not assess how these intentions translate into public responses. Crouse (1972) provides excellent descriptions of why journalists chose to structure their stories in particular ways, but his considerations of the social consequences of these choices are based on speculation. The Langs (1970) demonstrated how TV network plans for political convention coverage can result in distinctive perceptions of convention action. In particular, such coverage can probably easily reinforce widely held stereotypes. For instance, coverage on one network stressed the view that all important convention decisions are made in secluded, smoke-filled rooms by a handful of individuals.

Data Collection and Analysis Techniques

A wide variety of data collection and analysis techniques can be found in events research. As we indicated above, some of this diversity stems from the fact that researchers choose to study events for a variety of reasons. Unless these motivations can be narrowed it is unlikely that events research will produce findings that are of cumulative usefulness. Cantril (1958: 291) conducted personal interviews with 135 persons, 100 of whom were selected because they were known to have been upset by the War of the Worlds broadcast. Several studies of the impact of the Kennedy assassination (Greenberg and Parker, 1965) relied on telephone interviews with random samples of urban populations. Meyer (1969) was in the field conducting personal interviews when the assassination of Martin Luther King occurred; he was able to conduct a second set of interviews to gauge the impact of the event. The Langs (1970) exposed selected groups of students to convention coverage of different TV networks to assess differences in perception; the students wrote reports of their perceptions and were interviewed. Sorrentino and Vidman (1974) used a student panel and a panel representative of an urban adult population, to gauge the long-term impact of two political kidnappings; a series of questionnaires probed changes in beliefs and attitudes.

Data analysis techniques are equally diverse. Sorrentino and Vidman (1974) tested the significance of shifts in attitudes and beliefs, finding few long-term changes that were significant. The

Langs (1970) organized their findings by categorizing the perceptions of their sample; persons who fell into the same category tended to have watched the same network broadcasts. Meyer (1969) constructed tables showing the percentages who held certain attitudes at two different points in time, to assess the extent of change.

We need to begin to organize a set of data collection and analysis procedures that will make research findings more compatible, or at least to provide some guidelines. Studies directed toward understanding the links between elite actions and public responses require that only a relatively small number of variables be intensively studied.

This does not mean that the "firehouse" research model[10] should be abandoned. On the contrary, we need to increase our capacity to do field studies rapidly and to coordinate work among researchers. Any given study will have its methodological flaws, such as the lack of baseline measures, or a sample that does not represent any generalizable population. But rapidly fielded research need not (in fact should not) be hastily planned. Just as fire departments are not formed on the spot to deal with particular fires, research capacities can be developed well in advance of events, even totally unexpected events. Categories of variables can be selected, data collection procedures can be planned, and data analyses can be anticipated. When data are to be collected using divergent techniques an effort can be made to design the study so that various findings can be integrated.

STATE OF THE ART

Some of these characteristics of previous events research result from inadequate planning and should be eliminated. Others result from constraints imposed by events, especially the manner in which events are created and reported. These constraints can hardly be eliminated, but future research must more directly investigate how the staging and reporting of events affects their impact on the public.

Several important new foci for events research are suggested by our discussion. First, attention should be given to the study of particular types of messages about public events. These are messages that do more than simply relate "bits" of information about public figures. A significant message (i.e., one that has broad impact) may portray an event in a strikingly dramatic way. Such messages should not be regarded as merely sensational or pandering to popular taste.

Rather, they may serve to put events into a context that facilitates public understanding and use (i.e., they communicate events in "human terms"). While it is true that such messages may distort events they may also communicate useful perspectives. We need a better understanding of how various media serve to transmit such events and how different types of individuals attend to and use the various types of dramatic messages transmitted by the various media.

Second, messages that portray events in a dramatic way can be expected to involve an inordinate amount of creative effort on the part of mass media practitioners. These messages are not simple lists of facts. The stage must be properly set in communicating such events. The motivations and objectives of various actors must be explained. The consequences of actions may be anticipated. The moral, political or economic context of the event may be considered. Future research should explore how this creative task is accomplished. How much consideration does a reporter, news editor or cameraman give to providing a dramatic context for events? What sources of information are used to guide this creative work? How does the media professional anticipate the response of his audience?

In addition, research should consider how the interplay between communicators and politicians affects the way the event is portrayed. The news media do not operate with total autonomy but are themselves an integral part of the political system (see chapter by Chaffee). The existence of communication channels exerts an influence on what elites feel they must disseminate, on how they act, and how they communicate with members of various other elites and sub-elites. The goal is to document how interplay during a particular event or episode affects the way "reality" is portrayed and how it influences the public imagery of elites.

Third, research should study the public's attention to and use of messages about dramatic events. It appears likely that entertaining television dramatizations might be used by some persons in much the same way as news content. A prime objective of this research would be to determine the conceptions of reality which individuals are constructing in their use of dramatic messages. A second objective would be to explore some of the purposes served by these conceptions once they are formed. In particular, the use of these conceptions to plan action or to select other types of messages would be given consideration. For certain types of individuals, dramatic events may become crucial points of reference by which other events are evaluated and personal actions judged.

Fourth, the credibility of mass media should be investigated as a link in a larger process. Previous research on credibility tends to focus only on this variable and its direct effects.[11] Public acceptance of messages that are highly selective in their dramatization of events may be a function of the degree to which the medium transmitting the message is perceived as a credible source. When media (or reporter) credibility is lacking, individuals may accept informative messages but reject dramatizations as biased. Do persons with particular preconceptions about events reject messages that contradict these preconceptions, by labeling these messages as "untrue" and the media that transmit them as "biased"? What are the consequences of these perceptions?

All of these foci stem from the position that research should examine the full social process in which elite actions are linked to public actions and social change. In the next section we sketch a design for a research effort that attempts to study several parts of this process simultaneously. This design illustrates the direction we believe future research should move.

A DESIGN FOR CRITICAL EVENTS RESEARCH

One way to implement the critical events approach would be to assess the long-term impact of a series of dramatic public events. A prime objective of this research would be to determine if the perspectives communicated by certain events make it more likely that other events will be attended to and used in specific ways. For example, the exposure of the Watergate cover-up may have set the stage for public interest in other, relatively minor, political scandals in state or local governments. Thus, critical events may initiate a cycle of sensitization to other similar, though less important, events. We might expect that if individuals are sensitized to political scandals they will try to assess the honesty and integrity of political candidates and then vote for those candidates who rate highest on these criteria (see Becker et al. chapter, re "agenda-setting").

Political events analysis can look for direct linkage between specific media content and change in individual vote intentions; between the media coverage of an event and change in the status among elites of a candidate; between use of the media in a campaign and the outcome of an election. The purpose of this type of research is to understand *how* these effects come about rather than to measure their precise magnitude. For this reason also, some event researchers are not exclusively or even primarily concerned with the way individual opinions shape up but rather with the sequence of circumstances that account for the formation and movement of public opinion as a set of collective images that all parties to the electoral process take into account.

The point is that the collective definition of a political event, like any public image, arises in the communication process. Imagery is collective to the extent that it is shared and incorporates those characteristics and aspects of a situation to which a plurality of persons or publics are oriented.[12] For example, the popularity or reputation of a candidate is a social fact. It is something that everyone, whatever his own feelings, has to acknowledge. Similarly and to the extent they receive public recognition, a candidate's record, his personality, his past and present affiliations, etc. add up to a public image. The more public any act, the more likely is it to become incorporated into such an image. Therefore, insofar as together they control what becomes public, the parts played by professional communicators and public figures are crucial to the process of social definition. Other objects whose meanings are collectively defined include the issue structure that develops in a political contest; the images of the parties; the agenda for future decisions; the mood of the public; the role assigned to the media of communication; and any links that people widely believe exist between any two or more of the above.

Noelle-Neumann (1974) has suggested a second way that critical events may initiate trends in public opinion. She argues that individuals constantly evaluate popular support for various opinions and are reluctant to discuss opinions that are perceived to be losing favor with the public (even if those opinions are held by a majority at present). She labels this phenomenon "the spiral of silence." Dramatization of critical events by the mass media may communicate impressions about the future of public figures, institutions or policies. For example, media reports of the Quebec Liberation Front (FLQ) involvement in the 1968 kidnappings may have communicated images that later accelerated loss of public support for this group. By communicating impressions about future trends, the media may, in fact, be creating those trends. Noelle-Neumann (1974: 50-51) has described this situation:

> Mass media are part of the system which the individual uses to gain
> information about the environment. For all questions outside his imme-

diate personal sphere, he is almost totally dependent upon mass media for the facts and for his evaluation of the climate of opinion. He will react as usual to the pressure of opinion made public (i.e., published). . . . For a considerable time now a scientific discussion has been going on as to whether the media anticipate public opinion or reflect it—whether they are the mirror or the molder of public opinion. According to the social-psychological mechanism here called "the spiral of silence," the mass media have to be seen as creating public opinion: they provide the environmental pressure to which people respond with alacrity, or with acquiescence, or with silence.

Critical Events Research Operations

Figure 1 is a simplified representation of the data-collecting operations we would propose for study of a critical event. In the center is the event itself. The activities of actors who are involved in the event, and the operations and output of the news media are depicted along the vertical axis. (It should be understood that the event also involves actors who may be trying to understand, manipulate, or react to it, and that the media act on the event as well as reporting it.)

Four basic data-gathering operations can be identified: (1) those at the site of the event; (2) those in communities chosen to represent the public; (3) the collection of the media output in both of the first two sites; and (4) the collection of polls and other indicators of opinion trends.

The locale. The operations indicated on the left side of the chart are tied to the locale of an event and call for a research team that can be quickly assembled at such a site. In some cases, events are not localized but our idea is to get as close to the actors as possible in order to obtain information on:

a) What happened. Events are typically complex involving many activities that go unreported; only on-site investigation can reveal these details.

b) What goals participants (e.g., candidates, spokesmen for organized groups, members of the public) pursued and to what audiences they saw themselves playing.

c) The operation of media personnel at the site—especially the interaction between news personnel and other participants, and the degree of concordance between their goals.

The focused interview with elites—actors and media personnel—and direct observation (including the use of unobtrusive indicators) are the two basic methods for on-site data collection.

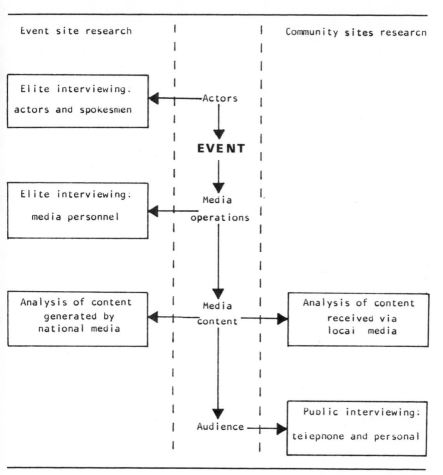

Figure 1: EVENT-CENTERED FIREHOUSE RESEARCH OPERATIONS

Public response. A second operation (right-hand side of Figure 1) is concerned with public response, which is in no way site-specific but which we assume to have something to do with the sources of information (media) available to persons in different localities. By means of interviews as close to the event in point of time as possible, an attempt is undertaken to obtain information on: (a) sources of information people used; (b) awareness and perceptions of what happened; (c) perceived changes in opinions or attitudes. One basis for site selection could be to choose cities with a maximum contrast in the media situation; that is to say, three communities that are "media-rich" and three "media-poor." Additionally, communities could be selected for their contrasting demography and/or politics.

Depending on resources, some combination of in-person and telephone interviews could be used. It is difficult to keep respondents on the telephone for more than about fifteen minutes, which limits the scope of such interviews. To exploit the obvious cost advantages of telephone interviewing, we suggest monitoring the media content continuously in order to design questions that refer directly to what was recently reported. Telephone interviews can be used to locate a subsample of individuals who report significant event influence. Face-to-face interviews with these persons can provide additional data. These interviews aid interpretation of the findings from the telephone survey.[13]

Collection of media output. A third operation involves the collection of media reports. This will serve two distinct but related purposes:

a) To compare "what happened" with media reports of what happened and to identify factual and interpretational discrepancies, including different media versions of the same event. This can be done, in effect, at the site of the event, somewhat broadly conceived.

b) To provide a record of what is made available to persons in the communities with their contrasting media situations. This calls for monitoring the local press and broadcast outlets, as indicated on the right-hand side of Figure 1.

A researcher could fairly easily collect a few influential national newspapers (e.g. the *New York Times* and *Washington Post*), the AP wire service output from the event site and input to the local audience-interview media, the major national news magazines, and at least the newspapers available at the community sites. Videorecording of network television coverage would be possible at some extra cost, as would be monitoring of local radio or TV news.

The collection of opinion trends indicators. A supplementary operation involves the continuous monitoring of opinion in order to place observations into the proper context. This is supplementary to the local audience interviews and is not shown in Figure 1; to a considerable extent these operations can be performed by existing national research organizations that in effect operate on a fire-house basis anyway; included are:

a) A record of major political, social and economic developments, including apparent shifts in the strategy or fortunes of candidates.

b) Poll reports and other assessments of trends in the public domain.

c) The possible piggy-backing of questions to a national poll, where continuing and nation-wide data seems useful.

The first point to be noted when it comes to analyzing these data is that each event can be viewed as a case study more or less complete in itself. The researcher should be able to say something about the event, about the aspects played up and ignored by the media, about the way media operations influenced both the coverage of the events and subsequent developments, and about the relationship between all these and the public reaction. This research model has built into it additional opportunities for comparison along both a spatial (the communities) and temporal (N events) dimension as well as between several combinations of the two. Thus, each set of data provides a baseline for examination of the impact of the next event. One objective can be to assess whether the effects of events are mostly ephemeral or are cumulative over time.

The following propositions are *illustrative* of working hypotheses derived from our conceptual framework that can be evaluated using this research organization:

1. Public

(a) The more spectacular an event and/or the more publicity it receives, the more will audience perceptions be responsive to media reports and therefore become homogeneous and resemble the event reports.

(b) The meaning of a "scheduled" event will be influenced more by expectations built up through media than will the meaning of an unscheduled event, because media will strive to make the event appear interesting to build an audience for it.

(c) People are likely to be more skeptical about the accuracy of media reports when the site is local and/or they have access to other "authentic" sources of information. Similarly media credibility will decline when media event reports conflict with each other.

2. Actors

(a) Event activities are staged more for the news media and the larger audience than for persons on the scene.

3. Media

(a) Media personnel shape their event reports to appeal to specific interests and concerns of their audiences.

(b) The national media (network TV and the prestige press) are significant in silhouetting the important stories. These media will be found to establish formulas for how events should be reported by other media.

4. Events

(a) "Major" events have impact more because of elaborations in subsequent news stories than because of what people remember directly.

(b) The presence of the media has greater effects on the behavior of participants when the event is scheduled than when it is unscheduled, because media professionals have more lead time to create a context for the story.

(c) Critical events serve to initiate or accelerate trends in public opinion or political attitude formation by highlighting the existence of significant support for such trends. During the most problematic critical events new social norms will be created or legitimated to the degree that they are portrayed by the media as widely supported (i.e., by reporting of opinion polls, support by respected public leaders, etc.).

5. Communities

(a) Selectivity processes operating during critical events may be related more to the *de facto* selectivity exercised by the mass media than to socio-psychological barriers within individuals. In media-poor communities the development of collective imagery during a critical event may be more clearly explained by media *de facto* selectivity than in media-rich communities.

CONCLUSION

Our initial attempts at defining this research approach led us to outline an integrated strategy that combines and integrates many existing research methods. The strength of this approach lies in the importance it attaches to analyzing an entire, complex social process. Previous research has tended to evaluate only isolated causal links in specific models. Such research may be eminently more practical than the research design we have proposed. However, even a study that considers only a few causal relationships should attempt to elaborate the model into which these relationships fit. For example, media credibility research is in part focused on understanding how individuals perceive media and whether these perceptions affect what people learn from media. Conclusions supporting such causal links are of limited usefulness unless they are understood as pieces of a social process that connects elite actions and public actions.

The conceptual framework we described to guide our own research design can hardly be viewed as one that will permit the deduction of all conceivable models of the social process it relates to. Instead, at best it will permit deduction of only a few useful models. It is useful primarily for the direction it indicates for future studies. In striving to conceptualize whole social processes and to evaluate empirically our models of these processes, we expect that mass communication research can approach its potential as a discipline that will contribute to constructive social change rather than as the recorder of communication crises.

NOTES

1. For example, Handlin (1954: 3) identified eight turning points in American history. In his introduction he stated that "the stories deal with men and women, with the clash of historical forces. They examine the motives that lead to action; and they describe the passions that action produces. They have the effect of drama. . . . From the incidents that form the substance of this book, great results followed."

2. Then-Senator John F. Kennedy (1955) sought to describe a characteristic that enabled some men to make events, which he labeled political courage. Those with this attribute shape history, he believed, because they are capable of ignoring public opinion and acting in the country's best interests.

3. This view of society was best elaborated by classical positivistic organicists. Martindale (1960: 87) quotes Emile Durkheim as describing this viewpoint in these words ". . . the social group precedes and constitutes the individual . . . it is the source of culture and all the higher values, and . . . the social states and changes are not produced by and cannot be directly affected or modified by, the desires or volitions of individuals."

4. We have greatly oversimplified in our brief introductory remarks here. Our choice is arbitrary and designed to serve our own purposes in this chapter. These two approaches as we have characterized them for purposes of contrast were not necessarily popular even when they enjoyed some acceptance.

5. See Brodbeck (1968: 280-303) for a discussion of the difficulties of making inferences from one level of analysis to another. She argues that it is necessary to define composition laws that "state what happens when several elementary situations are combined in specified ways. These combined situations are the macroscopic (molar) complexes referred to by the group terms of the reduced area." She goes on to argue that if the correct composition laws could be defined, "the reduction of sociology to psychology is a purely logical matter." Thus, generalizations made at higher levels of analysis using data collected at lower levels are possible only if composition laws exist which permit the two levels to be linked logically.

6. Ironically, it is some of the best journalism that is most prone to this failing. Reports that simply describe but do not generalize cannot be accused of it.

7. Rivers et al. (1971: 67-89) provide an excellent summary of libertarian views.

8. Campbell (1963) discusses such designs and their usefulness in understanding social

9. Berelson to Kraus, telephone conversation, May 16, 1975.

10. Firehouse research methods have been described by Katz and Feldman (1962: 186) as that "quality of rousing a few volunteers, assessing the extent of the fire and devising a strategy for coping with it."

11. Media credibility studies abound in the mass communication literature. See Edelstein and Tefft (1974) for a recent consideration of credibility.

12. A more elaborate treatment of this can be found in Lang and Lang (1961).

13. Rogers (1975) conducted an experiment to determine the effects of in-person and telephone interviews on the quality of responses and field performance. She found that "the quality of data both on complex attitudinal and knowledge items as well as on personal items is comparable to that collected in person. Moreover, field techniques for contacting the respondent and for conducting an interview as long as one hour in length need not be modified."

REFERENCES

BERELSON, B. (1962) "What missing the newspaper means," in D. Katz et al. (eds.) Public Opinion and Propaganda. New York: Holt, Rinehart and Winston.

BRODBECK, M. (1968) Readings in the Philosophy of the Social Sciences. New York: Macmillan.

CAMPBELL, D. T. (1963) "From description to experimentation: Interpreting trends as quasi-experiments," in C. W. Harris (ed.) Problems in Measuring Change. Wisconsin: University of Wisconsin Press.

CANTRIL, H. (1958) "The invasion from Mars," in E. E. Maccoby, T. M. Newcomb and E. L. Hartley (eds.) Readings in Social Psychology. New York: Holt, Rinehart and Winston.

CROUSE, T. (1972) The Boys on the Bus. New York: Random House.

EDELSTEIN, A. and D. TEFFT (1974) "Media credibility and respondent credulity with respect to Watergate." Communication Research 1 (October) 426-439.

GREENBERG, B. S. and E. B. PARKER (1965) The Kennedy Assassination and the American Public. Stanford: Stanford University Press.

HANDLIN, O. (1954) Change or Destiny: Turning Points in American History. New York: Little, Brown.

HOFSTETTER, C. R. (1969) "Political disengagement and the death of Martin Luther King." Public Opinion Q. 33 (summer):160-173.

KATZ, E. and J. FELDMAN (1962) "The debates in light of research," in Kraus (1962).

KENNEDY, J. F. (1955) Profiles in Courage. New York: Harper and Row.

KRAUS, S. (1962) The Great Debates. Bloomington: Indiana University Press.

LANG, K. and G. E. LANG (1960) "The unique perspective of television and its effect: A pilot study," in W. Schramm (ed.) Mass Communications. Urbana: U. of Illinois Press.

——— (1961) Collective Dynamics. New York: Thomas Y. Crowell Co.

——— (1970) Politics and Television. Chicago: Quadrangle.

LEVER, H. (1969) "The Johannesburg Station explosion and ethnic attitudes." Public Opinion Q. (summer):180-189.

MARTINDALE, D. (1960) The Nature and Types of Sociological Theory. New York: Houghton Mifflin.

McGINNISS, J. (1969) The Selling of the President, 1968. New York: Trident.

MEYER, P. (1969) "Aftermath of martyrdom: Negro militancy and Martin Luther King." Public Opinion Q. 33 (summer) 160.

NOELLE-NEUMANN, E. (1974) "The spiral of silence: A theory of public opinion." J. of Communication 24 (spring) 43-51.

RIVERS, W. L., T. PETERSON and J. JENSEN (1971) The Mass Media and Modern Society. New York: Holt, Rinehart and Winston.

ROGERS, T. F. (1975) "Interviews by telephone and in person: An experiment to test quality of responses and field performance," presented to the American Association for Public Opinion Research, Itasca, Illinois.

SORRENTINO, R. M. and N. VIDMAN (1974) "Impact of events: Short- vs. long-term effects of a crisis." Public Opinion Q. 38 (summer) 272-273.

TICHENOR, P. J., G. A. DONOHUE and C. N. OLIEN (1970) "Mass media and differential growth in knowledge." Public Opinion Q. 34 (summer) 158-170.

———, J. RODENKIRCHEN, C. N. OLIEN and G. A. DONOHUE (1973) "Community issues, conflict, and public affairs knowledge," in P. Clarke (ed.) New Models for Mass Communication Research. Beverly Hills: Sage Pubns.

WAX, M. (1970) "TV news: Wrong mix." The Nation (April) 433-435.

GOVERNMENT AND THE MEDIA

William L. Rivers, Susan Miller
and Oscar Gandy

THE STUDY OF GOVERNMENT and the media is a paradox. When a teacher attempts to summarize the research, he or she finds large amounts: many studies of government—elections, characteristics of officials and their performance—and many studies of media content or of the characteristics of media and practitioners. It may seem that one is surrounded by research. But when a person tries to bring together studies of the government with studies of the media, one finds great gaps. There are relatively few studies that have examined both media and government. Consequently, there is relatively little research that can give us a better understanding of the relationship between these institutions.

Let a teacher try to focus on, say, state government officials and reporters. In California, there is little more than Garcia (1967). It was a fine study, but a narrow one, a master's project focusing on the attitudes and opinions of 27 correspondents. It is now nearly ten years old. Yet to uncover further findings, one must mine "fugitive" publications, looking here and there for something related. Thus, the teacher usually ends up lecturing without a complete picture, or anything near it.

This is but a small example of the enormity of the problem. The governmental institution is multi-layered: municipal, county, state and federal. What is typical of one does not necessarily hold for the others. The problem is confounded by the tremendous variations among units within each level. The teacher can lecture from his or her own perspective, but cannot know how generalizable or typical this experience has been. For research, the would-be investigator has a vast opportunity, but very little in the way of a framework to guide new studies.

In an effort to pull together what is known about media-government relationships, we have devoted almost a year to searching out, reading and analyzing various studies.[1] We uncovered more than 300 that were directly relevant to our particular areas of interest. We were interested in all forms of government—local, state, and national—that are headed by elected representatives, and in all services that are provided and/or administered by these bodies. We included all officials who administer government agencies, departments, institutions, functions, and services—whether elected, appointed or civil servants.

As for news media, we included only those media that carry public affairs news on a regularly scheduled basis—newspapers, magazines, radio, and television but not films or books. We confined our study to news of public affairs, i.e. news about the activities of government and government officials.

As we began to compare, contrast and summarize the studies we were uncovering, we found it essential to develop a categorization scheme. We eventually settled on four major divisions that provided us with a useful framework for discussing media-government relationships. Our categorization scheme was as follows:

A. GOVERNMENT IMPACT ON MEDIA
  1. The mechanisms of control
    a. Laws and court action
    b. Regulatory agencies
    c. Informal techniques and pressures
  2. The exercise of control
  3. The impact of control
    a. Economic
    b. Newsgathering behavior
    c. Outputs

B. GOVERNMENT INFORMATION SYSTEMS
  1. The nature of information channels
    a. Formal channels
    b. Informal channels
  2. The nature of the participants
    a. Characteristics of government information personnel
    b. Attitudes of officials and government information personnel about the release of information
  3. How they do their job

C. MEDIA IMPACT ON GOVERNMENT
1. Officials' use of and attitudes toward the news media
    a. Reading and viewing habits
    b. Attitudes about news coverage
    c. Utilization of the news media in their work
2. Impact of the news media on the behavior of officials
    a. National government
    b. State government
    c. Local government
    d. The judicial system

D. THE NATURE OF THE NEWS MEDIA
1. The setting in which they operate
    a. The media as members of social systems
    b. The internal structure of news organizations
    c. Institutional norms
    d. Ownership
    e. The nature of the social setting and audience
    f. Economic factors
    g. Technological factors
    h. Professional standards and formulas
    i. The nature and characteristics of sources
2. How the news media operate
    a. Sources used by the media
    b. How information is obtained
3. The characteristics of journalists
    a. Demographic characteristics of reporters
    b. Journalistic philosophies of reporters
    c. Characteristics and philosophies of executives and editors
    d. Attitudes about their work
    e. Conflicts between attitudes and performance
4. The nature of news content
    a. Amount of news content
    b. Similarities among media
    c. How content varies with subject matter
    d. How content varies over time

The Impact of Government on the News Media includes all formal and informal techniques and processes by which officials exert influence on the news media—legislation, licensing, regulation, judicial rulings, the issuing or withholding of information, or officials' threats and pressures. This area includes research on all of the various mechanisms and types of impact, such as staffing, newsgathering behaviors, and outputs.

Government Information Systems includes all channels, tech-

niques, and processes by which government officials either disseminate information to the news media or compete with the news media
for public attention. This section includes research on formal and
informal systems, the characteristics and attitudes of government
information personnel, the attitudes of other government officials
about government information systems, and how these systems
operate.

The Impact of Media on Government includes all the ways in
which the news media influence official attitudes or behavior—
newsgathering techniques, behavior of news personnel, and use or
suppression of information, opinions, and criticism. This section
includes research on various types of impact and on officials' use of
and attitudes about public affairs news.

The Nature of the News Media includes research on the structure
of news organizations, how the news media operate, the characteristics and attitudes of public affairs reporters, the attitudes of their
superiors about public affairs news, and the nature of public affairs
content. To some extent these divisions and subdivisions simply
reflect the nature of existing research. For example, the reason there
are so many subdivisions within the Nature of the News Media is that
this is the area which has received the most research attention.

However, we feel that this scheme is also an appropriate and useful
means of conceptualizing media-government relationships, in that it
incorporates several useful distinctions: It differentiates between (1)
research focusing on the nature of institutions vs. research focusing
on their impacts, (2) research on institutional, social and structural
factors vs. research on individual, personal, and psychological factors,
(3) research on attitudes and personal characteristics vs. research on
behavior, (4) research on the nature of impacts vs. research on the
outcomes of impacts, and (5) various levels of government and
various types of media. We do not mean to imply, however, that all
these distinctions have been adequately researched or that they are
adequately understood. In fact, we found that all of our categories
have been inadequately studied, with the impact of government on
media studied least of all.

Lacking adequate analysis is the whole area of how media coverage
affects the behavior of officials once in office, and how it affects
official proceedings such as jury trials, Congressional hearings, and
the like. There also has been little research on the impact of government information systems on news coverage. Although the behavior
of reporters and editors has been somewhat better researched, most

studies have failed to identify relevant structural or institutional factors that can be generalized across a variety of situations.

The Impact of Government on the Media

When one looks for studies on ways in which government has an impact on the media, one finds that a number of studies have focused on the Federal Communications Commission. Perhaps this is because the FCC's decisions are readily available for study in a semi-public form. Krasnow and Longley (1973) have produced a picture of how the FCC makes decisions. They concluded that the FCC is at the mercy of the broadcast industry, citizens' groups, the courts, the President, the Congress, and congressional subcommittees. They believe the success of FCC policies is usually dependent on either industry or congressional support, but the picture changes when citizens, the President, or the courts become involved. Consequently, the FCC focuses on short-range gains and immediate problems, building policy through strategies of sequentialism and incrementalism.

Weaver (1974) has examined some causal relationships among variables related to freedom from governmental controls, using data across nations and over time. He offers a model of technological development-media-government forces in interaction, based on indicators of government behavior in a number of countries in 1950, 1960, 1965 and 1966. He concluded that accountability—which he defined as executive and legislative dependence on public support and votes—was a crucial factor in the increase of press freedom; increases in accountability came *not* during periods of quiescence, but during periods of social stress. His findings raise questions about our traditional models and theories, which predict that periods of social calm lead to a lessening of government control (see chapter by Stevens on this point).

Noll et al. (1973) noted the *stated* policy of the FCC is that local ownership, public affairs programming, and local program origination are favored. But these factors were found to be negatively correlated with receiving a license from the FCC. The amount of programming (in hours) was the most powerful predictor of getting the license; cross-media ownership was a near guarantee of rejection.

The remainder of studies in this area are either largely anecdotal or narrow in their focus. Anecdotal studies focus on extreme cases, but rarely give us any indication of how often such situations arise.

Narrow studies—such as case studies of a single subject—rarely identify relevant characteristics or offer generalizations in a form that permits comparisons between cases. Consequently, although we have heard much about the impact of government on media, we have little evidence about how often it occurs or to whom—and even less about why.

Government Information Media

Several studies of government communication efforts warrant attention. Nimmo (1964) is a relatively thorough study of interaction between information officials and reporters. He interviewed 38 public information officers (PIOs) who were spokesmen for executive agencies and departments, and 35 newspapermen covering them. Nimmo found that a crucial factor in the selection, outlook and performance of information officers was the type of agency for which the person worked. Regulatory agencies tended to employ civil servants who were oriented toward the public and served primarily as information-conveyors. In contrast, executive departments tended to employ political appointees oriented more to the political careers of their superiors. These PIOs also had higher status within their organizations and served more as political advisors—helping to formulate strategies and policies and to make decisions. We should note, however, that Nimmo's work was not based on a representative sample of PIOs, and is now some 12 years old. In the interim, public information programs have expanded tremendously, and information officers increasingly have taken on duties other than straightforward information conveying.

Shaffer (1973) focused on the press secretary of the Mayor of New York City, examining relations with the working press, use of journalistic techniques (press releases, leaks, and conferences), and use of the ethnic media. She found that the mayor's image was heavily dependent on the abilities of his press secretary, and that the role of the press secretary was that of a political advisor, not an in-house journalist. She concluded the American public may become distrustful of press secretary communiques; this suggests that research should focus on credibility dilemmas, which in part appear to have grown with the contemporary press secretary. There is no comparable study with which we can compare these conclusions.

Chittick (1970) carried out an excellent study using interviews with stratified random samples of State Department policy officers, information officers, foreign affairs reporters, and leaders of nongovernmental organizations. He found all groups felt that the basic reason to release information was to improve public understanding of existing programs and policies; all supported the "public right to know," and all agreed that it was legitimate for the government to release information in order to strengthen its image, increase domestic support, reduce speculation, or serve other governing needs. All agreed that secrecy might be necessary for security reasons; but organization leaders, reporters, and even information officers were less likely to accept the withholding of information merely to protect the images of allies.

However, it must be pointed out that, as with all studies of attitudes, Chittick's findings do not necessarily predict behavior. Glick (1973) found that the State Department's informational output had considerable diversity, covering 11 different subject areas. But of 57 releases analyzed, only four dealt with public affairs.

Bagdikian (1972) has provided numerous examples of the reliance of reporters on government-provided information. Schiller (1973) emphasizes the government's role in propaganda on its own behalf and on behalf of U.S. corporations. However, neither of these studies is quantitative in the sense of ascertaining how many people are involved, or how often such activities occur.

Some studies have quantified the amounts of government-provided information used by the media. Sigal (1974), for example, found that the Washington Post and New York Times relied on information obtained at press conferences for roughly one-fourth of their front-page stories over the period 1949-69. Another 18 per cent of the stories relied on information from press releases. However, these studies, valuable as they are, do not tell us anything about the amounts of information the government was issuing during these periods. As a result, we know relatively little about the success rates of various information sources and information-issuing techniques.

Impact of the Media on Government

This is another inadequately researched area, although some of the soundest studies are to be found here. Davison (1974) has written a solid article based on interviews with 23 European diplomats, 14 European journalists, and 11 U.S. diplomats as well as memoirs of other journalists and diplomats. He focused on the impacts—positive and negative—of publicity on international negotiation. Among his findings was the conclusion that diplomats' information about world development came primarily from the mass media, being merely supplemented by diplomatic or intelligence channels. Also, the media were apparently highly important to nations that censored their own media; countries that restricted outflow apparently also restricted the inflow of information. And despite contentions about the need for private negotiations, most negotiations were semi-public because the diplomats themselves leaked information—some of it deliberately inaccurate in order to favor their own negotiating positions. Furthermore, diplomats occasionally used a press release as an excuse to distribute copies of a statement or opinion to other diplomats; or they used an interview as a "trial balloon" to signal interest in negotiating. This study places the role of media coverage in a new light. Publicity may occasionally hamper negotiations by undermining a negotiator's image or confidence, or inter-diplomatic trust, or by providing inaccurate information. However, the primary impact is positive; in fact, diplomats would have great difficulty functioning without the resource of media publicity.

Weiss's (1974) study of 545 opinion leaders in government and other sectors of society is similarly useful. She concluded that the media serve to link the leaders in these various sectors of government and society. Cited as the most valuable media were: (1) news magazines, (2) New York Times, Washington Post, Wall Street Journal, (3) columnists, and (4) TV. Opinion leaders said they relied heavily on the media for information about foreign policy, urban problems, and culture and values, but not so much for economic problems or welfare and poverty. Her study is especially useful in identifying which media are most likely to have an impact—and on which issues.

Wilcox (1968) has set forth the most thorough review of behaviorial research on the effect of pretrial crime news on jurors. Laboratory and simulated-jury studies have found that pretrial publicity has immediate effects, which may dissipate during the trial procedure. Report of a confession looms as the single most potent pretrial publicity element. Willingness of potential jurors to prejudge increases with the amount of media information offered. The cognitive (informational) aspect of pretrial publicity is more important than affective (emotional) character. This is one of the most effective syntheses we have; however it is limited because it has not been possible to test the experimental conclusions against evidence from actual jury trials.

Cohen (1963) sought to determine the relationship between the formulation of foreign policy and the coverage and evaluation of issues in the press. After interviewing 62 officials and journalists, he concluded that the press often plays a major role in setting the agenda of public officials. Coverage could establish the comparative importance of issues in the minds of policy-makers, or establish public priorities that require responses from policy-makers. Furthermore, anticipation of reporters' questions could prompt officials to spend extra time on certain topics. Cohen concluded that the media may not necessarily tell us what to think, but they do tell us what to think *about,* especially when they are the primary source of information about a topic such as foreign affairs.

A thorough local study by Fielder (1974) analyzed events following the broadcast of a two-part documentary on illegal gambling and prostitution in Louisville, Kentucky, by a local TV station. Fielder concluded that a local documentary can contribute to community understanding and alleviation of a problem if it (1) strongly establishes the presence of the problem and possible solutions, (2) follows up with continuous news reports, (3) convinces and/or pressures officials to act, and (4) is produced by a station willing and able to withstand pressure and criticism from local officials. Her study is chiefly valuable in that it seeks to identify characteristics that can be measured and compared across a variety of situations. Fielder's work can serve as a general model for the examination and analysis of the impact of local programming on the behavior of local officials. Unfortunately, her study is almost unique in this regard. The authors of most case studies have been content to limit their analysis to specific, rather than generalized, characteristics.

The Nature of the News Media

The studies of the news media are by all odds the most comprehensive we have. Although far from complete, they are satisfyingly strong in certain areas. Leading is a fine study by Johnstone, Slawski and Bowman (1972-73). It is based on a questionnaire to 1,313 journalists—the first large-scale, nation-wide survey of characteristics and attitudes of American journalists. The questionnaire asked about their values, and also gleaned data on professional and social characteristics and the relationships between these factors. Johnstone et al. found substantial variation in education, political, and sociological orientation, philosophy, job satisfaction, working conditions, and salary. They found positive correlations among education, youth, advocacy reporting, job dissatisfaction, and mobility. Among women, they found low job status and salary, but surprisingly high job satisfaction. Although useful for identifying characteristics that lead to differences in hiring and assignments, the study does not relate these factors to the actual coverage that different kinds of reporters produce.

Wiggins and Yarborough (1973) have focused on political reporters as part of the legislative process. They interviewed 26 reporters covering the 1973 Iowa State Legislature, adding random samples of legislators and lobbyists. They concluded that personal values and amount of education are key predictors of the behavior of reporters. Just as important, however, are the expectations of their editors. Their study is valuable for illustrating the need to consider both individual and institutional factors.

The institutional characteristics of news organizations are the central focus of three important recent studies. Argyris (1974) carried out a three-year observation of on-the-job work of forty top executives plus reporters, editors, and deskmen at the New York Times. He found that there was poor interpersonal communication, with numerous barriers and misunderstandings; authoritarian leadership, in which subordinates refused to accept responsibility for decision-making and felt free to second-guess the decisions that were made; and a win-lose aspect permeating virtually all interpersonal contacts. Argyris believes the institutional system was not solely responsible for these problems, though. The newspaper had attracted individuals with such personal characteristics as a high desire for intellectual challenge and for meaningful "essential" work; high task orientation; and authoritarianism. The pressures and competitiveness of newsgathering and news production brought out such behaviors as deception, authoritarianism, mistrust, and cynicism. Argyris's report, although confined to a single newspaper, is a good example of a case study that identifies characteristics in a way that permits comparison with other situations. It is essential that other such studies be made before researchers attempt to generalize about interpersonal relationships in news organizations; the New York Times is, after all, a highly unusual newspaper.

Furthermore, the study does not attempt to find evidence of a systematic relationship between professional behavior and news coverage. Sigal (1974) observed internal operations and studied content of the New York Times and the Washington Post. He concluded that the perspective of the individual journalist was determined primarily by his position. Citing the observation, "Where you stand depends on where you sit," Sigal noted that editors were oriented to their readers, and deskmen to their reporters. In turn, reporters' loyalty was to their desks, not to the organization as a whole. In an effort to minimize conflict among desks, the newspaper editors tended to divide up front-page space evenly among the local, national, and foreign staffs, rather than responding to the relative importance of the day's events. This study provides an important example of how interpersonal relationships can have a measurable impact on content—but in unexpected ways. "Common knowledge" says that editors impose their biases and preferences on reporters, but Sigal concluded that more influence was coming from the opposite direction.

Sigal also looked at the relationships between newsgathering behaviors, professional formulas, and the structures of news organizations. In analyzing the source of information for page one stories in the Washington Post and New York Times, he found that almost half used a U.S. government official; approximately one-quarter used a foreign or international official; and approximately 15 per cent used U.S. citizens not affiliated with any level of government. Sigal suggested that this reliance on official sources stemmed from journalistic formulas about "objectivity" and "newsworthiness"—formulas that, in turn, simplify the allocation of resources and reduce the amount of effort that must be devoted to preparing the finished product. For example, the stress on "objectivity" reduces the problem of deciding how a story should be written. Focusing on the activities of government officials simplifies the task of deciding what topics to cover. Relying on government officials as the primary source of information reduces the amount of time and effort the reporter must devote to acquiring publishable information.

Tunstall (1971) conducted a mail survey of 207 special correspondents for 23 British news organizations. He examined the characteristics of correspondents, news sources, and news organizations for factors that explained differences in newsgathering behaviors and outputs. He found that the organization controlled the definition of the job and general content orientation, appointment of the correspondents, and editorial changes in copy. The correspondents controlled newsgathering techniques, timing of the submission of copy, and degree of free-lancing. Tunstall distinguished between two types of autonomy of correspondents. Within the news organization, autonomy increased with the degree of specialization, focus on professionalism, and cooperative relationships with competitors/ colleagues. Autonomy outside increased with the number of sources, turnover in sources, and desire for reporter-initiated coverage. Thus, political reporters had higher autonomy within their news organizations because of their cooperative relationships with other reporters and the focus on "hard" news, but lower autonomy outside of their organization because of their dependence on a few official sources. Although confined to Britain, Tunstall's findings provide a source of hypotheses and a basis for comparison with U.S. news organizations.

Tichenor, Donohue and Olien (1973) have produced a valuable review of the literature that focuses on community structure and communication. They conclude that the socioeconomic structure of a community determines media content. For instance, a small-town editor is less likely to report conflicts because it would harm his status, and small-town residents and officials are less likely to want conflicts reported. The socioeconomic base also helps determine the size of the newshole, by determining the number of ads, and hence, the number of pages there will be in the day's paper.

Their work points up the need to look beyond the institutions of media and government in attempting to explain media-government relationships. All of these latter studies illustrate a promising trend in research, the effort to examine unobvious—as well as obvious—sources of influence. The characteristics and behavior of reporters, editors, and officials are important topics of research. However, in order to understand media-government relationships, we need to look at institutions as well as individuals, and at exterior as well as interior factors.

WHY WE DON'T KNOW MORE

These summaries of what we know by no means fully summarize the research that has been done. The examples we have described were chosen to illustrate the kinds of research that have been conducted so far, and the problems inherent in many of these approaches. We should add that the studies we have described are among the very best research that exists. In general, we feel that research on media-government relationships has suffered from the following flaws:

(1) There is too much focus on individual attitudes and individual characteristics. There is too little attention to institutional characteristics that might limit individual freedom of choice. Too many studies give the impression that journalists, information officers or officials are free to do whatever they please, and that it is their personal goals alone that determine how they act. Too few studies

take into account institutional pressures, socialization processes and limitations imposed by roles, regulations, and norms.

(2) There is too much attention to attitudes, and too little to actual behavior. Too many researchers seem to imply that an individual's tastes and preferences, philosophies, and personal goals are an accurate predictor of his behavior. Several studies—such as Wilhoit and Drew's (1973) survey of editorial writers—have found that people sometimes believe one thing, but do another.

(3) There is too much reliance on interviews, questionnaires, or other subject-supplied information. There is too little effort to cross-check the validity of these data with other measures (such as public records, content analyses, and researcher observation).

(4) There is too much taking-for-granted of theories about governmental operations (i.e., how government actually operates, and too much acceptance of anecdotes as evidence of the ways journalists operate). There is too little attention to ascertaining whether government and the media in fact function the way the theories or "common knowledge" say that they do. If accepted descriptions are inaccurate or atypical, many of our theories about how officials and reporters operate may be irrelevant, and many of our common-sense assumptions about media-government relationships may have to be reanalyzed.

WHAT WE NEED TO KNOW

In suggesting specific topics in need of research, we are focusing on those that seem most relevant to current problems in media-government relationships. We have reviewed what prominent contemporary journalists, officials, political scientists, and others see as areas of conflict between journalists and officials. We base our selection of research topics not merely on filling in the gaps in the research that exists, but on identifying the kinds of information that seem to us to be most relevant to current problems. Thus, we believe that it is more important to know about impacts than to know about characteristics *per se.* Our list of research topics reflects this bias.

We recognize that, in order to understand impacts, it is often necessary to find out more about the nature of the people and the institutions one is studying. Studies about characteristics are a valuable source of hypotheses about how the media and government interact, and they often shed light on why certain impacts occur.

Studies of impacts can provide data that allow researchers to identify significant characteristics. Thus, the two types of research go hand in hand, each contributing to the other. Still, it is difficult to specify what characteristics are relevant to impacts until one has some knowledge about the nature of impacts. Without this knowledge, a researcher runs the risk of studying certain characteristics that may later prove to be irrelevant. Consequently, it seems to us that the logical first step in future media-government research is to focus more on impacts than on the nature of people and institutions.

The Impact of Government on the News Media

Perhaps the most important questions about government impact on media are those that look at the result of impact vis-a-vis news content. *Among the questions we might ask about regulatory agencies are:*

—Under what conditions do regulatory policies and standards affect the amount and diversity of news and editorial content?
—What is the impact of FCC policy on the development of new communication technologies?
—What is the impact of the development of new communication technologies on FCC policy?
—Are differences in content between print and broadcast media due primarily to licensing and regulation, or to other factors?

In studying the courts and the legal system, we might ask:

—What is the impact of permissive or restrictive legislation on news content? For example, how do statutes such as the Newspaper Preservation Act or the Fair Campaign Practices Act affect the amount and nature of news and editorial content?
—How does the lack of legislation guaranteeing protection of reporters' sources affect the amount and nature of news and editorial content?
—Under what conditions do lawsuits or legislation about hiring, promotion, and other employer-employee relationships lead to changes in news and editorial content? For example, does antidiscrimination legislation have a discernible effect on news content?

In examining the informal pressures brought to bear by officials, we should look at:

—Under what conditions do efforts by officials to pressure or manipulate the news media lead to differences in the treatment of topics and points of view?
—Under what conditions do efforts by officials to withhold informa-

tion, or to provide inaccurate information, lead to differences in news and editorial content?

The Impact of News Media on Government

In looking at the impact of media on government, what we are ultimately concerned about is the impact on the behavior of officials. Thus, *in doing research on officials' use of and attitudes toward media, we might ask:*

—Under what conditions do officials rely more on the media than on their internal channels of communication for information?

—Under what conditions do differences in (1) reading and viewing habits, (2) the use of particular media, and (3) exposure to particular journalists, affect the governmental decision-making process?

—Under what conditions do officials' attitudes about news coverage or about journalists affect the decision-making process?

—Under what conditions does reliance on the media for internal information change the decision-making process?

Research on the behavior of officials might address the questions:

—Under what conditions does publicity alter personal and departmental resources in ways that affect the decision-making process?

—How does publicity create problems that affect the nature of the decision-making process or the ability of officials to carry out their duties?

—Do the space and time limitations of news coverage—or other limitations inherent in the nature of the news media—affect official decision-making processes?

In research on the courts and the legal system, we might ask:

—Under what conditions does publicity, either prior to or during a trial, affect courtroom proceedings or the verdict that is reached?

Government Information Systems

Perhaps the most important research on government information systems is that which focuses on the utilization of the information by the media. *Research on structural aspects of information systems might ask:*

—How does the output of various departments and levels of government compare with the utilization of these messages by the media?

—What are the relationships between the techniques and processes used to issue information and the utilization of information by various media?

—What factors in the nature of governmental units lead to systematic differences in the amount, nature, or accuracy of the information they provide?

Research on the characteristics of information personnel or officials might ask:

—What factors in the personal characteristics of information officers or officials lead to systematic differences in the amount, nature, or accuracy of the information they provide?

Nature of the News Media

The most basic questions about news media are those directly focused on the nature and diversity of news and editorial content. *Research on societal factors might address the following questions:*

—Under what conditions does the number of media affect the range of topics or opinions expressed in a particular area?

—What factors in the nature of the audience or social setting most affect the selection or treatment of topics and point of view? Under what conditions do these factors lead to differences in selection or treatment?

—Under what conditions are individuals, groups, or institutions conscious of exerting pressures on journalists or news organizations? How do journalists cope with these pressures and how successful are they in resisting them?

Research on news organizations might look at:

—How do institutional characteristics common to news organizations affect the selection and treatment of particular topics and points of view?

—What institutional characteristics not common to all news organizations (patterns of decision-making, distribution of power and resources, degree of competition among departments or differences in goals) lead to differences in news content among various news organizations?

Research on the characteristics of journalists might consider:

—How do the personal characteristics and attitudes of journalists lead to systematic differences in the selection, treatment, and publication of topics and points of view?

—To what extent are the attitudes of journalists determined by the nature of their jobs and/or the nature of the institutions for which they work?

—What differences in the natures of relationships between reporters and news sources lead to systematic differences in the nature of information provided?

—What types of information and points of view are excluded from coverage or slighted because of journalists' reliance on official sources and on official-controlled channels of information?

Research on news content might focus on:

    —What factors best account for the lack of diversity in news content?
    —Under what conditions does the nature of the subject affect the selection and treatment of topics?
    —Under what conditions does news coverage vary over time?

HOW WE CAN FIND OUT MORE

Two projects currently underway at Stanford University illustrate how research might address these kinds of questions in ways that would avoid some of the pitfalls that have plagued past research efforts.

One project will examine the nature and degree of agenda-setting in congressional investigations. It will assess how often and under what circumstances the press plays a major role in the convening of congressional hearings, and congressional hearings play a major role in. press coverage of events. Cater (1959) and others have suggested hearings are sometimes convened for publicity. Recent events (Watergate, the CIA, and FBI probes) suggest the press can tip Congress's agenda. This study will assess the frequency of these events, the topics most open to agenda-setting, and the perceptions and willingness of the participants. It will include:

    • Study of a sample of the written records of congressional hearings from the 93rd Congress to establish how many were convened in response to prior press coverage of topics and how this varies by chamber, committee, topic, and other factors.

    • Study of press coverage of a sample of congressional hearings from the 93rd Congress, using the Bell & Howell and New York Times indices, to establish how many were covered, how many involved agenda-setting, and how this varied by chamber, committee, topic, and other factors.

    • Survey of current news coverage of congressional committees to uncover apparent examples of the press setting Congress's agenda, and Congress setting the press's agenda; this will be discussed with correspondents and congressmen during interviews in Washington, D.C.

    • Interviews with correspondents for the prestige, agenda-setting media—Washington Post, New York Times, Los Angeles Times, Chicago Tribune, wire services, Time, Newsweek, etc.—to determine how they decide what topics and committees to cover, their relationships with congressmen and congressional staff members, their perceptions about the nature and extent of agenda-setting by the press of Congress and agenda-setting by Congress of the press, and their accounts and perceptions of the processes involved in apparent instances of agenda-setting in which they were involved.

• Interviews with congressmen and committee staff members from a sample of congressional committees to determine how their committees decide what to investigate, their perceptions and evaluations of press coverage, their relationships with reporters, their perceptions about the nature and extent of agenda-setting and their accounts and perceptions of the processes involved in apparent instances of agenda-setting in which they were involved.

It is important to note several things about this project: (1) It will rely on written records (the text of hearings and news stories) as well as subject-supplied information, to provide a cross-check on the validity of the data. (2) The written records will be analyzed BEFORE the interviews are conducted. Thus, the researchers will be able to question participants about specific events, rather than general habits. Furthermore, they will be prepared to challenge any responses that seem totally out of line with the written records. (3) The project will analyze institutional as well as personal characteristics. Congressmen and reporters will be asked about their personal interests, philosophies and perceptions. They will also be asked about institutional pressures, obligations and responsibilities. (4) The focus is on behavior rather than attitudes, and on impact rather than on performance per se.

As an illustration of how research could focus simultaneously on government information media and the nature of the news media, consider another Stanford project:

Why do different news organizations produce different accounts of the same event? We propose to trace coverage from a single source through various media to the public, using events like speeches and press conferences where a transcript is available to give a constant starting point for our search.

Among the methods of data collection will be: interviewing public figures and their press representatives to determine the source's priorities; interviewing the press corps to determine their emphasis in reporting; acquiring these reporters' copies of their stories again, before they are edited; telephone-interviewing editors in charge of placing the story in the paper or on the air to determine their judgments of the relative emphasis to be placed on the story and items within it; collecting the accounts of the event in print and recording them off the air; telephone-interviewing a sample of the public to determine which parts they can recall.

In addition, we will collect information about the news organizations themselves, such as: individual or chain ownership, medium, size of market or circulation, advertising rate, geographical distance from the event. We will thus be able to study differences within and between classes of newsgathering organizations.

The significance of the project lies in its scope. While past works have focused on the news selection processes of individual gatekeepers, groups of correspondents, or individual organizations, this investigation will examine the coverage of events across the entire range of media and organizations.

Thus, it will assess the comparative importance of various factors that have been found to influence news content and information recall. It will examine both individual and structural factors, and elements internal as well as external to the news organizations themselves.

With a little thought and ingenuity, comparable studies could be designed for almost every other aspect of media-government relationships. We concluded our review of media-government research with the belief that the biggest barrier to knowledge has not been the unavailability of data but, rather, the lack of creativity in research design.

NOTE

1. This work was supported by the John and Mary R. Markle Foundation, through a grant to the first author.

REFERENCES

ARGYRIS, C. (1974) Behind the Front Page. San Francisco: Jossey-Bass.

BAGDIKIAN, B. H. (1972) The Effete Conspiracy, and Other Crimes of the Press. New York: Harper and Row.

CATER, D. (1959) The Fourth Branch of Government. Boston: Houghton Mifflin.

CHITTICK, W. (1970) "American foreign policy elites: attitudes toward secrecy and publicity." Journalism Q. 47 (winter) 689-696.

COHEN, B. (1963) The Press and Foreign Policy. Princeton: Princeton University Press.

DAVISON, W. P. (1974) "News and media and international negotiation." Public Opinion Q. 38 (summer) 174-191.

FIELDER, V. (1974) "The social and political effects of locally produced television documentaries: a case study of WHAS-TV, Louisville, Kentucky." Presented to Assn. for Education in Journalism, San Diego, Calif.

GARCIA, A. (1967) "A study of the opinions and attitudes of California's capitol correspondents." Journalism Q. 44 (summer) 330-332.

GLICK, E. M. (1973) The Federal Government-Daily Press Relationship, Washington, D.C.: American Institute for Political Communication.

JOHNSTONE, J. W. C., E. J. SLAWSKI and W. W. BOWMAN (1972-73) "Professional values of American newsmen." Public Opinion Q. 36 (winter) 522-540.

KRASNOW, E. G. and L. LONGLEY (1973) The Politics of Broadcast Regulation. New York: St. Martins Press.

NIMMO, D. (1964) Newsgathering in Washington. New York: Prentice-Hall.

NOLL, R., M. PECK and J. McGOWAN (1973) Economic Aspects of Television Regulation. Washington, D.C.: The Brookings Institution.

SCHILLER, H. (1973) The Mind Managers. Boston: Beacon Press.

SHAFFER, C. (1973) "The Press Secretary in the Office of the Mayor of New York City: 1898-1972." Ph.D. dissertation, New York University.

SIGAL, L. (1974) Reporters and Officials. Lexington, Mass.: D. C. Heath.

TICHENOR, P. J., G. A. DONOHUE and C. N. OLIEN (1973) "Mass communication research: Evolution of a structural model." Journalism Q. 50 (autumn) 419-425.

TUNSTALL, J. (1971) Journalists at Work. London: Constable and Beverly Hills: Sage Pubns.

WEAVER, D. (1974) "The press and governmental restriction: A cross-national study over time." Presented to Assn. for Education in Journalism, San Diego, Calif.

WEISS, C. H. (1974) "What America's leaders read." Public Opinion Q. 38 (spring) 1-22.

WIGGINS, C. and P. YARBOROUGH (1973) Political reporters and the legislative process. A proposal to the National Science Foundation.

WILCOX, W. (1968) The press, the jury, and the behavioral sciences. Journalism Monographs No. 9.

WILHOIT, G. C. and D. DREW (1973) "The politics and community participation of editorial writers." Journalism Q. 50 (winter) 638-644.

Chapter 8

ON THE USE OF MULTIPLE METHODS AND MULTIPLE

SITUATIONS IN POLITICAL COMMUNICATIONS RESEARCH

Michael L. Rothschild

THE EFFECTS of the mass media on voting behavior have long been a source of interest in the field of communications research.[1] Most of the past research in this area has relied upon the use of (1) survey methodology and (2) the examination of high-level election races. These foci have contributed, at least in part, to acceptance of what Blumler and McLeod (1973) have termed the "limited effects" model of mass media effects on voting behavior (see also chapters in this volume by Becker et al. and Kraus et al.). The model has been predicated on research showing great stability in the political process, but Blumler and McLeod observe that ". . . the world of politics no longer appears so stable" (p. 2).

Dreyer (1971), for example, has noted a steady decline since 1952 in the capacity of party identification to predict voting behavior in presidential elections. It is possible that television and its characteristic short-term information flows have led to this greater volatility. As party ties lose their salience, the power of the media may increase in importance. Mayer (1958) presented a similar view when he wrote that in the 1952 presidential election television advertising began to be a factor.

Rothschild (1974) found that during the period 1952-1974 the

AUTHOR'S NOTE: This research was supported by the American Assembly of Collegiate Schools of Business and the Graduate School of Business, University of Wisconsin, and was aided by the comments of Gil Churchill, Gay Leslie and Steven Chaffee.

voting age population increased by 40 per cent, while all political expenditures increased by 290 per cent, political broadcast expenditures increased by 600 per cent, and presidential campaign expenditures increased by 690 per cent. While some proportion of this increase in spending could be attributed to a "keeping up with the opposition", and some to inflation, there must also have been some belief in media effectiveness behind these expenditures. This increase in campaign spending is perhaps the key change in the political environment over the past 20 years. This radical transformation of the political process due to advertising and other types of promotion indicates a need to reassess the earlier work that led to the limited effects model.

When research was first done in this area, prior to massive political advertising, it is quite possible that the media had only a limited effect on the electorate. But modern advertising has added a new dimension, one that has such subtle and situation-specific effects that the investigator must turn to more subtle measuring instruments (than the survey questionnaire) and examine more varied situations (than the presidential race). Blumler and McLeod in effect share this point of view; they write that, although there are some recent developments to challenge the limited effects model, there are more untested hypotheses than there are techniques and supporting results. This chapter offers a framework for examining and developing new techniques, and some data that support a new look (Blumler and McLeod, 1973). This new look, however, can be seen as an extension of the limited effects model rather than a replacement for it.

Hypothetically, there are at least four states of the world with which one should be concerned in evaluating the effects of the media (and especially the impact of controlled media such as advertising) on voting behavior. These four states are concerned with high or low level elections, and high or low levels of expenditures. One could argue that in the early stages of political communications research only the low expenditures condition existed, and that only the high-level race, low expenditure state was examined. To understand the full range of media effects, research should cover all four states. The limited effects findings were probably due in part to limited situation exploration and limited methods. In defense, it should be noted that without high levels of expenditures as an incentive, there was no clear-cut need to enlarge the scope of investigation.

It is typical of many fields to rely on a single method for most of their work. For example, much of academic psychology is limited to experimental laboratory techniques; more than 90 per cent of all applied social science research relies on survey methods (Webb et al., 1966); some 80 per cent of marketing research is based on the interview (Ray and Sherrill, 1973). Since political communications research has grown out of these latter fields, the predominance of survey-interview methods is no more surprising that it is unusual, but one can also profitably look to these other fields to learn of viable alternatives. For example, marketing communications, which had relied extensively on survey methods in the past, is now employing more laboratory experiments, field experiments and unobtrusive measures.

There has been a gradual shift to these other methods such as econometrics (e.g. Palda, 1964) and experimental design (e.g. Ray and Sawyer, 1971). In order to develop valid and reliable sets of data and findings, this chapter advocates the use of both multiple methods and multiple situations. In particular, the use of experimental work and of lower level election settings is proposed and illustrated.

EVALUATING ALTERNATIVE METHODS

In order to separate and evaluate methods, one must first consider what is the relevant problem. For studying *existing* cognitive, affective or conative development, introspective responses common to survey methods might produce the desired information. On the other hand, if one were studying *the effects of communications* on cognitive, affective or conative development, then it would be preferable to use some sort of experimental design, to separate the effects of the key independent variable(s) and eliminate contamination from other elements of the environment. This latter task is more relevant to the development of the field of political communications. Much of the early work in the field was concerned with the first of the two problems and appropriately employed survey methods; any attempt to look at the second problem via survey/interview methods would have only limited chances for success.

There are four major types of data-gathering techniques available: laboratory experiments, field experiments, unobtrusive methods, and field studies and survey research.[2] This chapter will primarily examine the neglected potential of the remaining three methods.

Laboratory Experiments

A *laboratory experiment* is a research study in which the variance of all or nearly all of the possible influential independent variables not pertinent to the immediate problem of the investigation is kept at a minimum. This is done by isolating the research in a physical situation apart from the routine or ordinary living and by manipulating one or more independent variables under rigorously specified, operationalized, and controlled conditions. . . .

The laboratory experiment has the inherent virtue of the possibility of relatively complete control. The laboratory experimenter can, and often does, isolate the research situation from the life around the laboratory by eliminating the many extraneous influences that may affect the dependent variables (Kerlinger, 1973, p. 398).

One must also consider that the laboratory experiment can be very artificial and contrived if proper care is not taken. Often the "cover story" or ploy necessary to produce a proper setting for communication processes to operate naturally in experimentation is quite elaborate. Given a proper setting, though, a reasonable level of external validity can be achieved. External validity can be further enhanced by the use of multiple methods, i.e. by the subsequent or simultaneous testing of the same hypotheses in more natural settings.

The primary reason for experimentation is that one can establish relatively high internal validity in the laboratory. That is, a highly controlled setting maximizes the investigator's power to eliminate possible alternative explanations—other than the communication "stimulus"—of the effect found. Problems of external validity, or the power to generalize the finding beyond the laboratory conditions, call for creative innovation in the development of laboratory settings. As Kerlinger puts it:

The aim of laboratory experiments, then is to test hypotheses derived from theory, to study the precise interrelations of variables and their operation, and to control variance under research conditions that are uncontaminated by the operation of extraneous variables. As such, the laboratory experiment is one of man's greatest achievements (p. 401).

Field Experiments

The second of the three neglected methods is the field experiment.

A field experiment is a research study in a realistic situation in which one or more independent variables are manipulated by the experimenter under as carefully controlled conditions as the situation will permit. . . . The control of the experimental field situation, however, is rarely as tight as that of the laboratory experimental situation. We have here both a strength and a weakness. The investigator in a field study, though he has the power of manipulation, is always faced with the unpleasant possibility that his independent variables are contaminated by uncontrolled environmental variables (Kerlinger, 1973, pp. 401-402).

The field experiment is a popular device in marketing research for the testing of different prices, promotional campaigns and channels of distribution. It has proven quite valuable for testing these marketing elements in a "real world" situation and can be used whenever there is a reasonable span of time available for testing.

To do a field experiment in political communications, one would ordinarily need to find at least one candidate in a major race (covering more than one geographically distinct marketplace) who would be willing to experiment. Given that any candidate is either going to win or lose in a short period of time, one might be hard pressed to find a candidate willing to participate in a field experiment.[3] Since the political marketplace differs from the consumer goods marketplace in distinct ways, the field experiment—however suitable in principle—may not be pragmatically appropriate here.[4]

Unobtrusive Methods

The last type of method to be considered is usually known as the unobtrusive measure (Webb, et al., 1966; Ray and Sherrill, 1973). This set of measures is used to collect data without the awareness of the person whose behavior is being observed, i.e. without any possible respondent contamination. Webb includes in the list of possibilities entrapment, archival records, observation, and physical trace (erosion and accretion). While such indicators often admit problems of low reliability and validity, when skillfully used and carefully interpreted they can provide important supplementary evidence.

Ray (1973a) employed *seventeen* different methods to obtain data concerning a local election in California. These included archival records (voting records, census data, letters to the editor); observation (poll watches, precinct observation); physical trace (bumper sticker counts, water pressure monitoring, long distance telephone calls); entrapment (lost letter technique, postcard request for support, postcard request for information, lost letter—bumper sticker field experiment); and five interview measures (movie theater straw poll, school children questionnaires, expert informant interviews, mail and telephone interview). In only the last two (interview) methods was the electorate disturbed by questioning, and the political process possibly affected in any way by the researcher.

Weaknesses of Survey Research

Table 1 lists 15 serious sources of research invalidity in the use of questionnaires common to most survey work.[5] By using other than survey techniques, at least some of these sources of invalidity can be avoided or controlled. Although direct questioning is sometimes a poor method for collecting valid attitudinal data, it is still the primary method used in political communications and in other pragmatic branches of social science. The problem is that it sometimes produces spurious "effects" that would not have occurred but for the obtrusive presence of the researcher.

An interesting manifestation of "measurement as change" was shown by Ramond (1974). He interviewed two sets of respondents on their attitudes towards oil companies. In one case, he merely asked for an attitude, to show degree of favorableness. In the second case, this question was preceded by a set of questions dealing with exposure to and recall of oil company advertising. There were significant differences in the attitudinal responses of the two groups. Ramond attributed the difference to the extended line of questioning in the second case and felt that attitudes were affected by the questions. It is not possible to conclude that one of these two measures is the more valid; the study points up the need for careful interpretation.

TABLE 1
COMMON SOURCES OF RESEARCH INVALIDITY IN SURVEY RESEARCH

1. *Reactive Measurement Effect*	3. *Varieties of Sampling Error*
a. Awareness of being tested	g. Population restriction
b. Role playing	h. Population stability over time
c. Measurement as change	i. Population stability over areas
d. Response sets	
	4. *Access to Content*
2. *Error from Investigator*	j. Restrictions on content
e. Interviewer effects	k. Stability of content over time
f. Change–fatigue/practice	l. Stability of content over areas

5. *Operating Ease and Validity Checks*
m. Dross rate (degree of superfluous measures)
n. Access to descriptive cues
o. Ability to replicate

Source: Ray and Sherrill, 1973.

The Ramond study is analogous to observational problems in subatomic physics. In that field, in order to view very small particles of matter, it is necessary to focus light on the matter, but the energy of the light causes the matter to shift so that when it is viewed it is not in its original configuration. In survey research, similarly, the asking of questions, which induces role-playing by the respondent, can lead to distorted responses that do not validly express the person's "normal" views. Field experiments have demonstrated complex political opinion displacements due to respondents' perception of the status and affiliation of the interviewer (Atkin and Chaffee, 1972; Allen, 1975).

One could easily add to Table 1. For example, another reactive measurement effect frequently found in political communications research has been the inability of the respondent to deal with the topic. One often reads of research where the respondent was required to evaluate political advertising messages or what effect they have on him/her. If the advertising has been persuasive, the respondent might not be able to make this type of evaluation. Krugman (1965) posits that the effects of advertising for certain product classes and for certain media are subtle and take place over an extended period of time. If the respondent is not "involved" with the product class in question, he does not put up perceptual defenses and evaluate incoming messages. His cognitive set may change over time, and lead, without his realizing it, to the desired action. If Krugman is correct, it would be fruitless to ask a respondent how he was affected by the messages. Ray and his colleagues (Ray and Sawyer, 1971; Ray, Sawyer and Strong, 1971; Heeler, 1972, Sawyer, 1971; Strong, 1972) have shown the impact of repetitious advertising over time through experimental work that supports Krugman's theory.

In another context, Ray, Ward and Reed (1974) examined the value of several testing techniques ranging on a continuum from natural to artificial. This included the field experiment in a natural setting where the response to different conditions could be unobtrusively observed. Unobtrusive measures of political behavior include voting records, expert witnesses and news stories; independent measures such as quality and quantity of communications can also be unobtrusively observed. This kind of design can be expanded to include several settings; the data then lend themselves to regression analysis. This technique was used by Palda (1973) to develop a demand (for votes) model to analyze data from 108 Quebec electoral districts for the 1966 and 1970 elections. Palda found that political advertising does have an effect in local elections. He also showed that variables such as incumbency, and being in the same party as the winner at the top of the ticket ("coat tails") are more important than advertising. This particular study was made possible by stringent Canadian laws concerning the reporting of political advertising expenditures. Similar work can be done in the United States, to the extent that new Watergate-stimulated reporting requirements provide this kind of data.

At the other end of the Ray-Ward-Reed continuum are highly artificial methods. These are recommended for early testing to develop directions for later work. Such a sequential notion also fits into the Ray decision sequence (discussed below) in which laboratory experimentation occurs early to enable one to establish a presumptive case for hypotheses that can later be tested in the field.

In summary, two major points favor the use of non-survey techniques for evaluating effects of political communications.

1. It is difficult to isolate the effect(s) of any key variable via the use of survey techniques. By using longitudinal survey techniques, one can note that a change has taken place, but one cannot attribute this change to specific variables without elaborate analyses that require tenuous assumptions. For causal inferences, it is greatly preferable to employ an experimental design.

2. The measurement problem is compounded when the respondent is not able to give an accurate introspective description of his orientation and/or retrospective evaluation of the effect(s) of the communication. Change can be measured through the use of the questionnaire, but the respondent should not be expected to be able to evaluate the cause of this change; the investigator often must make serious inferential leaps to do so. Experimental designs are clearly preferable in such situations, and unobtrusive observation can provide important checks on the validity of traditional measurement.

MULTIPLE METHODS AND MULTIPLE SITUATIONS

Not only must different methods sometimes be employed in the study of political communication, but some format for the use of multiple methods must be established. One should also be ready to consider multiple situations, i.e. to look at a wide range of political races ranging from the presidential election down through ballot propositions. Research that employs a single methodology or a single operationalism of terms leaves its findings open to question. One test doesn't prove; it merely probes. Conceptual replications are needed to confirm. Despite its espousal by behavioral scientists such as Campbell (Campbell and Fiske, 1959), Webb (Webb, et al., 1966) and Ray (Ray and Heeler, 1971; Heeler and Ray, 1972; Ray and Sherrill, 1973), however, this multiple methods and measures format is rarely used in practice.

This chapter does not advocate the use of any single method, nor will it take the stringent approach of the Campbell and Fiske (1959) multitrait-multimethod matrix. This scientific ideal is not pragmatically feasible in most research situations. A middle path is chosen here, one that stresses that some confirmation via multiple measures, methods and situations is necessary. In effect, this involves a multitrait-multimethod matrix with some empty cells. To increase the resultant confidence in one's inferences, the methods used should be as divergent as possible.

A Multiple Methods Research Sequence

Ray (1973c) and Katz, Maccoby and Morse (1951) have argued for an ordered research sequence that can be efficiently implemented. Although the two sequences they suggest are similar in their ends of attempting to cross-validate findings, their means are quite different, as Figure 1 indicates.

Ray's suggested research sequence in Figure 1 is to examine a problem and develop a microtheoretical notion that can be tested in highly controlled experimentation where the key variables can be closely watched and manipulated. Later research moves to less controlled settings until the problem is eventually observed in the field.

Katz et al. propose almost the opposite sequence (Figure 1). They take a much broader initial problem area and identify suspected relationships through field studies. Interesting hypotheses are later studied in controlled experimental settings.

Figure 2 shows how the two sequences might be combined into a framework of continuous work as theories are expanded and new problems arise. The notion of a continuous sequence of work with simultaneous field and laboratory work is ideal; the notion of multiple methods, measures and situations is a necessity. Without multiple methods one may not recognize artifactual errors; without multiple situations one cannot generalize. These are the limitations which, in part, led to the limited effects model. Although internal validity had been achieved, there may not have been external validity or complete tests of reliability.

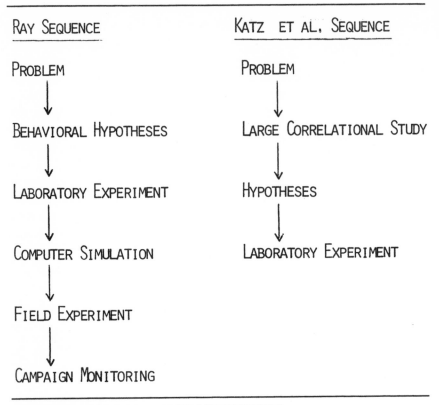

Figure 1: TWO ALTERNATIVE RESEARCH SEQUENCES

The Bounds of Reliability

In order for a body of generally accepted findings to become established over time, it is necessary to consider these problems of validity and reliability. This has been the case in political communications research, but only on a partial basis. The studies of Lazarsfeld (Lazarsfeld, Berelson and Gaudet, 1948; Berelson, Lazarsfeld and McPhee, 1954) and Campbell (Campbell, Gurin and Miller, 1954; Campbell and Cooper, 1956; Campbell, Converse, Miller and Stokes, 1960; 1966) have been replicated (and re-reported) many times (Nimmo, 1970; Lang and Lang, 1962; Rossi, 1966; Benham, 1965; Key, 1966; Sears, 1969; Trenaman and McQuail, 1961; Blumler and McQuail, 1969). Such a large and well respected body of literature certainly established a feeling of reliability of inferences. Considering the scope of these works (major elections, primarily before large-scale television advertising) there was also a certain level of external validity generated by what were at the time intuitively acceptable sets of findings.

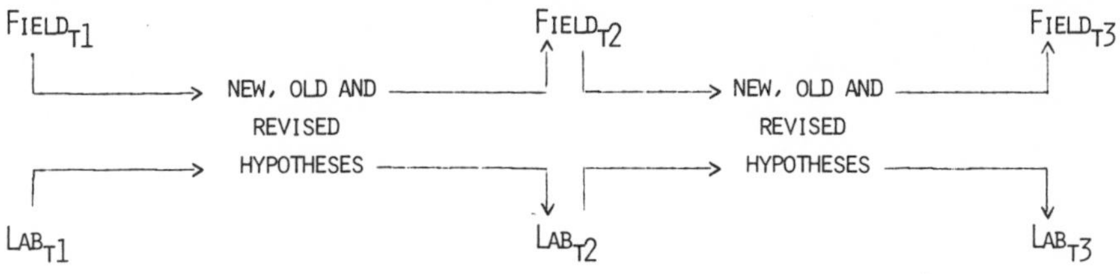

$FIELD_{T1}$ $FIELD_{T2}$ $FIELD_{T3}$

     ⟶ NEW, OLD AND ⟶   ⟶ NEW, OLD AND ⟶
          REVISED   REVISED

     ⟶ HYPOTHESES ⟶   ⟶ HYPOTHESES ⟶

LAB_{T1} LAB_{T2} LAB_{T3}

Figure 2: A SEQUENCE FOR CONTINUOUS RESEARCH

For 20 years these works were examined in their one context and so were not seriously questioned. But viewed in a broader context, and retested with different methods and in new situations, the limited effects model becomes less viable.

It is standard to treat *measurement reliability* via either a test-retest procedure or an equivalent-form procedure. Early findings (of limited effects) were confirmed by using similar tests of replication. In virtually all cases, the tests used survey designs and examined only the high level race, low level advertising situation. Yet an equally important concept is that of the *reliability of an inference*. This calls for a test of the bounds of the situations examined. Without multiple-situations replication, research becomes suspect as possibly due to a "situation artifact."

Kline (1972) was one of the first to report on key differences in communications effects as a function of the level of the election race. He presented a review and re-analysis of data from several national and local election field survey studies which generally examined the agenda setting function of the media. Kline concluded that there are two types of elections. *Presidential elections* affect people of varying involvement levels in similar ways, and voting tends to be quite stable. *Party elections* (i.e. below the presidential level) are quite unstable situations for the low-involvement voter. Here people rely on simple presentations and deviate from party identification as a result. Because they did not have enough information to make rational decisions, people relied on their simple recall of images; consequently, in Kline's scenario, the predominant image received the vote. This finding is important in demonstrating that, while the limited effects model holds in the high level election, the media can have considerable power in a low level race. More studies of the latter type of situation could reorder thinking that has been conditioned by the limited effects inference; this is a strong argument on behalf of the multiple-situations philosophy.

IMPLEMENTING THE NOTIONS

Several desiderata have been proposed for expanding the methodological bounds of political communications research. The remainder of this chapter is devoted to presenting an application that provides (1) an example of such methods and (2) data that support the exceptions to the limited effects model that have been taken here. The primary data collection device in the project was a laboratory experiment. Data were also collected via a field panel study, a series of field surveys, public and private archival records, and expert witness questionnaires. There were 11 election situations; the laboratory elections were further expanded via the use of several levels of advertising for each race. Table 2 gives an overview of the three

TABLE 2
SOME CHARACTERISTICS OF THE THREE STUDIES

Dimensions	Laboratory experiment	Field panel	California poll surveys
Control of environment	Artificial	Natural	Natural
Number of situations (races)	3	1	7
Levels of advertising	6	1	2
Depth of analysis of each situation	Medium	Deep	Shallow
Number of dependent variables	3	c.20	2
Respondents	Same throughout	Same throughout	New with each wave
Operationalizations of key measure	3	3	2
Principal method of analysis	Analysis of variance	Cross lagged correlations	Analysis of variance
Collection method	Controlled exposure and interview	Interview + Archival + Expert witness	Interview + Archival + Expert witness
Advantage of method	Controlled exposure	Natural exposure	Natural exposure
		(No control over method in these cases; data collected by outside source.)	
Disadvantage of method	Artificial	Not controlled; obtrusive measurement	Not controlled; obtrusive measurement

Source: Rothschild (1974).

studies comprising the project. In all, it contains one of the few laboratory experiments showing the effects of political advertising, several measures and methods in an attempt to validate the findings, and data on several levels of election races (situations).

The project examined the effects of political advertising on voting behavior, based on a behavioral model of decision-making styles under varying degrees of involvement. This model is referred to below as the "project" model, to separate it from the limited effects model discussed previously. Detailed discussions of the behavioral model, the data collection methods, and the findings can be found in Rothschild (1974, 1975) and Rothschild and Ray (1974). Involvement was defined as having three levels:

1. *No involvement:* no behavior due to lack of interest.
2. *Zero order involvement:* concern with the issue. There is a need to behave that does not relate to deciding between alternatives.
3. *Higher order involvement:* commitment to a position or concern with a specific stand on an issue; behavior reflects a decision based on concern or commitment.

Furthermore, involvement is a function of both the situation (situation involvement) and the individual's prior cognitive/affective development (enduring involvement). The model also postulates that two hierarchies of effect (Lavidge and Steiner, 1961; Ray, 1973b) exist, dependent on the level of involvement. These hierarchies differ in the internal relationships between affective development and conative development.

THE SEVERAL DATA COLLECTION METHODS

There are many ways in which one might implement the notions discussed above. Those reported here provide one example that proved to be effective for the author. The key point is that the notions are implementable with some degree of success, not that these particular methods are necessary or vital in order to fulfill the positions espoused in this paper.

The Laboratory Experiment

The experiment was 6 x 3 x 2 posttest-only control group factorial design. The independent variables were the number of repetitions of the advertisements; type of election race (situational involvement);

and involvement level of respondents (enduring involvement). Dependent variables, separately measured, were recall of the advertising, formation of an attitude concerning the candidate, and voting intentions. The experiment took place in a large shopping mall during mid-September 1972. The purpose was to attempt to observe changes in the dependent variables in a controlled environment by varying the subject's exposure to the messages of political candidates. Candidates in the experiment were those running at the time for president, and for congress and state assembly in the district of the shopping mall location.

Subjects were self-selected volunteers who happened to be in the shopping center. This method, in effect, consists of bringing a controlled "laboratory" environment to the subjects; 161 subjects saw the entire demonstration and completed the questionnaire sufficiently to give usable data.

Materials. The subjects were randomly assigned to one of six presentation sequences so that each sequence was seen by 23 to 31 subjects. Each sequence was a constrained random ordering of 49-53 slides showing messages for two products/candidates in each of six consumer product classes and three election races. In any particular sequence, messages for a product/candidate might be seen zero to six times and messages for the direct competitor could also be seen zero to six times. Twelve filler ads unrelated to the study were randomly inserted into each sequence to mask the concentration of test messages and to reduce any effects of primacy and recency on the learning of the messages being studied. Product/candidate ("A") messages and competitor ("B") messages were shown in conditions that ranged from 0 "A" and 6 "B" to 6 "A" and 0 "B", with more balanced ratios (1-4, 2-2, 4-1) and a control condition (0-0). In each sequence, one-third of the ads were political and two-thirds were consumer goods.

Procedure. Prospective subjects came to the shopping center auditorium in response to signs placed about the shopping center announcing a demonstration of shopping in the future. Upon entering the auditorium "laboratory" each prospective subject was given a leaflet describing the shopping demonstration and shown literature on field tests of shopping in the home via interactive computer systems. Subjects were told there would be a questionnaire to fill out and the entire procedure would take 20 to 25 minutes. If they wished to participate, they were then shown a demonstration of what that phenomenon might look like in their home. Subjects were told that due to the technical limitations of the shopping center, the demonstration was of more limited scope than an actual system would be, but that the purpose was to expose them to its concept and to get their reactions.

The presentation consisting of one of the six experimental conditions described above, was shown to not more than six subjects at any one time; it lasted eight minutes. After the demonstration, each subject completed a questionnaire that asked for opinions of the system demonstrated, and for recall (unaided) of the messages, attitudes toward the sponsors, purchase/voting intentions, and demographics.

Subjects were then asked for five more minutes to fill out a political science questionnaire supposedly unrelated to the demonstration. This questionnaire measured political involvement via a set of political efficacy and citizen duty statements (Campbell et al., 1954), and also included a set of assistance to candidates statements (Ray, 1973a). These were used to determine enduring involvement. Situational involvement was assumed to be based on the election level. Jennings and Ziegler (1970) have shown that national elections evoke high involvement, state elections low involvement, and local elections slightly higher than low involvement. The questionnaire also dealt with party loyalty and voting history.

The shopping of the future cover story and the basic design of the experiment are due to Ray and his colleagues (Ray, 1973b) and have been used successfully in nine other studies of consumer product and public service advertising. In this study, it was hoped that the cover story would attract people without regard to their election involvement, while at the same time producing as natural a viewing situation as possible. Debriefing indicated that in all but a few instances, for which data were discarded, the cover was successful.

The Field Panel Study

The field panel study was conducted in a midwestern state from August to November 1972. Data were collected by a political research firm in conjunction with its work for one of the candidates in the race being studied—a race for a United States Senate seat. Along with the panel study, there was also an expert witness questionnaire and an archival analysis.

The panel study consisted of three waves: pre-, during-, and post-campaign (August, October, and November, respectively). Sample sizes in these waves were 769, 466, and 172. Attrition of panel members was severe, but there is no indication that the 172 differed from the 769 on any important dimensions other than that they consented to be interviewed three times. The sampling procedure that was used was a two-stage area cluster sample (Kish, 1965). The first wave respondents were contacted in person. For the second wave, the same respondents were interviewed by telephone; in the third wave, those who had been recovered in the second wave were again interviewed by telephone.

Information sought from respondents dealt with involvement towards the political process, awareness of the candidates and issues, attitudes concerning the candidates and issues, behavior toward the candidates (how will you vote; how did you vote), voting history and party loyalty, demographics, and exposure to news and advertising. The panel study basically attempted to examine the same relationships in a natural environment as the laboratory experiment did in a controlled environment.

The expert witness questionnaire. This item was sent to people in the panel's state who the researchers felt would be knowledgeable and insightful with regard to the senatorial race studied. They were asked to compare the candidates' real personalities, news portrayals, and advertising images on several dimensions of judgment that corresponded to those of the field panel study. This method was also used to assess the candidates' stands on key issues.

Analysis of news and advertising. During the campaign (mid-August through Election Day), relevant news and advertising content was collected from the two largest newspapers in the state (one from each of the two largest cities). Both candidates provided data concerning expenditures and media allocations. One candidate provided a film of all television commercials.

The California Poll Data

This project used a subset of the data collected by the California Poll during the 1972 election campaigns. One thousand to 1500 potential voters responded in one of three polls and gave opinions concerning seven propositions on the California ballot. Data concerned voting intentions (direction and concreteness of intent) for the propositions. Supplementary information was gathered from two sources. Several California newspapers were reviewed during the period in question to obtain public archival data; and several experts on California politics were interviewed to get their feelings on key points not available from either of the other data sources.

The newspaper archival data and the expert witnesses provided,

TABLE 3
DATA USED TO DETERMINE INVOLVEDNESS OF THE PROPOSITIONS IN AUGUST 1972

Proposition number	Proposition issue	Expert consensus on involvedness of issue prior to campaign	Author's interpretation of poll press releases	Newspaper content analysis	Undecided responses Calif. Poll (8/72) a	Number of news stories concerning the issue prior to the campaign (7/72-9/72) b	Involvedness level of the issue prior to the campaign
11	Taxes	H	Z^d	—	H (.07)	H (20)	H (3 of 4)^c
17	Death penalty	H	H	—	H (.08)	Z^d(6)	H (3 of 4)
18	Obscenity	Z	Z	Z	Z (.17)	Z (5)	Z (5 of 5)
19	Marijuana	H	H	Z^d	H (.06)	— (10)	H (3 of 4)
20	Coastal	H	Z^d	—	H (.06)	H (34)	H (3 of 4)
21 Busing	Busing	H^d	Z	Z	Z (.17)	Z (5)	Z (4 of 5)
22	Farm labor	Z	Z	—	Z (.20)	H^d(20)	Z (3 of 4)

a. Figures represent proportion undecided, higher values indicate less involvement

b. Figures represent number of news stories dealing with general issue from 7/72 to 9/72 in major California newspapers.

c. 3 of 4 represents consistency of measures in row

d. Represents divergent view in row

Z = zero order involvement

H = higher order involvement

Source: Rothschild, 1974.

respectively, somewhat objective and highly subjective information on the involvedness of each of the seven ballot propositions and their advertising levels. Table 3 shows how these data from several weak sources were combined to make stronger determinations as to an important missing variable, that of involvedness. These unobtrusive measures were used to create a measure that could not be obtained via survey work. This measure would have suffered from low validity without the use of multiple methods, since it would have been difficult to place much confidence in any of the individual measures. Nevertheless, Table 3 shows fairly good agreement across measures, a convergence that enhances overall validity of the index. The suspect archival and expert sources were used in this case because without them an excellent data source (the California Poll) would have been discarded for want of information concerning one key variable.

THE FINDINGS

The results were both plausible and intuitively pleasing. Furthermore, at least in the laboratory experiment, the findings were not ones that would be self-reported by respondents in an introspective survey situation. The findings presented here are not complete, but are meant (1) to support the use of other-than-survey and multiple methods and (2) to support an expanded view of the political communication effects model.

The Laboratory Experiment

The experiment showed that political advertising can have an effect and that this effect is dependent on the involvement of the race and the voter. The major concern of the study was with direct changes in voting intention as a result of advertising levels; the effect here was pronounced. The data show that political advertising has a strong positive effect on voting intention in a zero order involvement race but not in a higher order involvement race, as shown in the right-most portion of Figure 3.

The importance of this first finding was heightened by a second finding. In the zero order involvement situation, it was possible to effect a change in behavioral intent without affecting attitude formation to the same degree. The data indicated the existence of a zero order involvement hierarchy wherein an individual might behave without developing a prior attitude. This can be seen in the overall

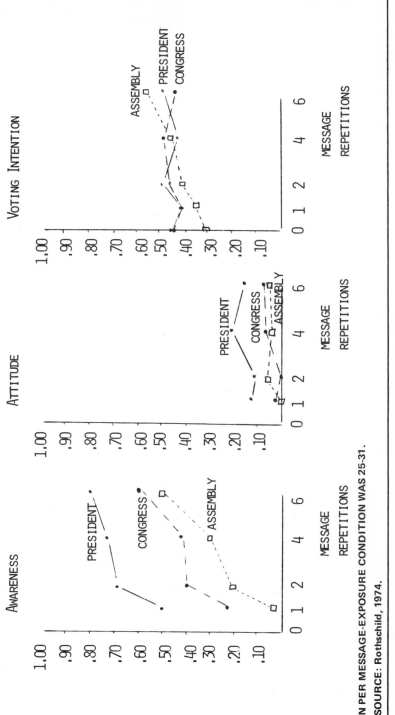

N PER MESSAGE-EXPOSURE CONDITION WAS 25-31.

SOURCE: Rothschild, 1974.

Figure 3: RESPONSE TO VARYING REPETITIVE ADVERTISING LEVELS

Figure 3. In the zero order involvement situation, this mode of decision making (or acting without decision making) held even for those individuals who might generally be thought of as having higher order involvement.

The experimental situation was especially appropriate to this project. Because involvement was such a delicate topic, it was felt that direct questioning would affect responses. (This may have occurred in the field panel study, where 85 per cent of the respondents reported that they were party loyal and had higher order involvement towards the political process.)

The Field Panel Study

Changes both within and between levels of the hierarchy were objectively analyzed through the time frame of the campaign. Analysis of the data examined the simultaneous, serial and cross-lagged relationships. It was found that:

(1) There was no significant change in intended behavior toward the candidates during the period of the campaign. This would be predicted from the limited effects model. Since the race under examination was a high involvement situation (senatorial race) the project model would not have made a different prediction. Logically, however, a null hypothesis like that of the limited effects model is untestable using statistical methodology.

(2) Changes over time in cognitive, effective and conative development were consistent with what the project model predicted for a higher order involvement situation. There was greatest stability in conative development and least stability in cognitive development.

(3) Decision-making style was predicted on enduring involvement plus situation involvement in a manner similar to that noted in the laboratory experiment.

The California Poll Data

The project model predicted that individuals with higher order loyal involvement toward an issue would be early decision makers; individuals with higher order information-seeking involvement would be late decision makers; and individuals with zero order involvement would decide at random times. This seems to have been the case.

In looking at the relationship between advertising level and situation involvement, one finds a significant effect due to advertising level, a slight effect due to situation involvement, and no interaction effect. If it is assumed that fraudulent advertising (as reported by the press) leads to greater information seeking, the data further support the project model. Those propositions determined to have higher order involvement had the least undecided voters at any point in time; those propositions determined to have fraudulent advertising had the most undecided voters at any point in time.

The methodologies and measuring instruments of the field panel study and the California Poll were not originally designed to test the project model, yet both of these pieces of research have supported different sections of this model. This support leads to increased confidence in the validity of the full set of inferences and the model that links them.

RELATING THE PROJECT TO THE PROPOSED RESEARCH SYSTEM

The physical sciences are fortunate to have some well-defined and accurate laws that govern the outcome of physical events; the laws of social science (if there are any) are complex and interactive with other laws. In the social sciences, proof is a very difficult concept; notions are tested, retested, confirmed, disproved, and re-examined in differing settings and using differing methodologies. So in social science one often must accept the premise that many weak findings pointing in the same direction lead to confidence in results.

The project described here examined involvement as it mediates between the stimulus of advertising and the response of behavior in a political context. Eleven settings and three methodologies were employed; overall, some consistent findings have emerged. Figure 4 shows the 11 settings as they appear in a 2 x 2 advertising/ involvement matrix over the several studies reported. Figure 4 concentrates on a key concern of the overall study: how do differing advertising and involvement levels interact? The project model has hypothesized that a zero order involvement/high advertising situation will lead to the greatest change, and that a higher order involvement/ low advertising situation will lead to the least direct or indirect change in a conative component. The data generally confirm this expectation. There is no documented change in any case of the lower left cell of Figure 4. There is, though, change in all of the cases in the upper right cell of the figure. The laboratory data fit the model very well; the only case in the panel data also fits. The California Poll data

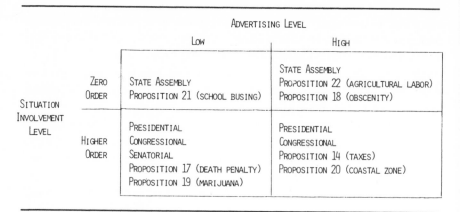

Figure 4: THE ADVERTISING/INVOLVEMENT MATRIX AS USED IN THE THREE STUDIES

showed slightly greater change in the high involvement situation, which is also consistent with the model. Most important, the data demonstrate the value of integrated multiple situation research.

Conflicting results were obtained in examining situation and enduring involvement. Modern psychological theory posits that behavior is situation-specific. In two of three applicable cases in the laboratory and panel data, that theory is upheld. In two of three cases a rival hypothesis also holds: the notion is that low involvement dominates, whether it be in the situation or in the subject's prior cognitive set. Due to the uncertainty of this result, judgment is withheld pending further research in this area. Use of multiple methods are shown in this instance to lead to the withholding of conflicting data, and, in turn, to generate ideas for further research.

A Final Assessment

The field panel study taken by itself would have been read as support for the limited effects model. It reinforced earlier findings that political communications have little effect on voting—that is apparently because the panel study uses a method (survey) and situation (high involvement race) similar to most of the earlier work. By combining the field panel study with the laboratory experiment, the California Poll data and the supporting unobtrusive methods, one finds that there is both (1) support for the notions of this chapter, and (2) reason for an elaboration of the limited effects model. The use of multiple methods has led to convergent findings (in the spirit of Campbell and Fiske, 1959) and external validity. One should note also that a few divergent results are not entirely unpleasant since they point to directions for further research.

The limited effects model is not incorrect, but it does seem to be incomplete. By using a richer set of data, one can see that the traditional model attempted to generalize from a small sample of homogeneous data sets to a larger set of heterogeneous situations. The traditional work looked primarily at higher order involvement situations and, in retrospect, situations with low advertising levels. This set of situations fits into the lower left cell of Figure 4.

This chapter has attempted to meet Blumler and McLeod's criticisms of the literature, which noted a need for new techniques and richer results. The work presented here is only one of a large number of possible ways of dealing with the problems confronted in this chapter. It is not meant to be an ideal solution, but rather it is an example of what can be done in the present circumstances to enrich the literature of the field.

NOTES

1. For fairly complete reviews, see Sears (1969); McCombs (1972); Weiss (1969); and several chapters in this volume.

2. An excellent discussion comparing the strengths and weaknesses of experimental and survey work can be found in Kerlinger (1973). Webb et al. (1966), is the seminal piece on unobtrusive measures.

3. As an alternative to relying on existing candidates, the social scientist could run for office and thereby have control over his own campaign. This was done by Kassarjian and his colleagues (Nakanishi, Cooper and Kassarjian, 1972). The research was more successful than the campaign.

4. Two distinctions come to mind: (1) the consumer goods campaign typically lasts for several years, thus allowing more time for experimentation; (2) the consumer good does not win or lose as dramatically—it typically has a change in market share and another chance to recapture any losses.

5. Table 1 is derived from Webb et al. (1966). For an expansion of these concepts of validity, see Campbell and Stanley (1966).

REFERENCES

ALLEN, R. (1975) "Response effects in the interview." Ph.D. dissertation, University of Wisconsin: Mass Communications Research Center.

ATKIN, C. K. and S. H. CHAFFEE (1972) "Instrumental response strategies in opinion interviews." Public Opinion Q. 36 (spring) 69-79.

BENHAM, T. W. (1965) "Polling for a presidential candidate: Some observations on the 1964 campaign." Public Opinion Q. 29: 185-199.

BERELSON, B. R., P. F. LAZARSFELD, and W. N. McPHEE (1954) Voting: A Study of Opinion Formation in a Presidential Election. Chicago: University of Chicago Press.

BLUMLER, J. G. and J. M. McLEOD (1973) "Communication and voter turnout in Britain," presented to the Assn. for Education in Journalism, Fort Collins, Colorado.

——— and D. McQUAIL (1969) Television and Politics: Its Uses and Influence. Chicago: University of Chicago Press.

CAMPBELL, A., P. E. CONVERSE, W. E. MILLER and D. E. STOKES (1960) The American Voter. New York: Wiley.

——— (1966) Elections and the Political Order. New York: Wiley.

——— and H. C. COOPER (1956) Group Differences in Attitude and Voters: A Study of the 1954 Congressional Election. Ann Arbor: Survey Research Center, Institute for Social Research, University of Michigan.

———, G. GURIN and W. E. MILLER (1954) The Voter Decides. Evanston, Ill.: Row, Peterson.

CAMPBELL, D. T. and D. W. FISKE (1959) "Convergent and discriminant validation by the multitrait-multimethod matrix." Psych. Bulletin 56.

——— and J. C. STANLEY (1966) Experimental and Quasi-Experimental Designs for Research. Chicago: Rand-McNally.

DREYER, E. C. (1971) "Media use and electoral choices: some political consequences of information exposure." Public Opinion Q. 35: 545-553.

HEELER, R. M. (1972) "The effects of mixed media, multiple copy, repetition, and competition in advertising: A laboratory investigation." Ph.D. dissertation, Stanford University.

——— and M. L. RAY (1972) "Measure validation in marketing." J. Marketing Research 9.

JENNINGS, M. K. and H. ZIEGLER (1970) "The salience of American state politics." Amer. Political Science Rev. 64(2) 523-535.

KATZ, D., N. MACCOBY and N. MORSE (1951) Productivity, Supervision, and Morale in an Office Situation. Ann Arbor: Survey Research Center, University of Michigan.

KERLINGER, F. (1973) Foundations of Behavioral Research. New York: Holt, Rinehart and Winston.

KEY, V. O., Jr. (1966) The Responsible Electorate. Cambridge: Harvard University Press.

KISH, L. (1965) Survey Sampling. New York: Wiley.

KLINE, F. G. (1972) "Mass media and the general election process: Evidence and speculation," presented at the Syracuse University conference on mass media and American politics, Syracuse, New York.

KRUGMAN, H. E. (1965) "The impact of television advertising: Learning without involvement." Public Opinion Q. 29: 349-356.

LANG, K. and G. E. LANG (1962) "The mass media and voting," in E. Burdick and E. Brodbeck (eds.) American Voting Behavior. Glencoe, Ill.: Free Press.

LAVIDGE, R. and G. A. STEINER (1961) "A model for predictive measurements of advertising effectiveness." J. Marketing 25: 59-62.

LAZARSFELD, P. F., B. R. BERELSON and H. GAUDET (1948) The People's Choice, 2nd ed. New York: Columbia University Press.

McCOMBS, M. E. (1972) "Mass communication in political campaigns: Information, gratification, and persuasion," in F. G. Kline and P. J. Tichenor (eds.) Current Perspectives in Mass Communication Research. Beverly Hills, Calif.: Sage Pubns.

MAYER, M. (1958) Madison Avenue, U.S.A. New York: Harper.

NAKANISHI, M., L. COOPER and H. H. KASSARJIAN (1972) "Voting for a political candidate under conditions of minimal information," presented to Pacific Chapter, American Assn. for Public Opinion Research, Asilomar, Calif.

PALDA, K. S. (1964) The Measurement of Cumulative Advertising Effects. Englewood Cliffs, N.J.: Prentice-Hall.

——— (1973) "The marketing of political candidates: An econometric exploration of two

Quebec elections," in T. V. Greer (ed.) American Marketing Association Combined Conference Proceedings. Chicago: American Marketing Assn.

RAMOND, C. (1975) "A new approach to monitoring corporate image: The one question survey," in W. W. Wells (ed.) Attitude Research at Bay. Chicago: American Marketing Assn.

RAY, M. L. (1973a) Final Analysis of a Multiple and Unobtrusive Measure Field Study of Attitudes and Behavior; Technical Report 35. Stanford, Calif.: Stanford University Graduate School of Business.

——— (1973b) "Marketing communication and the hierarchy of effects," in P. Clarke (ed.) New Models for Mass Communication Research. Beverly Hills, Calif.: Sage Pubns.

——— (1973c) "A proposal for validating measures and models for highly competitive situations," in B. W. Becker and H. Becker (eds.) Dynamic Marketing in a Changing World. Chicago: American Marketing Assn.

——— and R. M. HEELER (1971) "The use of the multitrait and multimethod matrix for trait development: Cluster analysis and nonmetric scaling alternatives." Stanford: Graduate School of Business, Stanford University.

——— and A. G. SAWYER (1971) "Repetition in media models: A laboratory technique." J. Marketing Research 8: 20-30.

———, ——— and E. C. STRONG (1971) "Frequency effect revisited." J. Advertising Research 11: 14-20.

——— and P. N. SHERRILL (1973) "Unobtrusive marketing research techniques," in S. H. Britt (ed.) Marketing Manager's Handbook. Chicago: Dartnell.

———, L. S. WARD and J. B. REED (1974) New Directions For Advertising Pretesting Research. Cambridge, Mass.: Marketing Science Institute.

ROSSI, P. H. (1966) "Trends in voting behavior research: 1933-1963." In E. C. Dreyer and W. A. Rosenbaum (eds.) Political Opinion and Electoral Behavior, Belmont, Calif.: Wadsworth, 67-78.

ROTHSCHILD, M. L. (1974) "The effects of political advertising on the voting behavior of a low involvement electorate." Ph.D. dissertation. Stanford University.

——— (1975) "Involvement as a determinant of decision making styles." American Marketing Assn. Conference Proceedings. Chicago: American Marketing Assn.

——— and M. L. RAY (1974) "Involvement and political advertising effect: An exploratory experiment." Communications Research 1(3) 264-285.

SAWYER, A. G. (1971) "A laboratory experimental investigation of the effects of repetition of advertising." Ph.D. dissertation. Stanford University.

SEARS, D. O. (1969) "Political behavior," in G. Lindzey and E. Aronson (eds.) The Handbook of Social Psychology, 2nd edition Vol. 5. Reading, Mass.: Addison-Wesley, 315-458.

STRONG, E. C. (1972) "The effects of repetition in advertising: A field experiment." Ph.D. dissertation. Stanford University.

TRENAMAN, J. and D. McQUAIL (1971) Television and the Political Image. London: Metheun.

WEBB, E. J., D. T. CAMPBELL, R. D. SCHWARTZ and L. SECHREST (1966) Unobtrusive Measures: Nonreactive Research in the Social Sciences. Chicago: Rand-McNally.

WEISS, W. (1969) "Effects of the mass media of communication," in G. Lindzey and E. Aronson (eds.) Handbook of Social Psychology, 2nd Edition, Vol. 5.

Chapter 9

HISTORICAL RESEARCH ON POLITICAL COMMUNICATION

John D. Stevens

THE HISTORIAN enjoys one tremendous advantage over others who study political communication, and that is his opportunity to apply hindsight in deciding what really was "political." Unfortunately, he often forfeits this advantage, dazzled by the glare of partisan politics, especially national politics.

"Political" has meant more than that. Contemporaries probably did not recognize that the rise of the modern corporation at the end of the 19th Century was "political," but it changed the landscape of American society more than any presidential election. Politics is the essence of every war, both in determining strategies on the field and in the capital. It is well to remember, too, that state and local governments have affected the individual citizen more throughout our history than has the federal.

The writing of history is "political," too. Not only are the histories written by the victors, they are written by males—almost always white males. Only recently have the political implications of that become obvious. In a real sense, any issue that is significant is, by definition, political.

THE CHANGING NATURE OF HISTORY

What is history? Eliminating such tongue-in-cheek definitions as George Bernard Shaw's "A lie agreed upon," the others boil down to history's being a systematic reconstruction of the past into some meaningful order. Although history traditionally has focused on the outcomes of events, some recent scholarship has sought to go beyond events, to discern and explain relationships among complex social, economic and demographic patterns.

That almost always involves quantification. The difficulties for historians in seeing beyond events are like those of journalists in reporting quiet, continuing developments, such as race relations or ecological decay. Today journalists, like historians, are using behavioral research techniques to locate these social indicators. Not all journalists and certainly not all historians agree that explaining broad patterns is what they do best or even adequately. Boorstin (1960) argues that the historian is peculiarly qualified "to note the rich particularity of experience, to search for the piquant aroma of life, as contrasted with the abstract, antiseptic dullness of numbers, 'cases,' and prototypes." Berkhofer (1969) says history can never be a social science "because we can study processes in history but not history as process"; Tuchman (1967) says selectivity is the key to history, and selectivity is normative. The list is long and some of the arguments tedious; yet it is fair to say most historians are more comfortable with description than with definition.

That is one (but only one) reason why they so frequently turn to biography. No one chronicles a "typical" person. Most individuals leave little to study, anyway; those who do leave manuscripts almost invariably look good in them. It is only by compressing vast amounts of census and similar data that one gets any picture of "typical" citizens.

History, like other disciplines, has been racked by the "machine-in-the-garden" debate. Statistical techniques, it is charged, will squeeze the life out of the rich diversity of human experience and leave a residue of tables and graphs. Aydelotte (1966) responded sensibly to such charges that ". . . what cannot be done with statistics cannot be done without them, either." Reasonable men know that any research technique is merely a means to an end, and that end should be answering meaningful questions. Good questions are the key to good research; no amount of statistical or other manipulation will produce valuable answers out of stupid questions. As Gottschalk (1963) commented: "Undismayed pursuit of the right answers to persistent questions is of greater importance than definitive answers to questions that no longer matter." Men never decided, after all, how many angels could dance on the head of a pin; they simply agreed it was not a very productive question to pursue.

Not only does quantification make it possible for the historian to test general propositions, it also broadens greatly the vistas for the kinds of questions which he can ask. There is a tradition in historiography of debating the difference between "facts" and "generalizations"; that semantic sophistry is summarized by Aydelotte (1963). It seems to be a distinction without a difference, he notes, since few modern scholars would argue that the facts speak for themselves; once the researcher helps them, he is generalizing—even only if in his choice of conjunctions such as "nevertheless" and "therefore." Historians usually limit their generalizations to the lower levels. If they are humble, they have a lot to be humble about; but many are anything but humble in the type of untested generalizing they indulge in, especially in their introductory sections.

Generalizations may stimulate further research, even if they are not supported in the particular work that inspired them. A case in point is the two "propositions" suggested by Siebert (1952) in the introduction to his monumental study of three centuries of controls on the British press:

> *Proposition I.* The extent of governmental control of the press depends on the nature of the relationship of the government to those subject to the government.

> *Proposition II.* The area of freedom contracts and the enforcement of restraints increases as the stresses on the stability of the government and the structure of society increase.

He proposed these as universal concepts, bound neither by time nor geography. Several scholars have suggested that Siebert's own research does not bear them out; nevertheless they have adapted the propositions, particularly the second, as a hypothetical framework. For example, Shaw and Brauer (1969) found that threats and overt actions increased against an outspoken North Carolina editor during the Civil War when the Confederate fortunes of war dimmed. His readers seemed willing to put up with his less-than-enthusiastic support for the war as long as things were going well; but when the Yankees began clearly winning, they stopped looking on him as a relatively harmless crank. My study of legal and extra-legal controls on expression during World War I (Stevens, 1969) seemed to indicate the same thing. The spring of 1918 was the low-point for American fortunes, and that was the time when legal and mob actions against alleged disloyalty were at their worst. Both of these studies involve short time periods, of course, whereas Siebert was surveying three centuries.

Just as a suggestive proposition may move a discipline along, so may a speculative essay. When Copernicus suggested that the sun and not the earth was the center of the universe, it made the careful measurements and observations of contemporary astonomers obsolete. Frederick Jackson Turner and Charles Beard generalized far beyond their data, much to the benefit of American history. Carey (1974) cited no data to chronicle the most glaring weakness of journalism historiography, namely its philosophical agreement about the press moving from a class to a mass medium, improving over time, and reflecting the democratization of the nation. Carey said it was not that the interpretation was necessarily wrong, only that it was worn out and that new viewpoints might bring fresh insights.

THE LITERARY TRADITION

Unlike the other social sciences, history was born and matured in the literary tradition. Its academic home until the end of the 19th Century was the English Department, while the widely read history books were produced by non-academicians. Bancroft, with his strident patriotic prose, dominated the scene for half a century after the publication of his first volume in 1834. By the time of his death, the romantic school dominated the writing of history on both sides of the Atlantic; certainly Parkman's sweep and grandeur seldom has been matched.

This is not the place to recount American historiography (see Kraus, 1953) but it is important to be aware of this tradition. Even with the coming of the new "scientific" historians in the last decade of the last century, there still was much attention to fine prose. While Henry Adams was seeking some philosophy or theory of history, his rhetoric was nearly flawless. Even today, the most widely read popular historians—the Barbara Tuchmans, the William Shirers, the Cornelius Ryans—write extremely well. Academic historians could take a lesson from them, but if historians need that lesson, then surely those from other social science disciplines need it even more. Almost all social scientists are guilty of spending too much time on their research and too little on their reporting of it.

While traditional historians might say their job ends when they present "the facts" about the past, more ideological historians insist on presenting a "useable past," one that illustrates the greater truths which they perceive. The generation we call the Founding Fathers were avid readers of history, but they saw it as a propagandistic tool, filled with illustrative moral lessons. Neither side in this historians' debate advocates lying or shoddy scholarship; they simply disagree as to their central purpose.

The parallel is striking between these debates among historians about the proper focus of history, and those of journalists about objectivity. Both arguments are eternal and erupt periodically. During the late 1960s and early 1970s, younger, ideological journalists questioned the desirability of objectivity. More traditional newsmen admitted absolute objectivity was impossible, but they insisted that its quest was essential. Certainly the traditionalists decried the invented dialogues and composite characters that the "new journalists" insisted revealed more Truth than did sticking to what could be absolutely documented. Like most fundamental debates, the issue was not resolved.

Historians have gone in many directions to deepen their studies. There is great need for comparative history, a kind of macroanalysis, both across societies and across time. But it is a wary historian who enters that thicket and often a wiser one who emerges. There are lots of booby traps. As a last resort, the comparative historian can resort to the old crutch of the economic forecaster: ". . . all other factors being equal." Since they never are, hindsight can always show that the unequal factor was, alas, the critical one. In spite of the hazards, excellent comparative studies have been published and many are summarized by Woodward (1968).

Another direction is microanalysis, in the sense of focusing on private aspects of thought and action. It is not that historians disregard the importance of what happens in the nursery, the bathroom or the bedroom; it is simply that they are not trained in psychological analysis, and if they were, there seldom would be sufficient preserved evidence upon which they could draw valid conclusions. The few attempts to apply psychoanalytical techniques to biographies of Hitler, Ghandi, Wilson and others have not been convincing.

THEORY AND THE HISTORIAN

Historians seldom apply what a competent behavioral researcher would consider rigorous methodology, and even less frequently espouse concepts, theories and models. "Rigor" in traditional historiography means covering appropriate sources, which Benson (1972) has denounced as "proof by haphazard quotation." Few scholars have gone even so far as Nelson (1964) who differentiated "guided entry" (starting with a well-defined question) from "immersion."

History is catching up with other social sciences in shifting its emphasis from implicit to explicit, and from deduction to induction. Historians still tend to argue that their crude and incomplete data will not support theories but that at some advanced stage of their inquiry they may "come up with a theory." That ignores the importance of organizing theories, such as the four prototypic models suggested by Siebert, Peterson and Schramm (1956). Their typology influenced much of the cross-national research that followed.

One historian who discusses theory construction is Hollingsworth (1974), who chided his fellow historians, "Whereas many historians are reluctant to create plausible hypotheses to explain the facts when they are without the facts, the scientist creates hypotheses in order to aid in discovering the facts." He urged historians to investigate the assumptions behind theories (e.g. the non-economic assumptions labor and developmental economists make about social structures) and pointed out that a scholar may not find enough cases in the contemporary world to test his theory. Longitudinal analysis, which is, after all, the natural home of the historian, is increasingly popular in all the social sciences.

One might investigate, for example, some of the non-economic assumptions involved in the Principle of Relative Constancy (McCombs, 1972), which suggests that for the last four decades, at least, the proportion of the nation's wealth that has been invested in the media marketplace is constant although the relative shares of this constant fraction that are allocated to different media change over the years.

Even the most descriptive historian talks about past public opinion, relying on newspaper editorials, letters to the editor, congressional and legislative votes, petitions, speeches, sermons, party platforms, legislative resolutions, election returns, letters and diaries and memoirs.

For more recent studies, he might quote opinion polls. All of these he uses selectively. Studies are replete with comments about how the "American press" or the "Northern press" felt about vital issues. More often than not the quotes are from the New York papers (if for no other reason than their ready availability on microfilm in so many libraries). This is like finding a Biblical quotation to support your position, in more than one way.

An equally serious problem is an assumption that "everybody knew" about an issue. Why should we assume that for the past, in the face of so many contemporary studies about dissemination, multistep flows, and media ineffectiveness?

Merritt (1963) demonstrated how imaginative content analysis could shed light on colonial opinion. He counted words and phrases colonial editors printed indicating a primary allegiance to England and those which indicated they were thinking of themselves as Americans. There was a steady increase in the latter in the 30 years before the Revolution.

While historical perspectives would improve almost any kind of study, we will limit discussion here to two phenomena, elections and wars. Both are manifestly political, and both leave much data for the serious historian.

ELECTION STUDIES

If historians have devoted a disproportionate share of their attention to presidential elections, it does not mean that there is nothing to research in that area. There are new concepts, new techniques to apply, and new relationship to examine in almost every election. Too much of what we "know" about them either is not true or has not been proven. Few elections have been analyzed more than Andrew Jackson's victory in 1828. Voting totals were the highest to date, and his 56 per cent of the popular vote was the highest of the entire 19th Century. This has invited the easy and general interpretation that he was swept in on a wave of voters who had not previously participated. McCormick (1960) explained the swollen vote totals by the newly-broadened definition to the franchise in several states and the fact that all but two of the states had recently changed their laws to permit popular election of Presidential Electors; until then, they had been chosen by the state legislatures. There were other contributing factors, including a vigorous (not to say mud-slinging) campaign between only two candidates. Four years earlier, there had been four candidates, all nominally of the same party. Jackson's was also the first election with an elaborate system of party newspapers and with broad solicitation of campaign funds. Remini (1971) points to a more basic problem in interpreting the results of 1828. He contends that even if Jackson's election *can* be explained in other than rise-of-the-common-man terms, it should not be, because that is how it was seen by contemporaries of all political stripes. He insists that "what is believed by the electorate is frequently more important than the objective reality."

"How many papers endorsed which candidate?" probably is the oldest and most repeated political communication question. All early studies assumed that editorials swayed vast numbers of voters, an assumption that Elmira and subsequent election studies called into question (see O'Keefe chapter). It became fashionable to dismiss entirely the possible effect of endorsements. Recently, though, Robinson (1974) found a solid correlation between the way people voted in the 1972 election and the endorsement of the newspaper they read. He then turned to secondary analysis on archived survey data from the preceding four presidential elections and found the same pattern, concluding that endorsements were important, after all. Although it covered five quadrennial elections, his study hardly qualified as "historical" in any traditional sense; rather, he was a social scientist using longitudinal analysis. Any historian would be remiss, of course, if he did not use all the information available in reaching his conclusions. This points up one basic difference between the historian and the social scientist. The historian uses "hard data" to corroborate other findings, but almost never as the sole basis of his conclusions. If the historian chooses to investigate periods before 1940, there are almost no survey data to which he could turn.

Research shows how stubbornly 20th Century voters cling to their presidential choices, so why should we assume that was any less true of voters in earlier periods? Did Horace Greeley or Joseph Pulitzer really sway that many voters, or did people read those newspapers for other reasons, perhaps even in spite of the editorials? Perhaps we cannot answer that question, but unfortunately much historical writing already has assumed that we could and that the answer was that those publishers did have great influence. Historical literature is filled with implicit assumptions.

Historians need to consider the wide range of research findings about recent electoral behavior, many of which are summarized by Sears and Whitney (1973), and to apply these insights to their studies of the past. (See also chapter by O'Keefe.) Frustrated social scientists, finding that most voters make up their minds quite early, were too quick to discount the political clout of the press. One reason they were misled was that their focus was on opinion change, rather than on information conveyed. The news media are primarily in the information business, after all. Many of the same studies cited to "prove" the impotence of the media in changing attitudes showed that people learned facts about candidates and campaign issues to which they were exposed, and they learned them whether they obtained them from message sources they trusted or distrusted. This literature is reviewed in the Becker, McCombs and McLeod chapter here.

The media are most effective in shaping lightly held opinions, and according to studies by Christenson (1959) and others, they may be much more influential in local than in national elections. (See Rothschild's chapter for evidence.) Chaffee (1972) and others have found the media role greatly magnified in non-partisan referenda. Remembering always that throughout most of óur history, the important political decisions have been made at the local level and that few nations in the world are so fond of resorting to votes on everything from public policies to baseball all-star teams, press influence takes on added significance. Comparatively little research has been done on referenda votes, but this condition may be corrected as archives make more of these results available in machine-readable form.

Rural areas have been under-studied by election (and most other social science) researchers. Conventional wisdom tells us that small towns have been the seats of reaction, but we have little evidence. Election and referenda analyses could provide some clues. Similarly, the weeklies and smalltown dailies have not received their share of attention, considering their numbers and possible influence. There is little doubt that they are more carefully and completely read than are big-city papers. Many rural editors have been political party activists, others have served in elective and appointive offices, while still others have benefited, directly or indirectly, from government printing contracts. History is rife with scandals connected with letting such contracts, which often were considered the rightful spoils for the newspapers that had backed the winning party. Historians once assumed that political pipers called all the journalistic tunes, but recent research on the content of subsidized papers in early Boston, Philadelphia and Washington throw considerable doubt on this. Yodelis (1975) found that for Boston papers during the Revolutionary period, government printing was far less important than religious printing. With the exception of one printer, she found profit came with or without government printing work. Lacking as she did the ideal measure of a printer's economic fortunes—his ledger book—she based her investigation on an index based on the annual mean number of items and pages of general printing turned out by each printer in the city, and the annual mean number and columns of advertisements published each week in the papers.

Ames and Teeter (1971) went to the preserved circulation account book of William Bradford's *Pennsylvania Journal* at the time of the Revolution, to show how widely the copies were distributed, and by implication, how this minimized the direct economic pressures local Philadelphia groups could bring to bear. They also found that even the avowedly partisan press of 1819-1846 Washington often had the political courage to criticize its benefactor. They added:

> One of the advantages of the patronage system—one frequently overlooked—was the quantity and quality of the reporting of the congressional debates and proceedings which the patronage-supported newspapers supplied. With less need to attract large audiences with popular reading fare, the publishers of patronage-aided papers could concentrate upon publishing in-depth reports and accounts of the proceedings in Congress and also in other agencies of government.

Certainly we need to know more about the effect of such subsidies on frontier printers. These romantic figures who followed the wagon trains westward have been pictured both as fiercely independent, ready to pick up their type and move on at the first hint of coercion—and as groveling journalistic prostitutes, beholden to local businessmen and afraid to publish even one discouraging word. No doubt, there were both kinds, plus many who fell between. How did these printers affect key local elections? We need studies of these men and the content of their scattered issues which remain in order to get some clearer answer.

Favorable postal rates, which are simply subsidies, have been inadequately studied; there is not even a good summary of what the rates for various classes have been through the years. At certain periods, books were published in a newspaper format to take advantage of reduced postal rates, but several times these loopholes were plugged. More recently, it has been asserted that favorable mail rates have kept alive opinion and special interest publications. Newspapers have enjoyed a sweetheart status with the Post Office, second only to the free franking privilege extended to congressmen. These arrangements date back to Benjamin Franklin, not only the first Postmaster General but also the first prominent "media baron" in American history. In many jurisdictions until recently, papers could be mailed absolutely free within a county and at highly favorable rates in adjacent counties. Certainly such considerations have affected not only marketing but content strategies of publishers.

Today's press is far less partisan than yesterday's. Today's editor is expected to air all sides of a political argument and allow the reader to draw his own conclusions; that concept would have appalled readers in the last century. They expected to subscribe to a journal that expressed their own prejudices, and they decried as gutless any editor who admitted there was another side. What caused the change? Shaw (1967) credited the telegraph. Press associations had to serve client papers of all political stripes, and therefore, had to play politics down the middle. Shaw believed that even the reporters preparing copy for the local papers toned down their partisanship, influenced by the non-partisan wire copy they were emulating. He found a striking time-coincidence relationship between the expansion of the telegraph system and the decline in partisan bias in the press.

Does an openly partisan paper influence more or fewer votes than one which pretends, at least, to be balanced? If all your readers are already committed, it is hard to imagine you will influence many; however, an important part of any campaign strategy is to kindle the enthusiasm of the committed. Does an endorsement from a paper that always endorses the same party influence independent voters as much as one from a paper that shifts from election to election?

The Scandinavian countries believe so strongly in the importance of party organs that they invest large sums in subsidies to keep them alive. Even with subsidies, their circulations are far smaller than these of "regular," less ideological papers. Does this indicate that Scandinavians are becoming less interested in political ideology, or does it mean that they always would have preferred a balanced or non-political paper if offered the choice? The obvious next question is whether this is (or was) true of Americans, as well.

While nearly everyone decries the decreasing competition among media, especially as it reduces the voices in the political system, we do not know that fewer newspapers or stations mean fewer viewpoints. Historical studies of multi-newspaper cities are needed to find out how much more news and opinion is brought in by a third, fourth or fifth daily paper or radio station. The more newspapers or stations, the more duplication, of course, so what level of redundancy is optimal? Good answers might help guide policy-makers in establishing guidelines for cable television. Seeing the same cop show—or even highly similar ones—on a dozen channels simultaneously has only limited social value. What are the implications for candidates seeking an audience if there are dozens of channels from which the viewer can choose, and consequently a very fragmented audience? And how can the historian help illuminate such a question?

The influence of broadcasting on elections has been almost ignored by historians, partly because of the lack of an archive comparable to the bound and microfilmed files of newspapers. A couple of pioneer stations broadcast the 1920 results, and many more covered the conventions and returns four years later. (The loser, Democrat John W. Davis, blamed his defeat on his poor radio voice.) By the time of the 1952 election, television had become a major source of information. A candidate's looks—and pocketbook—became an important consideration. Each election received increased attention from researchers. Several studies, for example, focused on the televised debates between Nixon and Kennedy in 1960 (see Kraus et al. chapter). Political advertising, both in style and amount, has been the subject of much study and debate recently. The federal government, along with many states, has attempted to impose legal limits on media campaign expenditures. The historian has encountered similar arguments about alleged bandwagon effects during earlier campaigns, and should be able to help provide some perspective on this policy question. On the other hand, the current debate should give the historian incentive to attempt to measure those effects during earlier elections.

If the media exert as much influence in agenda-setting as recent studies indicate (see Becker et al. chapter), then historians can test these findings in many contexts, including election campaigns. Even the earliest researchers went to the archives to describe how much "play" various editors gave certain stories. Cohen (1963) suggested that the press is more successful in telling the public what to think *about* than it is in telling what to think, and research generally bears him out; certainly, the landmark election studies do. Some elections seem much more ideological than others; that is, certain issues (as opposed to candidates) seem to dominate. Relatively simple content analysis on issues discussed in the press during those campaigns might provide some new insights into these key elections. Again, the greatest need is for local and state election studies, but even some Presidential elections offer interesting possibilities. What issues attracted public attention in 1852 and 1856? Were they the same as those presented in platforms and preserved speeches of the candidates in those turbulent years before the Civil War? By 1860, the die may already have been cast.

Few elections have been more bitterly contested than 1896, dominated as it was by the gold-silver issue, surely one of the most complex questions ever to heat up the political masses. (If it did.)

How much discussion of this issue was there in the media, aside from the candidates' exhortations? It is nearly impossible for us to imagine unlettered men "going to the barricades" over the proper ratio for the valuation of silver. The more historians "explain" it, the less likely the entire incident seems. The media agenda might give us some helpful clues.

Lasswell (1942) complained how difficult it was to separate "political content" from the rest of the media; we are not much closer to a solution one-third of a century later. This is partly because in certain situations, an event has political salience for some people that it would not otherwise. A story about street crime or burglaries in certain contexts may be quite "political," as may a sports story or a comic strip. The self-image of a nation (and popularity of its government) may rest on the performance of its Olympic team. A town may hang its head for a year after a loss by its high school team to a traditional rival. Comic strips can be overtly political, such as "Pogo" in the 1950s or "Doonesbury" in the 1970s, or represent a political ideology such as "Little Orphan Annie." They can also have implicitly political overtones, as in the way they depict racial, social or sexual roles, an inherent problem because cartoons must resort to stereotypes for simplicity. Sports or social stories that deal with race have inevitable political ramifications. They were the raison d'etre for the black press, and their publishers still consider them their most important content (LaBrie and Zima, 1971). Religious reports also are political and once were much more so. The inventive historian can link his study of political election campaigns to a far wider range of archived media content than has been utilized to date.

CRISIS STUDIES

Why focus on crises, which by definition are atypical? Because it is only in times of social upheaval that the outlines are clear enough to permit study. Wars and crises leave indelible impressions; "normal" times do not. The red spurs of war not only speed the pace of social change, they make it obvious and memorable.

Anyone over the age of 40 can tell you how he spent December 7, 1941, but don't count on his recalling the same date in 1951, 1961, or 1971. Former soldiers remember their combat experiences vividly, but their families who stayed home have only a hazy general recollection of the same period. More to the point for the historian, soldiers often make and save diaries. The Civil War was the first one in which a substantial share of the rank-and-file of the military could write; almost every archive in the country has several of those narratives, but much less about the home front during the same years. Not only are the military events more dramatic, they are recognized by the participants (and their heirs) as having historical importance. The availability of material is another reason why historians study crises.

One of our most cherished beliefs is that, somehow and however imperfectly, American public policy on significant issues reflects public opinion. If this is true, then logically there should be some relation between the content of the media and what the public thinks. The problem is more difficult for the historian, seeking to gauge public opinion at some time in the past. Benson (1967-68) concluded that for all their imperfections, voting totals are about the only surviving documents from which an historian can safely draw direct inferences about public opinion.

Certainly any historian working in the recent period will make what use he can of opinion polls, many of which are summarized regularly in Public Opinion Quarterly. Any major war effort requires substantial public support, or at least acquiesence. It is in this regard that Vietnam, and to a lesser degree Korea, offer interesting settings in which to study the relationships among media content, public opinion and public policy.

These "little wars" were not the first unpopular ones in American history. It has been estimated that fully one-third of the colonists opposed the original break with Great Britain, and sizable numbers spoke out against the War of 1812, the Mexican War, and the Spanish-American War (Morison, Merk and Friedel, 1970). The anti-draft riots of the Civil War dwarfed the similar protests of a century later, and thousands of dissenters were silenced by laws and by mobs during World War I.

For a citizenry taught to think in World War II terms of territory captured, it was difficult to understand the nature of essentially guerilla wars of more recent decades in Asia. The media had great difficulties reporting it, and remarks from the White House and from generals in briefings about villages captured and enemies killed only complicated the task. While officials talked about the "light at the end of the tunnel," what really may have turned the public against the war was the light at the end of the tube, the television tube. They had the war in their living rooms every night, in living, bloody color. There are few more important questions to ask than whether this did, indeed, color public opinion.

A nationwide survey in 1971 found that children who read newspapers and watched television news knew significantly more about the Vietnam War than their fellow 7-to-15-year-olds who did not; however, media use did not seem to have anything to do with their attitudes toward the war, which instead correlated with opinions held by their parents and teachers (Talley, 1973).

Although wars always have whetted the public's appetite for news, the Civil War was the first in which a really large proportion of the populace could read. In that sense, the Civil War was the newspaper's "first war," in the same sense that World War II was radio's first, and Vietnam was television's first. No one has assessed adequately the impact of those changes on the perception of the wars by either the public or the participants.

Certainly technological changes shape messages. The uncertainties and the high per-word costs of the telegraph probably dictated the organization of the modern news story. Reporters could use the telegraph during the Civil War only at times when the military had nothing to send. They could not take a chance on the traditional chronological way of telling a story, since they might be cut off before they reached the conclusion; they began sending the most important facts first. The high cost of telegraph news spurred co-operative newsgathering ventures, which in turn led to a steady decrease in the amount of political bias carried by the wire services, serving as they did a wide variety of clients.

The difficult task for any serious scholar is to find a topic worth pursuing—a "Moby Dick," if you will. If he finds one, he must be prepared, like Captain Ahab, for a long and frustrating quest. In my case, I want to explain why toleration for unpopular expression expands and contracts. While Siebert's Proposition II is suggestive, it is too general. My white whale has led me into varied waters. Three examples must suffice.

First, I tried to explain why dissent was so ruthlessly suppressed in some Wisconsin counties during World War II, while it was being tolerated to a much higher degree in nearby and apparently similar counties. Once the counties had been paired on a number of Census and constructed variables, their newspapers' coverage was compared on a series of events that had civil liberty overtones. My study (Stevens, 1969) found that where the papers were more tolerant, both before and during the war, so were the citizens. The correlations were higher for 1900-1916 events than for those during the war itself, indicating the need to examine the effects of regular press diets on the populace. (This content analysis was only one aspect of the study, which drew heavily on more traditional material sources, such as documents, manuscripts, diaries and even interviews.) Whether the newspapers caused this tolerance or were reflecting the dominant attitudes of their readers is, of course, a more difficult question.

Second, I examined the press reaction to the West Coast Japanese-Americans at the beginning of World War II and found that except for the traditional anti-Oriental voices, it was remarkably restrained at the time of Pearl Harbor. It picked up momentum only under the impetus of Congressional and other rabble rousers some three months later. There was little questioning of the military claims for the security requirement of removing the Japanese-Americans, two-thirds of whom were U.S. citizens; still, even in the Army's own official history there is an admission that by the time the evacuation took place in the spring of 1942, there was no longer a real need for it. After examining the pressures on the Japanese-language papers in those difficult months, I pursued the question of policies and practices on the newspapers published in the relocation centers (Stevens, 1971). Based on governmental reports, interviews and the published content of the papers themselves, I concluded that personal characteristics of the editors and the camp administrators had far more to do with the freedom permitted than did any laws or official policies delivered from Washington.

Finally, I combined a long-time interest in the black press with my concern for wartime restraints, producing a *Journalism Monograph* (1973) that described the work of 29 war correspondents who were accredited to black weekly newspapers. The first stage was a careful reading of the four major black weeklies for the World War II period; not only did this provide an overview, it gave me a checklist of the correspondents and their assignments. I managed to locate all of those who were still alive and interviewed them, either in person or by mail. Most reported they were treated well by the military and by the white correspondents; however, they also reported their problem of serving as a conduit between the black enlisted men and their white officers. Often their articles criticized the segregated policies of the military, but they suffered little direct censorship. Frankly, this ran counter to my expectations when I had started the study. I'm sure my Moby Dick has some more surprises in store.

For whatever reasons, there was much more tolerance for civil liberties during World War II than there was in World War I. This is especially striking since the geopolitical dangers to the United States were more grave and the later war saw three times as many Americans under arms and killed in battle. The U.S. was also at war for nearly three times as long (45 months as opposed to 16). Although the Japanese Americans were treated despicably (and worse, the treatment was sanctioned by a decision of the Supreme Court of the United States) in the second war, Americans of Italian and German descent suffered few reprisals, blacks made significant social and economic gains, and anti-semitism diminished.

The explanation may be as simple as that we learned from the World War I experience. One specific illustration was Congress's refusal to enact censorship and mail restrictions on the foreign-language press; the folly of this policy in 1917-1918 was cited in the debate. Ekirch (1956) concluded the only reason for such toleration was that the dissenters were so few and posed so little threat. Blum (1968) attributed it to the wartime prosperity. Others have suggested the unity of the citizenry behind the war, which was precipitated directly by an attack, rather than by abstract principles of the rights of neutral ships as in World War I. Still others argue that the Roosevelt administration, especially the Attorney General, was more tolerant and more sensitive to the civil liberty issues than Wilson's had been.

Throughout history, even when wars (or military preparedness for war) have been popular, paying the taxes to finance them have not been. The states had great difficulty raising even the niggardly funds for George Washington's army, and the Federalists probably lost the election of 1800 as much because of the $2 million tax imposed to ward off the alleged threat of a French invasion as for any widespread revulsion against the excesses of enforcement of the Alien and Sedition Acts. In modern times, only a few people object to the principle of taxes, although almost all complain about the way they are assessed and allocated.

Taxes have long been used to punish or silence unpopular ideas, but they are only one of many administrative methods that can be used that way. In the United States, postal officials have been the most repressive, insisting they know what is good for the public, whether for peoples' morals or for their loyalty. When Postmaster General Kendall refused to deliver Abolitionist tracts, Congress in 1836 made it clear that the use of the mails was a right, not just a privilege. Congress told the Post Office to worry about the mechanics of delivery but not about the contents; it was, however, a lesson that did not stay learned. Anarchists ran afoul of the postal laws at the beginning of this century, but their problems were minor compared with the radicals and anti-war groups during World War I. Then Postmaster General Burleson was ruthless in suppressing publications or, equally effective, in holding them up for extended investigation—thus acquiring grounds to remove their second-class mailing permit because of their failure to publish on schedule. There were a few small publications expressing unpopular views that got halted by similar tactics during World War II and later. (No one knows how many times the Post Office or the Customs Bureau used alleged obscenity as an excuse to punish what were really offensive political or social views.)

At the local level, the unpopular speaker may find it difficult to rent a hall, or that there is suddenly a flood of applicants for use of public facilities—all of which must be carefully (and slowly) investigated. Applications for parade permits may get lost on some official's desk. Anyone who feels he has been discriminated against can appeal to the courts, of course, but that takes time.

Even more effective than laws in stilling dissenters are the extra-legal restraints, ranging from silent disapproval expressed by one's neighbors to the crudest kind of mob action. Most of us want to be liked and approved; a whole range of research confirms this desire to conform to the norms of our peer groups. For those who are a bit more bold, the threat of physical reprisals usually keeps them in line. One does not need to feel the wrath of a mob personally, only to know of others who have. A little terror, like Chinese mustard, goes a long way. Cheney (1938) concluded that popular passion silenced far more Tories, Abolitionists, Mormons and anti-capitalists than all the laws in American history.

It is sometimes suggested that vigilantes spring up in places where the legal system is not dealing with a problem. In my study of Wisconsin, that was not the case during World War I. Mob actions, at least as reported in the local newspapers, were most frequent in counties with the most federal and local legal prosecutions. Further, mobs and courts were punishing essentially the same kinds of anti-war remarks, most frequently some sort of praise for Germany. If the speaker were of German ancestry, his remark was even more likely to cause him problems. The most frequent offending phrase cited in the federal indictments was the hackneyed socialist shibboleth about its being a rich man's war but a poor man's fight. (Interestingly, the German government was prosecuting socialists for using the same phrase.) The point is, legal and extra-legal restraints form a kind of seamless web, the same mood supporting both.

The one pragmatic test for the level of freedom in a society is how much freedom there is to criticize its most sacred institutions. Disregard the endless attempts to distinguish dissent from heresy and mavericks from disloyalists; ask instead how much freedom there is to criticize those in power. No society ever has been confident enough to permit absolute freedom to criticize during a national emergency, but debate, discussion and criticism pose less threat than does placing any topic, policy, man or institution above criticism. Dissent, and more specifically the toleration of it, is the true sign of political maturity.

REFERENCES

AMES, W. E. and D. L. TEETER (1971) "Politics, economics, and the mass media," in R. T. Farrar and J. D. Stevens (eds.) Mass Media and the National Experience. New York: Harper & Row, 38-63.

AYDELOTTE, W. O. (1963) "Notes on the problem of historical generalization," in L. Gottschalk (ed.) Generalization in the Writing of History. Chicago: University of Chicago Press, 145-177.

––– (1966) "Quantification in history." Amer. Historical Rev. 71 (April) 803-825.

BENSON, L. (1967-68) "An approach to the scientific study of past public opinion." Public Opinion Q. 31 (winter) 522-567.

––– (1972) Toward the Scientific Study of History: Selected Papers. Philadelphia: Lippincott.

BERKHOFER, R. F. Jr. (1969) A Behavioral Approach to Historical Analysis. New York: Free Press.

BLUM, J. M. (1968) "World War II," pp. 315-327 in C. V. Woodward (ed.) The Comparative Approach to American History. New York: Basic Books.

BOORSTIN, D. J. (1960) America and the Image of Europe. New York: Meridian Books.

CAREY, J. W. (1974) "The problem of journalism history." Journalism History 1 (spring) 3-5.

CHAFFEE, S. H. (1972) "The interpersonal context of mass communication," in F. G. Kline and P. J. Tichenor (eds.) Current Perspectives in Mass Communication Research. Beverly Hills: Sage Pubns.

CHENEY, E. P. (1938) "Freedom and restraint: A short history." Annals of the Am. Academy of Pol. and Soc. Science 200 (November) 1-12.

CHRISTENSON, R. M. (1959) "The power of the press: The case of the Toledo Blade," in R. M. Christenson and R. O. McWilliams (eds.) Voice of the People. New York: McGraw-Hill.

COHEN, B. C. (1963) The Press and Foreign Policy. Princeton: Princeton University Press.

EKIRCH, A. A. (1956) The Civilian and the Military. New York: Oxford University Press.

GOTTSCHALK, L. (1963) Generalization in the Writing of History. Chicago: University of Chicago Press.

HOLLINGSWORTH, J. R. (1974) "Some problems in theory construction for historical analysis." Historical Methods Newsletter 7 (June) 225-244.
KRAUS, M. (1953) The Writing of American History. Norman: University of Oklahoma Press.
LA BRIE, H. G. and W. J. ZIMA (1971) "Directional quandaries of the black press in the United States." Journalism Q. 48 (winter) 640-644.
LASSWELL, H. D. (1942) "The politically significant content of the press: Coding procedures." Journalism Q. 19 (March) 12-23.
McCOMBS, M. E. (1972) Mass media in the marketplace. Journalism Monographs No. 24. Lexington, Ky.: Assn. for Ed. in Journalism.
McCORMICK, R. P. (1960) "New perspectives on Jacksonian politics." Amer. Historical Rev. 65 (January) 289-291.
MERRITT, R. L. (1963) "Public opinion in colonial America: Content analyzing the colonial press." Public Opinion Q. 27 (fall) 356-371.
MORISON, S. E., F. MERK and F. FREIDEL (1970) Dissent in Three American Wars. Cambridge: Harvard University Press.
NELSON, H. L. (1964) "Guides to morasses in historical research." Journalism Educator 19 (spring) 38-42.
REMINI, R. V. (1971) "Election of 1828," in A. M. Schlesinger Jr. (ed.) The Coming to Power. New York: Chelsea House.
ROBINSON, J. P. (1974) "The press as king-maker: What surveys from last five campaigns show." Journalism Q. 51 (winter) 587-606.
SEARS, D. O. and R. E. WHITNEY (1973) "Political persuasion," in I. Pool and W. Schramm (eds.) Handbook of Communication. Chicago: Rand-McNally.
SHAW, D. L. (1967) "News bias and the telegraph: A study of historical change." Journalism Q. 45 (summer) 326-329.
——— and S. W. BRAUER (1969) "Press freedom and war constraints: Case testing Siebert's Proposition II." Journalism Q. 46 (summer) 243-254.
SIEBERT, F. S. (1952) Freedom of the Press in England 1476-1776. Urbana: University of Illinois Press.
———, T. PETERSON and W. SCHRAMM (1956) Four Theories of the Press. Urbana: University of Illinois Press.
STEVENS, J. D. (1969) "Press and community toleration: Wisconsin in World War I." Journalism Q. 46 (summer) 255-259.
——— (1971) "From behind barbed wire: Freedom of the press in World War II Japanese centers." Journalism Q. 48 (summer) 279-286.
——— (1973) From the back of the foxhole: Black correspondents in World War II. Journalism Monographs No. 27. Lexington, Ky.: Assn. for Ed. in Journalism.
TALLEY, H. (1973) Children and War. New York: Teachers College of Columbia University.
TUCHMAN, B. (1967) "The historian's opportunity." Saturday Rev. 50 (February 25) 27-31.
WOODWARD, C. V. (1968) The Comparative Approach to American History. New York: Basic Books.
YODELIS, M. A. (1975) Who Paid the Piper? Publishing Economics in Boston, 1763-1775. Journalism Monographs No. 38. Lexington, Ky.: Assn. for Ed. in Journalism.

Chapter 10

LEGAL RESEARCH AND JUDICIAL COMMUNICATION

Donald M. Gillmor and Everette E. Dennis

LAW IS A RICH and limitless process of negotiation which, Ovid said in his *Fasti,* prevents the strong from always having their way. Only a small part of it—what Roscoe Pound called its "pathology"— ever becomes a case in litigation. Its sources are a concatenation of custom, convention, constitutional mandate, statute, executive order, court opinion, social fact, historical accident, and the predilections of judges, lawyers, clients, and legal scholars.

A full understanding of the allocation of political power depends upon legal research and theory. "Scarcely any political question arises in the United States," Alexis de Tocqueville observed acutely, "that is not resolved sooner or later into a judicial question."[1] The Supreme Court, Bernard Schwartz wrote, "is primarily a political institution, in whose keeping lies the destiny of a mighty nation. Its decrees mark the boundaries between the great departments of government; upon its action depend the proper functioning of federalism and the scope given to the rights of the individual."[2] And in his engaging Irish-American dialect, Mr. Dooley put it succinctly, "No matther whether th' constitution follows th' flag or not, th' supreme coort follows th' iliction returns."[3]

Beyond its apparent political characteristics, the United States Supreme Court, with its institutionalized and stately sense of independence, strives to make "fairness" central to the proper adjustment of interests in a "lawful" society. The Court is guided by the Fifth and Fourteenth Amendments to the Constitution, which guarantee concrete rights under a less-than-concrete expectation of *due process* or essential fairness.

[283]

There are at least two kinds of due process. Procedural due process is offended when generally accepted notions of fairness in form are violated, such as the right to notice of charges against one and a fair hearing concerning those charges. Substantive due process is assaulted by legislative acts abridging fundamental rights enumerated in the first ten amendments to the Constitution and effectively protected by the due process clauses of the Fifth and Fourteenth.

For a full understanding of politics and political communication, it is necessary to study the judicial component of that larger process. This chapter offers a perspective on legal research and suggests what the versatile communication researcher may want to include in his methodological armamentarium. He or she confronts two methodological traditions, one documentary, the other social scientific. While the documentary method dominates and looks for its hypotheses in myriad legal materials, there is a quantitative approach which seeks behavioral explanations and draws from a range of social science methodologies. This chapter explores the utility of both approaches.

It is largely in public law (government-to-citizen and government-to-government relationships) that legal research, both traditional and behavioral, fulfills its functions of "clarifying the law through analysis of procedure, precedent, and doctrine; reforming old laws and creating new ones; providing a better understanding of how law operates in society; and furnishing material for legal education."[4] In constitutional law particularly, legal research may have profound importance. It may help determine whether a case will be heard and how it will be decided.

There is a productive tension between traditional and behavioral methodologies in legal scholarship. Most legal research is problem-oriented and reflects the lawyer's adversarial needs. Frequently it is unabashedly normative and reformist. The legal researcher often makes a discrete problem of law "the prime object of inquiry [and] runs a strong bent toward law reform, guided by notions of desirable public policy."[5] Perhaps this is what Ralph S. Brown, Jr. of the Walter E. Meyer Research Institute of Law meant when he said:

> Many scholars might call themselves positivists, in order to avoid a natural-law label on the one hand or an uncritical identification with social engineering on the other. But there are few indeed who would live with positivism and consider their task finished when they had synthesized and rationalized a collection of sovereign commands. A series of undertakings with essentially that aim, the "Restatements" of the American Law Institute, have been most criticized when they left the law as they found

it; they were well-received only when, under the influence of reporters and advisers with ideas of their own, they attempted to mold doctrine toward what these men and their critics (mostly scholars on both sides) thought socially preferable results.[6]

It is this linkage of problems and policies that pushes traditional legal research toward normative analysis. As long as one deals with the case as the unit of analysis and regards the legal system as self-contained, this approach has rigor, but "the method falters when it is forced to reach outside the legal system itself for data and values to justify the ends that the researcher seeks to advance."[7]

Traditional jurisprudents depend largely on deductive logic and analogy in assessing the degree to which a rule or precedent governs a current case. The case may represent an unreplicable legal issue leading to what Morris L. Cohen has called "that wilderness of single instances."[8] But seldom are litigable issues unique; frequently they are variations on the themes of earlier attempts to accommodate interests. Jurisprudents see the appellate process as an interaction of self-perceived judicial roles, a judge's values, and the availability of clear and applicable precedents, doctrines and statutes. In this system the implicit goal is an objective, impartial and just decision.[9]

Judicial behaviorists—although seldom in the mainstream of judicial decision-making—assert that objectivity and impartiality are not to be found in shifting, theory-free and transcendental interpretations of cases and constitutions. Lee Loevinger, a former state supreme court judge, Federal Communications Commissioner, and early proponent of "jurimetrics" (the scientific investigation of legal problems), has noted that "In every other field of activity, knowledge has remained primitive until the adoption of scientific methods. . . ."[10] Perhaps this is what Justice Oliver Wendell Holmes, Jr. had in mind when he wrote that "An ideal system of law should draw its postulates and its legislative justification from science."[11]

Traditional legal scholars, working in isolation within their own self-contained system, may actually render misleading results if they are not cognizant of the potential contributions of other systems of thought. Traditionalists deny, however, that the dead hand of precedent (*stare decisis*) rigidly directs their deliberations. They see law as a living, breathing body of doctrinal rules and remedies which can be and are adapted to the evolving norms of a complex society.

Behaviorists, on the other hand, contend that "the problems of jurisprudence are formally 'static' problems which presuppose the existence of one final authoritative answer while the questions of jurimetrics are 'dynamic' in form in that they allow for changing answers as our knowledge increases. Indeed, in jurimetrics the questions themselves change as the body of knowledge grows, since the problems are constantly reformulated in terms of prior data."[12]

Vilhelm Aubert, a legal sociologist, believes that any excursion into new modes of legal research necessitates a thorough recognition of the structure of legal thinking. In an attempt to synthesize new and old methodologies, Aubert suggests six characteristics of traditional legal thinking that set it apart from the epistemological mode of the natural and social sciences:

(1) "Scientific approaches tend to emphasize, often to the exclusion of everything else, that aspect of a phenomenon which is general. Judicial opinions, and also legal theory, tend . . . to stress the unique aspects of the case. . . .

(2) "The web of relationships which legal thought throws over the facts of life is not a causal or functional one. Legal thinking, legislation and judicial decision-making are [only] peripherally touched by schemes of thought in terms of means and ends. . . .

(3) "Legal thinking is characterized by the absence of probabilism, both with respect to law and with respect to facts. Events have taken place or they have not taken place. A law is either valid or invalid. . . .

(4) "Legal thinking is very heavily oriented to the past. . . .

(5) "Law is a comparison process. . . . The legal consequences, in the terminology of the law, are not those factual consequences expected to follow a certain action. . . .

(6) "Legal thinking is dichotomous. Rights or duties are either present or absent. . . ."[13]

These properties of the traditional legal method do not necessarily inhibit systematic scholarship. Yet the scholar must remember that in dealing with the law "the goal of judicial processes is not always knowledge. Indeed, the judicial process, in innumerable ways," says political behaviorist S. Sidney Ulmer, "actively suppresses the search for 'truth'." He adds:

In choosing among hypotheses concerning historical fact, the lawyer seeks victory not truth. The adversary process repels evidence as do delays in litigation. In making decisions the judge recognizes (1) that the case must be decided one way or another, whether or not the evidence is sufficient for a "scientific" conclusion; (2) that judicial fact-finders are not bound by rules of consistency; and (3) that facts may be bent by the judicial process to serve an ulterior purpose.[14]

Justice Tom Clark, in his opinion for the Court barring cameras from courtrooms, alluded to some of these problems:

> The State contends that the televising of portions of a criminal trial does not constitute a denial of due process. Its position is that because no prejudice has been shown by the petitioner as resulting from the televising, it is permissible; that claims of "distractions" during the trial due to the physical presence of television are wholly unfounded; and that psychological considerations are for psychologists, not courts, because they are purely hypothetical. . . . It is true that our empirical knowledge of its full effect on the public, the jury or the participants in a trial, including the judge, witnesses and lawyers is limited. However, the nub of the question is . . . "the insidious influences which it puts to work in the administration of justice. . . ." The conscious or unconscious effect that this may have on the juror's judgment cannot be evaluated, but experience indicates that it is not only possible but highly probable that it will have a direct bearing on his vote as to guilt or innocence. . . . But we cannot afford the luxury of saying that, because these factors are difficult of ascertainment in particular cases, they must be ignored. . . . Our judgment cannot be rested on the hypothesis of tomorrow but must take the facts as they are presented today.[15]

The communication researcher, then, in using legal materials and methods, needs to be cautious in drawing inferences or in broadly generalizing from judicial propositions without full recognition of the narrow assumptions upon which they may rest. At the same time, underestimating the complexity of the legal process may create hazards for the social scientist.

Theodore Becker, in evaluating the work of pioneer judicial behaviorist Glendon Schubert,[16] uncovers a serious misperception of the judicial process in his conceptualization. Schubert treats the *case* (his stimulus or independent variable) as the facts as stated in the judicial decision. The vote of the court (its decision) is the response or dependent variable. The judge and his attitude set serve as intervening variable.

Facts stated in the published opinion, however, are not the same facts presented to the court prior to its decision in order to influence that decision; they are not in reality the stimulus but rather part of the response. They are not the same facts that are "filtered through the attitude net" . . . but . . . "a distillation of the stimulus which was the actual fact situation presented to the court," says Becker:

> If Schubert is going to employ factor analysis techniques to present a set of actual factors (stimuli) that relate to an ultimate decision which is an

output from a psychological process of decision-makers, then he must go to the *actual fact sources* themselves in order to maximize the potential validity of his findings . . . after-the-fact facts are not the real thing.[17]

Recognizing the problem of access to certain kinds of judicial information, Becker nevertheless argues that the "facts" of a case—Schubert's stimulus—are to be found only in the briefs presented to the court, the verbatim record of the oral arguments, and a transcript of what the appellate judges said to one another in conference. Simply put, Schubert has misconceived response as stimulus in his decision-making model.

UTILITY OF LEGAL RESEARCH IN COMMUNICATIONS STUDIES

Legal empiricism and realism, symbolized by the "Brandeis Brief,"[18] a legal argument rich in socio-psychological data, has over a period of six decades stimulated an inductive, theory-construction approach to law which attempts to explain why and how judges decide as they do, and to predict what they will decide—the latter itself a definition of law used by Justice Holmes. Such an approach is useful and intellectually rewarding. It is not all of law, however: it does not help one in challenging a broadcast license renewal; nor in testifying knowledgeably against a proposed rule of criminal procedure which would close preliminary hearings in criminal cases to the public; nor in convincing a court that post-publication accountability imposed by judges upon journalists covering criminal trials is tantamount to prior restraint, and therefore is forbidden by the First Amendment; nor in drafting a statute for a legislative session which would make restrictions on obscenity comport with Supreme Court standards.

Most communications research, whether documentary or social scientific in methodology, follows the same steps from problem identification to discussion of research findings. When integrating data into the totality of communication research, both documentary researcher and social scientist ought to provide a contextual explanation. If legal scholarship is adversarial in nature, i.e., if it stems from a value-laden hypothesis which assumes that certain changes in the law or in legal interpretation must follow, this should be fully stated. The adversarial researcher, like the lawyer defending a client, may depend upon dissenting opinions and deviant commentaries related to particular cases or trends in the law to solidify his argument. Similarly, in analyzing the work of a legal scholar who links process with policy, inherent value judgments ought to be fully identified and explained.

The failings of documentary methods can be serious. Traditional jurisprudents have shown "an extreme tolerance for low accuracy results"[19] in fact-finding. As a subset of this problem, courts, which frequently rely on legal scholarship, have difficulty generating their own sources of information, of getting information from available sources, of understanding information they do get, and of applying it logically to particular cases.[20]

In a leading case in which the Supreme Court rejected the journalist's First Amendment claim to a right to withhold the identity of source when under grand jury subpoena,[21] both majority and minority opinions took notice of empirical evidence on the effect of subpoenas on the flow of news and of the opinions of journalists on the efficacy and advisability of "shield" laws.[22] In dissent, Justice Potter Stewart elaborated on the relationship between empirical studies and constitutional decision-making:

> Empirical studies, after all, can only provide facts. It is the duty of Courts to give legal significance to facts; and it is the special duty of this Court to understand the constitutional significance of facts. We must often proceed in a state of less than perfect knowledge, either because the facts are murky or the methodology used in obtaining facts is open to question. It is then that we must look to the Constitution for the values that inform our presumptions.[23]

If empirical studies "can only provide facts" (!) as Justice Stewart says, to proceed without facts is to proceed, in Abraham Kaplan's words, "as we did in physics before Galileo. . . . We do not bother to look because we imagine that we already have a fundamental understanding of the nature of things."[24]

It is difficult to honor the decisions of judges or the declarations of legal scholars who persist in remaining oblivious to available evidence. How can the Supreme Court, in fashioning a revised (and incomprehensible) standard for the punishment of obscene publication,[25] ignore the broad empirical findings of a Presidential Commission on Obscenity and Pornography, the recommendations of which will surely form the rational basis for future legal rules in this emotive area?[26] How can a federal judge in a 1974 article estimating the effectiveness of judicial instructions to jurors in criminal cases fall back upon a hoary quotation from an opinion written by Supreme Court Justice Robert Jackson in 1949—"The naive assumption that prejudicial effects can be overcome by instructions to a jury . . . all practising lawyers know to be unmitigated fiction"[27] —

and ignore evidence to the contrary in a systematic ten-year study of the American jury?[28]

If traditional legal methods are so fraught with difficulty, why use them at all? First, traditional legal research is tied to one of the most comprehensive information storage and retrieval systems ever devised. Although not yet computerized, legal literature is a codified system of laws, court decisions, and commentaries that are cross-indexed and referenced in a most ingenious manner.[29] Such a complete and readily usable organization of research materials does not exist in the social sciences or humanities.

Second, the quality of thinking and of logical reasoning found in traditional legal research is often singularly impressive. Some of our best minds use the method to urge change in both procedural and substantive law. Their suggestions for reform are not the musings of isolated scholars in academic settings, but instead the "stuff" that judges, especially at appellate levels, use to chart new pathways in dealing with complex social problems. Law review articles, treatises, and other scholarly commentaries are cited by American judges with great frequency and have had an unusual influence on the direction of the law.

Third, traditional legal research provides an especially important linkage for mass communication scholars who do not wish to deal with legal issues narrowly. For example, a researcher attempting to understand libel laws as they relate to "private" persons may need a broader background in civil procedure, while one who studies the constitutional conflict between free press and fair trial may need to know more about criminal procedure. Still others will need to understand property law, equity, contracts, and other legal subjects.[30] The unified system of legal research materials allows one to move with dispatch and with an assurance of completeness. A substantial law library is a massive resource base for the communication scholar.

Finally, the benefits to the student of communication of painstaking, systematic legal research within a theoretical framework is evident in the work of Zechariah Chafee,[31] Alexander Meiklejohn,[32] Fredrick Siebert,[33] Leonard Levy,[34] and Thomas Emerson, to name only some of the more eminent. In his classic study of freedom of expression which enhances our understanding of political communication, Emerson says:

> [A]n effective system of freedom of expression requires a realistic administrative structure. It is not enough merely to formulate the broad principles or simply to incorporate them in general rules of law. It is necessary

to develop a framework of doctrines, practices, and institutions which will take into account the actual forces at work and make possible the realistic achievement of the objective sought. Although we have had long experience with these aspects of the problem we have done little to explore the dynamics of operating a system of free expression. This interrelated set of rights, principles, practices, and institutions can be considered a system, at least in a rough way, because it has an overall unity of purpose and operation.[35]

Using traditional methods within a theoretical framework and organizing case law around legal concepts, Emerson has provided a means of understanding how freedom of expression has been and should be articulated with other constitutional rights. Law, as Emerson implies, is not simply a matter of Supreme Court opinions. One must also know how an issue develops. How do statutes and administrative rulings impinge upon freedom of expression, for example? What social interests were at work in developing a particular law? How do the values and thought-patterns of attorneys affect litigation involving the law? On what legal grounds and on whose initiative do cases move through the appellate process? And, finally, what part of a judge's opinion is ruling law and what part "dicta" or philosophical speculation?[36] In short, how does the system of freedom of expression, or any other system involving communication, work?

If traditional legal research is sometimes short-sighted in terms of process and has problems with unexpressed normative assumptions and a deficiency of facts, behavioral studies in the law can often be said to be too narrow, too limited in scope. Sidney Ulmer, in demonstrating what he believes to be the virtues of behavioral over traditional scholarship in his work on the voting record of Justice Hugo Black on civil liberties issues during the whole of his long career (1937-1971), admits the severe limitations of his own work but says that "on the whole [my work is not] discouraging to those who may wish to explore the extent not only of judicial reliance on 'election returns' but the impact of the entire panorama of social events and relations on the behavior of judges."[37]

Long a platitude, less often a practice, is the notion that the communication researcher should use the methodology most appropriate to the problem at hand. Because communication law researchers are usually more interested in the substance of law than in methodological issues, they have been slow in aligning method with problem. Most communication law studies use traditional methods. To some extent this is dictated by the law reviews, the most prestigious publishers of legal scholarship. The reviews, essentially outlets for law student scholarship, are also conduits for sophisticated legal philosophy and analysis.[38] Increasingly the reviews are opening their pages to behaviorists, and a number of them specialize in the sociology of law.[39]

The communication law researcher, in isolating the focal variables of his study, should like other communication researchers seek out the methodology most conducive to generalizable results. Even in instances where the researcher is investigating the impact of a single case, he should find the method that will provide the richest interpretation, the most sanguine explanation. This may involve an exhaustive search of applications of the case to other cases, a purpose to which traditional methodologies are well suited. In other situations a survey of newspaper editors or a field experiment in various media management settings may yield more useful explanations. If, for example, the researcher suspects that a particularly repressive court ruling has had a "chilling effect" on free expression, thus making reporters overly cautious in their writing, it would be more appropriate to ask a reporter than to search the law library for cases in point.[40]

Although certain modes of research into interpersonal communication (for example, coorientation studies) might be useful in ascertaining a kind of "person-other perception" view of a legal concept such as "the public interest," the fact remains that most communication law research is institutional in character. The most compelling problems seem to be in the public law arena where mass media institutions and government do battle. Most of the major concepts of communications law have sociological dimensions. Research has to do with the impact of communication law on particular industries (e.g., broadcasting stations or magazines) and particular practitioners (e.g., reporters). Because law and its processes are dynamic, the researcher must take care not to focus exclusively on the ephemeral, soon-to-be-discarded case of the moment. Instead one should seek out pervasive problems, lasting research arenas. In an effort to move toward this goal, this chapter offers a number of general parameters for research using (a) traditional and (b) social science methodologies.

This is not to suggest that there cannot be an interrelationship of the two, or that certain problems might not be confronted in diverse ways. Indeed, if communication law scholarship has one great need, it is probably a greater infusion of creativity into the process of research itself.

For the mass communication researcher both methods can be

nourishing. Traditional methods promise a rich and detailed resource base; behavioral methods a theory for explaining and predicting judicial behavior. A fusion of the two promises a systematic theory-building within the vast literature of the law. On the latter point Felix Cohen said, "A failure to recognize that the law is a vast field, in which different students are interested in diverse problems, has the unfortunate effect of making every school of legal thought an *ex officio* antagonist of every other school."[41]

Traditional legal scholars and behavioral scientists need to know more about how each approaches his problems. When their methodologies merge, new models of communication research may appear, and important questions of social policy can then be addressed.

RESEARCH AGENDA: TRADITIONAL METHODS

Since much of their concern focuses on interpretations of the First Amendment, students of communication law have been preoccupied with constitutional and administrative law which account for the largest categories of cases ultimately heard by the United States Supreme Court through the process of judicial review.

Loosely defined, constitutional law is that branch of public law which deals with the structure of government, the organs and powers of sovereignty, the distribution of political and governmental authorities and functions, and—most germane to mass communication—the fundamental principles which regulate the relations of government and citizen.

An enduring concern of constitutional scholarship is an understanding of how judicial doctrine is applied by divisions of the Court to define and balance individual against social or collective rights. Comparisons of the consequences to First Amendment freedoms, for example, of a doctrine of "preferred freedoms" on the one hand and a doctrine of "judicial restraint" on the other expose the political roots of judicial review.

Nowhere is this more evident than in the Supreme Court's sometimes subtle shift of emphasis from personal to societal rights and from judicial to legislative law-making which began in the 1969 October term with the new Burger Court. Changes in political values and in judicial constructs supporting those values have been most clearly reflected in cases involving legislative reapportionment, criminal law, and, to a lesser extent, First Amendment, Fourth Amendment, and "equal protection" cases.

The Court on occasion would seem to be divided between those deferrent to the "democratic" mandate of legislatures and the prerogatives of state courts, and those who would protect "preferred" or "fundamental" freedoms against lawmakers and state courts in most circumstances. The former frequently constitute the new Court majorities, the latter the "activist" Warren Court holdovers.

In a series of cases beginning with *Younger v. Harris*[42] in 1970 the Court divided on the question of when the federal courts should interfere with pending state criminal proceedings. Justice William O. Douglas in a minority opinion declared that the latitude given state courts by the majority would have a "chilling effect on the exercise of First Amendment rights." And in a case in which the majority held that an accused's constitutional rights are not infringed by permitting a jury to impose the death penalty without any governing judicial standards, dissenting Warren Court holdovers Douglas, William Brennan and Thurgood Marshall, said that "The Court errs at all points from its premises to conclusions."[43]

Justice Marshall, dissenting vigorously in a 1972 picketing case, acknowledged the philosophical split on these kinds of issues when he observed that "The vote in *Logan Valley* was 6-3, and that decision is only four years old. But, I am aware that the composition of this Court has radically changed in four years."[44]

In the term ending June 28, 1973, the four Nixon appointees— Warren Burger, Harry Blackmun, Lewis Powell and William Rehnquist—had voted as a cohesive bloc in 70 per cent of all cases decided. The Eisenhower appointee, Potter Stewart, and Byron White, appointed by Kennedy, held the balance of power. Minorities have a way of becoming majorities, however, as political fortunes ebb and flow. And a justice may influence from the grave. John M. Harlan's notions of federalism are apparent in Court opinions of the present.

Where a conflict is not finally settled by the Supreme Court—and that is true of most conflicts—decisions of lower federal and state courts must be consulted. Legislative decisions are found in state and federal statutes. Executive orders and the regulations and rulings of more than 200 state and federal administrative agencies are found in the widely scattered and untidy literature of administrative law.

Administrative law, a fluid amalgam of constitutional, statutory and common law, affects more people more intimately than any other part of law because it deals with such matters as utilities, broadcasting, advertising, consumer safety, food and health, bank deposits, unemployment, welfare, old-age security, and labor unions.

For example, the National Labor Relations Board alone reviews at least eight times as many cases as the Supreme Court, writes nine times as many opinions, and publishes four times as many pages of opinions.[45] In 1963, the number of civil trials in all federal district courts was 7,095; the number of cases disposed of by federal agencies in the same period, and for which there was a written transcript, was 81,469.[46]

Administrative agencies have quasi-executive, quasi-legislative and quasi-judicial powers. They get their money and their mandate from the legislature;[47] their personnel come from the executive (high appointments also require legislative ratification); their rulings can be reversed by the judiciary. Lawyers and judges have wondered for a long time whether this "fourth branch" of government affords litigants adequate due process.[48]

Whatever its strengths and weaknesses, the administrative process is part of a larger political process. One cannot comprehend the influence of politics on broadcast and advertising communication without knowing something about the functioning of the Federal Communications and Federal Trade Commissions.[49] Nor can one comprehend the "politics of monopoly" without help from the anti-trust Division of the Department of Justice.

Using delegated executive, legislative and judicial power, the administrative agencies altogether issue perhaps 100,000 rulings a year—frequently without benefit of public hearings, sworn testimony, or other traditional safeguards of due process.[50] Whatever autonomous power the regulatory agencies enjoy they derive from their technological proficiency; yet it has been said that Congress has found no way to make "experts" out of political appointees.[51] And, of course, their "expertise" is to be used in the public interest.

The communication scholar must be bound to some extent by the general organizational framework of his field. Communication law has traditionally been concerned with libel, privacy, newsman's privilege, copyright, access to information and other topical areas. Any major hornbook[52] or casebook[53] reflects these interests. Because these standard divisions are well indexed in law libraries, traditional methods of legal scholarship are particularly appropriate in dealing with them.

Some communications scholars have combined legal methods with historical scholarship.[54] At the same time straightforward updating and reinterpretation of legal developments are always appreciated. Other investigators have selected areas that are likely to be of interest to particular segments of the communications industry. William Francois of Drake University, for example, offers regular commentaries on the impact of changes in communication law on the magazine industry and the freelance writer.[55] The Magazine Publishers Association[56] and the American Newspaper Publishers Association[57] have commissioned studies of special interest to them. Scholars have sought to build a legal-historical theory of freedom of expression.[58] J. Edward Gerald studied press-government relations during the period of the New Deal.[59] Focusing more narrowly, Harold L. Nelson studied libel in news of Congressional investigating committees.[60] Journalist Anthony Lewis gave us a fascinating, though impressionistic, step-by-step account of how an impoverished prison inmate, who had been tried and convicted of a felony without benefit of counsel, brought a landmark case to the Supreme Court and won.[61]

There is a considerable distance between the examination of a single case and a theory of the First Amendment, and along the way communication scholars have concerned themselves with contextual studies of communication law problems as well as general area studies. For example, a study of press-government relations in purloined papers controversies such as the 1971 Pentagon Papers case thrusts the scholar into the thicket of property law, especially that part of it concerned with public or government property.[62] Copyright, conversion theory, criminal laws against receipt of stolen goods, and even espionage law, become pertinent. Contextual studies of necessity probe deeply into general areas of communication law. As students of privacy have pointed out, only a segment of privacy law has any relevance to mass communication, yet the careful researcher must see his problem in context if he is to make effective and appropriate judgments.

As we indicated earlier, some traditional researchers openly advocate legal reform. Jerome Barron called for a new theory of the First Amendment in order to expedite public access to the major media of mass communication. His argument was unanimously rejected by the Supreme Court.[63] Others have sought to change particular state laws.[64] Some communication law scholars work closely with state bar associations in an effort to reform and improve the administration of justice as it relates to the communication industry.[65]

Finally, descriptive studies may help define legal practices and illuminate concepts that recur in the law. Such routine problems as access to police blotters[66] and the journalist's privilege to protect the anonymity of his sources and the integrity of his notes and tapes require descriptive treatment. Here traditional methods of legal scholarship provide rapid assembly of information.

In a broader conceptual frame, notions such as the "public interest," a term frequently used in administrative rulings and court decisions, requires definition.[67] In pursuing definitions, scholars look both inside and outside the law, but ultimately it is the legal definition which the courts use that has the definitive impact. One can, after all, read dozens of theories about the public interest in political science, economics and sociology, but the actual adjudication using public interest definitions in the context of press-government disputes is in the hands of the courts.

In most of the interest areas referred to above, painstaking traditional legal research would seem the best method of understanding and resolving problems. Sampling techniques or inference theory will not work. One cannot sample libel cases and then generalize about the nature of the law in that area. Each case has a specific and sometimes peculiar meaning that interlocks and interrelates with all others. Here the "wilderness of single instances" has to be welded into a meaningful whole. Traditional legal methods are best suited to the task.

RESEARCH AGENDA: SOCIAL SCIENCE METHODS

We have discussed and criticized the application of social science methods to studies of judicial behavior. The judge's vote becomes the unit of analysis and it is examined over time in a variety of topical contexts.

The work of Schubert, Ulmer and others in this area provides a new dimension to our understanding of the political behavior of courts generally, as perceived through the behavior of individual judges or philosophical blocs of judges on appellate courts specifically. Communication law scholars have not been active in this field of study and seem not to have been influenced much by the work of political behaviorists.

One segment of the field that has attracted considerable attention is public opinion and the legal process. Here the methods of survey research are applicable as scholars probe the relationship between public understanding and support and sanction of the operation of the courts, especially the U.S. Supreme Court. Years ago Chief

Justice Charles Evans Hughes spoke of the "self-inflicted wound," when the Court moves counter to public opinion.[68] Fred P. Graham reintroduced this concept in his 1970 book about public opinion and the criminal defendant cases of the Warren Court.[69] Other scholars have examined public opinion and the Court, and this is obviously a productive area for continuing study.[70] Both survey methods probing public attitudes and content analysis examining court decisions for references to public opinion are useful methodological tools. In addition, various scaling methods might usefully be tested.

In addition to public opinion in the broadest sense, the attitudes of jurors and prospective jurors tempt communication researchers. Jury studies in communication law are rare except in the free press-fair trial area.[71] That vexing problem has stimulated considerable research, using both traditional and social scientific methodologies.[72] Communication scholars also take note of the use of social science data by the courts. Such evidence gained respectability in the great school desegregation decision of 1954.[73] Appellate courts, however, still lack any formal fact-finding resources. Survey and experimental research data, although they still have to run the gauntlet of the "hearsay" rule, are now being used sparingly in criminal cases, especially in considering 'motions for a change of venue and in the selection of jurors. A federal district court in Puerto Rico, for example, was willing to listen to expert testimony on attitude formation, to a review of the research evidence on jury influences, and to the results of an opinion survey of prospective jurors in a terrorist bombing case. Although the judge did not find the empirical evidence sufficiently persuasive to benefit the defendant, he did give it his close attention.[74]

Social scientists helped attorneys choose jurors for the trials of Angela Davis and the Harrisburg Seven,[75] and there have been similar alliances in other "political" trials. Survey and experimental research data are no strangers to administrative law generally and to patent, trademark and copyright infringement cases in particular.[76]

Not unrelated to the work of the judicial behaviorists are studies of role relationships and organizational structure and process within the judiciary. Of special interest to communication scholars are studies of the courts as communicators,[77] especially the reportorial practices and information policies of the Supreme Court and the manner in which it is covered by the media.[78] Some work has been done at the lower federal court level, but there are few studies of press coverage of the courts generally, both in terms of what gets reported and the relationships between the bench, the bar and the press.

SUMMARY AND CONCLUSIONS

The communication researcher who uses either the traditional or social scientific approach to legal research as practised by jurisprudents and behaviorists will probably always be frustrated. It should be remembered that neither group is particularly interested in communication problems. Instead they probe policy questions or examine behavioral patterns for purposes of explanation and prediction. Communication researchers study the law in the context of freedom of expression or for the purpose of identifying communication patterns within judicial structures. And for this they need a new model, one which has a communication research perspective.

No doubt there are many paths one might follow in searching for a new model. The creative researcher will find one best suited to his own needs. However, some considerations are immediately evident. In order for legal scholarship to become part of the totality of communication research it must:

1. Adopt the systematic, step-by-step procedures of the scientific method from problem formulation to hypothesis development, methodological strategy, data collection and analysis, and discussion of findings;
2. Frame hypotheses that move away from normative, adversarial positions and are instead based on a preponderance of evidence growing out of a complete review of the relevant literature;
3. Present the often-important dissenting views of judges in their full historical context so that they can be understood as part of the fabric of judicial behavior and not simply as exercises in legal reasoning (it is here that the distinction must be made between holdings and dicta);
4. Make efforts to temper normative assumptions when analyzing the admittedly normative behavior of jurists. That is, while recognizing the value-laden quality of court decisions, the communication researcher should nonetheless seek systematic and value-free modes for dissecting and discussing them and their implications.

While recognizing the necessity of documentary methodologies, we are suggesting that the philosophical bases for legal research be scientific, that the communication scholar discard adversarial hypotheses and the case-building reformism of his law school colleagues. We are asking the communication scholar to adopt a standard that meets the rigorous tests of scientific methodology. Once this has been done, the communication researcher should be free to utilize either documentary or social science methods, mixing and blending them where appropriate.

Policy-oriented legal research will continue to have immediate application to administrative, legislative and judicial decision-making and will therefore attract some communication researchers. Those with an interest in the˙ advancement of knowledge, however, will have to break away from the traditions of normative scholarship if they wish to do work which relates to the rest of communication research.

To some extent legal historians have already accepted this view, but for the most part communication law scholarship stands in disarray, with a fragmented borrowing from others and no clear direction of its own. The need is obvious and the tools are available for the robust development of a communication law method.

APPENDIX

There are a number of basic law library resources which the researcher ought to know about. Legal librarians and treatises on legal research can provide specific guidance on how these and other sources are used. Begin with COHEN, M. L. (1971) Legal Research in a Nutshell. St. Paul: West Publishing Co. See also, RAOLFE, W. R. (1965) How to Find the Law. St. Paul: West Publishing Co.; JACOBSTEIN, J. M. and R. M. MERSKY (eds.) (1973) ERVIN H. POL-LACK'S Fundamentals of Legal Research. Mineola, N.Y.; The Foundation Press; PRICE, M. O. and H. BITNER (1970) Problems for Effective Legal Research. Boston: Little, Brown.

(1) The American Digest and Key Number Systems. All reported U.S. cases are organized in digest form under key numbers which represent precise points of law. This system is composed of the General Digest which cumulates all reported state and federal cases in 10-year segments (decennials) and the Century Digest for older cases. When a key number is found which relates to the legal issue you wish to examine, all other relevant cases can be uncovered. A Cumulative Table of Key Numbers will assist you in this task. There is a Descriptive Word Index to the entire set. The Modern Federal Practice Digest is a rapid way of locating digests of Federal court decisions by key number. The cases in full are reprinted in the Supreme Court Reporter (S.Ct.), U.S. Supreme Court decisions; the Federal Supplement (F. Supp.), Federal District Court cases; the Federal Reporter (F. and F. 2d), U.S. Courts of Appeals; and various regional reporters reprinting decisions of state appellate courts (e.g., N.W. and

N.W. 2d containing appellate decisions of the courts of Minnesota, Wisconsin, Michigan, Iowa, North and South Dakota, and Nebraska).

(2) United States Supreme Court Reports (L. Ed.). Annotated reports of United States Supreme Court decisions and summaries of lawyers' briefs. There is an index to the annotations.

(3) American Law Reports (A.L.R., A.L.R. 2d and A.L.R. 3d). Selected appellate court decisions annotated by lengthy essays discussing their legal significance. Annotations are kept up to date by supplements. There is an index here also.

(4) U.S. Law Week (L.W.). Earliest reports of significant court decisions, including full texts of U.S. Supreme Court opinions, new statutes and agency rulings.

(5) United States Code Annotated (U.S.C.A.) and Federal Code Annotated (F.C.A.). Multi-volume codifications of federal laws updated by cumulative pocket parts. Annotations include summaries of court decisions interpreting the law, opinions of attorneys-general, and occasionally citations to law reviews or other secondary sources. There are also annotated codes for most states.

(6) U.S. Code, Congressional and Administrative News (U.S.C.C.A.N.). Useful in constructing the legislative histories of federal statutes and a good source of committee reports.

(7) Code of Federal Regulations (C.F.R.). Regulations of Federal administrative agencies, codified and organized by subject matter. Supplemented by the Federal Register.

(8) Pike and Fischer Radio Regulation (R.R. and R.R. 2d). One of many loose-leaf services invaluable in the study of administrative law. This one is the most comprehensive source of F.C.C. decisions and regulations, statutes and court decisions pertaining to telecommunications. There are digest volumes to the series. For an introduction to broadcast research see J. M. FOLEY (1973) "Broadcasting regulation research: a primer for non-lawyers." Journal of Broadcasting 17 (Spring); and D. R. LeDUC (1973) "Broadcast legal documentation: a fourth-dimensional guide." Journal of Broadcasting 17 (Spring).

(9) Shepard's Citations. Traces of "life history" of a case, a statute or an administrative ruling. How a case has been treated by the courts. Has it been followed or overruled? What have attorneys-general and law review writers said about it? Has a statute been amended or repealed? How has it been treated by courts and in periodicals? This is sometimes a crucial final step in legal research.

(10) Corpus Juris Secundum (C.J.S.) and American Jurisprudence (Am. Jur. and Am. Jur. 2d). Legal encyclopediae which summarize and suggest the parameters of substantive and procedural issues in law. Sometimes recommended as a place to begin legal research. Volumes kept up to date with pocket supplements, a device used in many legal materials. Check inside back covers for updating information.

(11) Black Law Dictionary. The best known of legal dictionaries. See also, Ballentine, Bouvier, Cochran and Gifis (paperback).

(12) Index to Legal Periodicals. A reader's guide to articles in scholarly and professional law journals. Also useful are Index to Periodical Articles Related to Law and the Index to Foreign Legal Periodicals.

REFERENCES

1. De TOQUEVILLE, A. (1966) Democracy in America (Trans. by G. Lawrence), New York: Harper, p. 137.
2. SCHWARTZ, B. A Basic History of the U.S. Supreme Court. Princeton, N.J.: D. Van Nostrand, p. 10.
3. DUNNE, F. P. (1968) Mr. Dooley on the Choice of Law. Charlottesville, Va.: University of Virginia Press, pp. 47-52.
4. Research News (1971) "How does the law change?" Ann Arbor: University of Michigan, Volume 8 (February):4.
5. BROWN, R. S., Jr. (1963) "Legal research: the resources base and traditional approaches," Amer. Behavioral Scientist 7 (December):5.
6. Ibid.
7. Ibid., 6.
8. COHEN, M. L. (1971) Legal Research in a Nutshell. St. Paul, Minn.: West Publishing, p. 228.
9. BECKER, T. L. (1964) Political Behavioralism and Modern Jurisprudence: A Working Theory and Study in Judicial Decision-Making. Chicago: Rand-McNally, p. 86.
10. LOEVINGER, L. (1965) "Some reflections on the jurimetrics conference at Yale, 1963." P. 11 in E. Allen and M. E. Caldwell [eds.], Communication Sciences and Law. New York: Bobbs-Merrill.
11. HOLMES, O. W. (1920) "Learning and science." Collected Legal Papers. New York: Harcourt, Brace, p. 139.
12. LOEVINGER, op. cit., p. 13.
13. AUBERT, V. (1963) "Researches in the sociology of law." Amer. Behavioral Scientist 7 (December):17.
14. ULMER, S. (1963) "Scientific method and the judicial process." Amer. Behavioral Scientist 7 (December):22.
15. ESTES v. STATE OF TEXAS, 381 U.S. 532, 541, 545, 550, 552 (1965).
16. SCHUBERT, G. [ed.] (1964) Judicial Behavior: A Reader in Theory and Research. Chicago: Rand-McNally.
17. BECKER, op. cit., 14.
18. MULLER v. OREGON, 208 U.S. 412 (1908) Then an attorney, Louis Brandeis furnished the Court with what for its time was overwhelming social scientific documentation of the deleterious effect on working women of long hours.
19. KORN, H. L. (1966) "Law, fact, and science in the courts." Columbia Law Rev. 66:1080, 1115.
20. An excellent study of the relationship of facts and values in judicial decision-making is J. C. ROBBINS (1970) "Social science information and first amendment freedoms: an aid to supreme court decision-making." Ph.D. dissertation. Minneapolis: University of Minnesota. See also, ROBBINS (1972) "Deciding first amendment cases: Part I, and "Deciding first amendment cases: Part II, evidence." Journalism Q. 49 (Summer and Autumn): 263-270 and 569-578.
21. BRANZBURG v. HAYES, IN THE MATTER OF PAPPAS, UNITED STATES v. CALDWELL, 408 U.S. 665 (1972).
22. See, BLASI, V. (1971) "The newsman's privilege: an empirical study." Michigan Law Rev. 70:229.

23. BRANZBURG v. HAYES, at 736.

24. KAPLAN, A. (1967) "Behavioral science and the law." Case Western Reserve Law Rev. 19:57, 67.

25. MILLER v. STATE OF CALIFORNIA, 413 U.S. 15 (1973).

26. Report of the Commission on Obscenity and Pornography (1970) [WILLIAM B. LOCKHART, chairman]. New York: Bantam Books.

27. KRULEVITCH v. UNITED STATES, 336 U.S. 440, 453 (1949).

28. KALVEN, H., Jr. and H. ZEISEL (1971) The American Jury. Chicago: University of Chicago Press.

29. See APPENDIX for a sketch of basic law library resources.

30. One of the best examples of how courts and the legal process relate to freedom of expression is M. A. FRANKLIN (1968) The Dynamics of American Law. Mineola, N.Y.: The Foundation Press.

31. CHAFEE, Z., Jr. (1954) Free Speech in the United States. Cambridge: Harvard University Press.

32. MEIKLEJOHN, A. (1948) Free Speech and Its Relation to Self-Government. New York: Harper.

33. SIEBERT, F. S. (1952) Freedom of the Press in England, 1476-1776. Urbana: University of Illinois Press.

34. LEVY, L. W. (1960) Legacy of Suppression: Freedom of Speech and Press in Early American History. Cambridge: The Belknap Press.

35. EMERSON, T. I. (1970) The System of Freedom of Expression. New York: Vintage Books, p. 4.

36. Some of the dangers involved in overemphasizing the impact of the United States Supreme Court on the law, and the greater danger of quoting excerpts from judicial decisions without concern for the nature of a particular statement (ruling law or simple "dicta") are discussed in H. J. ABRAHAM (1968) The Judicial Process. 2d ed., New York: Oxford University Press, Chapt. 4.

37. ULMER, S. (1973) "The longitudinal behavior of Hugo LaFayette Black: parabolic support for civil liberties, 1937-1971." Florida State Law Rev. 1:131, 153.

38. MILLER, A. S. (1973-1974) "The law journals." Change 5 (Winter):64-66.

39. For example, the Law and Society Review, published by the Law and Society Association, State University of New York, Buffalo.

40. See, for example, S. S. GOLDSCHLAGER (1971) "The law and the news media." Senior thesis. New Haven: Yale University Law School. Includes a survey of managing editors' attitudes toward Supreme Court reporting.

41. COHEN, F. S. (1935) "Transcendental nonsense and the functional approach." Columbia Law Rev. 35:809-849.

42. 401 U.S. 37 (1970).

43. McGAUTHA v. CALIFORNIA, 402 U.S. 183, 249 (1971).

44. LLOYD CORP. v. TANNER, 407 U.S. 551, 584 (1972).

45. DAVIS, K. C. (1960) Administrative Law and Government. St. Paul: West Publishing, Chapt. I, pp. 11-54.

46. ——— (1973) Administrative Law. St. Paul: West Publishing, p. 4.

47. The Administrative Procedures Act, 60 Stat. 237 (1946), as amended by 80 Stat. 378 (1966), as amended by 81 Stat. 54 (1967), 5 U.S.C. § § 551-559, 701-706, 1305, 3344, 6362, 7562, governs the federal administrative agencies.

48. See, for example, M. SHAPIRO (1968) The Supreme Court and Administrative Agencies. New York: Free Press, Chapt. 2.

49. See KRASNOW, E. G. and L. D. LONGLEY (1973) The Politics of Broadcast Regulation. New York: St. Martin's Press, for an account of the political influences which impinge upon the Federal Communications Commission.

50. KOHLMEIER, L. M. (1969) The Regulators. New York: Harper & Row, p. 31.

51. Ibid., p. 8.

52. For example, H. L. NELSON and D. L. TEETER (1973) Law of Mass Communications. Mineola, N.Y.: The Foundation Press.

53. For example, D. M. GILLMOR and J. A. BARRON (1974) Mass Communication Law, Cases and Comment. St. Paul, Minn.: West Publishing.

54. Studies of communication law using the historical method combined with legal scholarship include F. SIEBERT, Freedom of the Press in England, 1476-1776, op. cit.; D. R. PEMBER (1972) Privacy and the Press. Seattle: University of Washington Press; E. G. HUDON (1963) Freedom of Speech and Press in America. Washington, D.C.: Public Affairs Press; P. MURPHY (1972) The Meaning of Freedom of Speech: First Amendment Freedoms from Wilson to FDR. Westport, Conn.: Greenwood.

55. See Francois's work regularly in the Writer's Digest.

56. One such study is D. L. SMITH (1969) The New Freedom to Publish: Trends in Libel and Privacy Law—Effects on the Magazine Industry—New Challenges. New York: Magazine Publishers Assn.

57. See, for example, H. L. CROSS (1953) The People's Right to Know, Legal Access to Public Records and Proceedings. New York: Columbia University Press; A. B. HANSON (1969) Libel and Related Torts, 2 Vol., New York: American Newspaper Publishers Association Foundation, Supplement, 1970; D. M. GILLMOR (1974) Judicial Restraints on the Press. Columbia, Mo.: Freedom of Information Foundation; J. B. ADAMS (1974) State Open Meetings Laws: An Overview. Columbia, Mo.: Freedom of Information Foundation; D. GORDON (1974) Newsman's Privilege and the Law. Columbia, Mo.: Freedom of Information Foundation.

58. See notes 31, 32, 33, 34 and 35. See also, T. I. EMERSON (1966) Toward a General Theory of the First Amendment. New York: Random House.

59. J. E. GERALD (1948) The Press and the Constitution, 1931-1947, Minneapolis, Minn.: University of Minnesota Press.

60. NELSON, H. L. (1961) Libel in News of Congressional Investigating Committees. Minneapolis, Minn.: University of Minnesota Press.

61. LEWIS, A. (1963) Gideon's Trumpet. New York: Random House. The case is GIDEON v. WAINWRIGHT, 372 U.S. 335 (1963).

62. See, E. E. DENNIS (1973) "Purloined information as property: a new first amendment challenge," Journalism Q. 50 (Autumn): 456-462, 474; also DENNIS (1974) "Purloined papers and information as property: a study of press-government conflict." Ph.D. dissertation. Minneapolis: University of Minnesota.

63. BARRON, J. A. (1967) "Access to the Press—a new first amendment right," Harvard Law Rev. 80:1641. See also, BARRON (1973) Freedom of the Press For Whom? The Right of Access to Mass Media. Bloomington, Ind.: Indiana University Press. The case is MIAMI HERALD PUBLISHING COMPANY v. TORNILLO, 418 U.S. 241 (1974).

64. For example, R. S. WARREN (1972) "Free press-fair trial: the 'gag order,' a California aberration." Southern California Law Rev. 45 (Winter):51.

65. For example, Prof. ALBERT PICKERELL at the University of California, Berkeley, and Prof. JAY WRIGHT at Syracuse University.

66. PETRICK, M. J. (1969) "The press, the police blotter and public safety." Journalism Q. 46 (Autumn):475-481.

67. See, E. E. DENNIS (1974) "The press and the public interest: a definitional dilemma." DePaul Law Rev. 23 (Spring):937.

68. HUGHES, C. E. (1928) The Supreme Court of the United States. New York: Columbia University Press, pp. 50-53.

69. GRAHAM, F. P. (1970) The Self-Inflicted Wound. New York: Macmillan.

70. For example, J. KESSEL (1966) "Public perceptions of the supreme court." 10 Midwest J. of Political Science 10:167; W. J. DANIELS (1973) "The supreme court and its publics." Albany Law Review 37:632, and DANIELS (1970) Public attitudes toward the U.S. supreme court." Ph.D. dissertation. Iowa City: University of Iowa.

71. Several studies are cited in Fair Trial and Free Press (1966) tentative draft of the American Bar Association Project on Minimum Standards for Criminal Justice, Standards relating to Fair Trial and Free Press, New York: Institute of Judicial Administration. See also, C. BUSH, W. WILCOX, F. SIEBERT and G. HOUGH (1970) Free Press and Fair Trial. Athens, Ga.: University of Georgia Press.

72. See, R. J. SIMON (1968) "Use of the semantic differential in research on the jury." Journalism Q. 45 (Winter):670-676; SIMON and T. EIMERMANN (1971) "The jury finds not guilty: another look at media influence on the jury." Journalism Q. 48 (Summer):343-344. A study using traditional methods is D. M. GILLMOR (1966) Free Press and Fair Trial. Washington, D.C.: Public Affairs Press.

73. BROWN v. BOARD OF EDUCATION, 347 U.S. 483 (1954).

74. MARTINEZ v. COMMONWEALTH OF PUERTO RICO, 343 F. Supp. 897 (1972).

75. SCHULMAN, J., P. SHAVER, R. COLEMAN, B. EMRICH and R. CHRISTIE (1973) "Recipe for a jury." Psychology Today 6 (May):37.

76. BARKSDALE, H. C. (1957) The Use of Survey Research Findings As Legal Evidence. Pleasantville, N.Y.: Printer's Ink Books.

77. GREY, D. L. (1968) The Supreme Court and the News Media. Evanston, Ill.: Northwestern University Press.

78. See, for example, C. A. NEWLAND (1964) "Press coverage of the United States supreme court," Western Political Q. 17:15, D. L. GREY (1966) "Decision-making by a reporter under deadline pressure," Journalism Q. 43 (Autumn):426-428; and E. DENNIS (1975) "Another look at press coverage of the supreme court." Villanova Law Rev. (Spring).

AUTHOR INDEX
(italics denote complete citations)